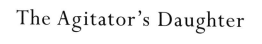

The Agitator's Daughter

The
Agitator's
Daughter

A Memoir of Four Generations of
One Extraordinary African American Family

SHERYLL CASHIN

PUBLICAFFAIRS
New York

Book Design by Timm Bryson

Library of Congress Cataloging-in-Publication Data
Cashin, Sheryll.
    The agitator's daughter : a memoir of four generations of one extraordinary African American
family / Sheryll Cashin. — 1st ed.
        p. cm.
    Includes bibliographical references.
    ISBN 978-1-58648-422-4 (hardcover)
    1. Cashin family. 2. African Americans—Alabama—Biography. 3. African Americans—
Alabama—Politics and government. 4. African Americans—Civil rights—Alabama—History. 5.
Cashin, John L. (John Logan), 1928- 6. National Democratic Party of Alabama—History. 7.
Alabama—Politics and government—1865-1950. 8. Alabama—Politics and government—1950-
9. African Americans—Alabama—Social conditions—19th century. 10. African Americans—
Alabama—Social conditions—20th century. 11. Cashin, Sheryll. I. Title.
    E185.93.A3C37 2008
    305.896'0730761—dc22
    2008011122
First Edition

10 9 8 7 6 5 4 3 2 1

For Marque Clark Chambliss,
my husband, my best friend.

CONTENTS

Cashin Family Tree

Virginia = William Henry Dorsey   Emma   John Thomas   Catherine Eveline

Herschel Brewster   Minnie Vivian "Aunt Vivi" = Carroll Napier Langston "Uncle Tode"   Newlyn Edward = Countess Harris   Lillian Emmett "Aunt Jack"

Carroll Napier, Jr.

Lillian Estelle Sykes "Lil"

John Cashin ═ Catherine Matilda Edwards

James — John Jr. ═ Lucinda Bowdre — Oswell — Mary Ann

Laura Francis — Herschel Vivian ═ Minnie V. Brewster — James

Patti (twin) ═ Leo Sykes — John Logan, Sr. (twin) ═ Grace Romania Brandon — James Blaine ═ Hortense Fears

Dr. Marcus Carpenter ═ Dr. Marie Rufin Carpenter

Herschel Brandon — John Logan Jr. ═ Joan Carpenter — James Blaine, Jr. "Blinny" — Elizabeth Virginia "Betty V."

Gigi Marie — John Marcus — Carroll Langston — Sheryll Denise

The Agitator's Daughter

My Inheritance

I t's August 11, 1969. Another hot day in Greene County, Alabama. I am seven years old, about to start the second grade. We are here to watch the swearing in of six men who were elected thanks to the NDPA. Daddy created the *National* Democratic Party of Alabama because he thought Alabamians deserved to vote for national Democrats rather than George Wallace for president. In 1964, he told me, Alabamians could not even vote to reelect Lyndon Johnson because his name did not appear on the ballot. Daddy also thought that black people needed a new party because they deserved to elect themselves. For the first time since 1816, when the Choctaw Nation had to give Greene County over to white people, some "colored" people will have a say. We have been driving down to the county a lot this summer. It feels different today, though. We are standing outside the old courthouse in Eutaw, the county seat. Everybody is laughing and smiling. I look up at this chubby woman standing next to me. Her skin is very dark. They call it "blue black." But I already know that black is beautiful. Her teeth stick out. She is wearing a loud royal-blue polyester dress and white plastic beads that spread across her large bosom. Her hair is fried greasy straight. Because she is sweating, it is starting to go back to nappy. She is shouting, like all the other people around us. "Yes-suh!" she says, affirming the inauguration speaker like she affirms her preacher on Sundays. "It's a new day in Greene County!" For some reason I will remember her and not Senator Birch Bayh, the man who has been invited here to validate this people's victory. She doesn't have much but her dignity. Today she is feeling her power. She's the kind of person the big men who own everything in the county never have to reckon with. Now they have no choice but to deal with black folks who can and will vote.

The courthouse looks tired. It was erected in 1869 and is about the oldest thing that I have ever seen. Something mossy and green trickles down its white plaster sides. Inside, I sense newness. In this courtroom black people used to sit with fear in their stomachs, Daddy told me, afraid of what judgment would bring. Today they are feeling like I feel on my birthdays: giddy because they know what's coming. It's time for the NDPA candidates to be sworn in. A white man with sagging jowls sits in the big chair in the courtroom, surrounded by other white, official-looking people. He gives this speech about how he is ready to work with the new (black) men coming in. He's looking everybody dead in the eye, like he really means what he's saying. Maybe he does want to try. I always want to see the good in people. But Daddy doesn't believe him. He is laughing because this is the same probate judge, Dennis Herndon, who left the NDPA candidates off the ballot last fall. Daddy's lawyers had to go all the way to the Supreme Court of the United States to get an order giving the NDPA the right to run candidates throughout the state. When Herndon disobeyed that order, the lawyers went back to the Supreme Court and it ordered a special election just for Greene County. On July 29, 1969, a week after we watched Neil Armstrong land on the moon, blacks shocked everyone in the state, maybe the whole country, when they swept the election.

Something begins to stir in me at the swearing in. Before then, all the NDPA really meant to me was time away from Daddy—and licking envelopes. We have a huge dining room table that seats about twelve people the two times a year we use it for eating meals: Christmas and Thanksgiving. Otherwise, that table is always piled with NDPA stuff. Mama gathers us around the table—me and my two older brothers, Johnny and Carroll—and some kids from the neighborhood. Mama is our commander and she teaches us how to fold, stuff, lick, and then stamp the NDPA mail. I never think to read what the mail says, or to ask Mama about it. In this courtroom, I begin to understand why my parents care so much about politics and civil rights, why they are always traveling, going to meetings, leaving us behind with babysitters, taking us along when they can. They think that the people of Greene County deserve to be treated like they are somebody and that helping other people be free is what our family is supposed to do.

I understand even more the following year when Dad decides to run for governor against George Wallace. I think he could win. Daddy can do anything. He's the only black dentist in Huntsville, where we live. He flies his own airplane. He seems smarter than anyone else in the world. The summer and fall of 1970 we are always going down to the Black Belt. Lowndes County. Marengo. Greene. Sumter. Wilcox. I remember most of the names and know that this is the middle part of the state. I also know, because I have been there so much, that it is poor, rural, and black. I always thought it was called the Black Belt because so many black people live there. My teacher tells me the area is named after its dark soil. I know that the dirt in other areas of Alabama tends to be red, so she could be right, but I still have doubts about her explanation.

On trips to the Black Belt we drive the back roads, sometimes in Daddy's gold Chrysler 300, sometimes in our camper van. Daddy always does the driving and he always breaks the speed limit, by a lot. Mama sits in the front seat with him. The three of us are in the back. Carroll is one year older than me, and Johnny is one year older than him. Our alliances shift constantly and when they gang up on me I tell Mama or Daddy, which usually works but guarantees that they will exclude me from their next conspiracy.

We play cow poker to pass the time. Grandma Grace, Daddy's mother, taught us this game. I count all the cows on my side of the road. Johnny or Carroll count all the cows on his side of the road. Whoever has the most cows when we get to our destination wins. A cemetery on your side kills all your cows and you have to start counting from zero, *if* your opponent sees the cemetery. A white horse or mule is worth five, but otherwise horses and mules don't count. A white cow costs you thirty points. It's an easy game to play in the Black Belt because most of the land is used for farms and open pastures.

I like these car rides. The green hills roll by. Mostly things are quiet and still. In the heat, the animals move slowly or not at all. Sometimes we pass an old plantation house, like Thornhill near the farm Daddy bought for the Black Muslims. At the top of a hill, white with pillars, the house stands grandly, defying time. I think only of its beauty, never about the slaves who used to work these fields. The car radio is tuned to a soul station. That song, "Oh Happy Day," plays constantly. *Oh happy day. Oh happy da-ay. When Jesus washed, he washed my sins away.* The chorus is the best part, a sea of black voices rising: *He taught me hoooow, to liiiiive—night and day—he washed my sins away.* The chorus washes over me. We are Unitarians but I still like the song.

Throughout Dad's campaign it seems like we go to every church in the Black Belt, sometimes three or four in a day. Sometimes we act up, embarrassing Mama, although Daddy laughs when she tells him what we did. Like the time one of us farted; it made a loud sound against the wood of the church pew while the minister was talking. All three of us giggled. We couldn't help it. Mama gave us that "stop it" look with her eyes. It was only partially effective. She doesn't have the power of Grandma, or Daddy. Her whippings are mild. Daddy learned from Grandma that whippings are supposed to hurt if a child is to mind because she "whipped him good" when he deserved it. When either of them is in charge, we usually behave. Poor Mama stops her whippings as soon as we start to cry, and crying is easy to fake. With her we can and often do run wild.

I watch Daddy give the same speech, and I never get tired of it. The point is to get people to go to the polls on Election Day and vote the straight NDPA ticket by marking their "X" under the party's ballot symbol, the eagle. The symbol for the George Wallace Democrats is a white rooster. Folks don't have to be able to read or write to know the difference. That rooster means everything bad that blacks have lived with in this state. Dad tells them that the "X" is the Greek letter chi, the symbol of Jesus Christ. They can mark their X and bear *His* cross in the voting booth. But they need a reason to believe that registering to vote and going to the polls will change things. Daddy tries to give it to them. My favorite part is when he quotes Frederick Douglass:

> *Those who profess to favor freedom and yet depreciate agitation are men who want crops without plowing up the ground, they want rain*

without thunder and lightning. They want the ocean without the awful roar of its many waters. This struggle may be a moral one, or it may be a physical one, and it may be both moral and physical, but it must be a struggle. Power concedes nothing without a demand. It never did and it never will. Find out just what any people will quietly submit to and you have found out the exact measure of injustice and wrong which will be imposed upon them.

Then Dad tells stories about people who won't do for themselves. A man has tight new shoes. They hurt his feet. He wants to take them off, he could take them off, but he chooses to look good even if it hurts. A woman sits down on a nail. She doesn't want to jump up and risk looking silly. Then Daddy's voice rises to a crescendo. "Well, if you won't get up then you deserve that nail in your tail!" The crowd begins to get into it. "Alright." "Speak, Doc Cashin." They like him and what he has to say. He is not one of them. He is from north Alabama, which may as well be Chicago. Yet they know he is with them and something is about to change.

I begin to express that optimism. My second-grade teacher, Mrs. Hovik, asks us to write stories in class. I write about family trips to "Muntgumery" and "Sante Lewis." I also write:

Why?

If I could vote I know who would get my vote. But why would he get my vote? Because he will give us better schools and jobs. He will give us better houses and bulidings [*sic*]. He will give us better bridges and highways. But I won't tell who he is but why. The end.

Mrs. Hovik is encouraging. She writes "Very Good Stories & Thoughts" on my paper. My activism is launched. I write President Richard Nixon to tell him how to solve the problems of "poulution": "I feel that we start it and have to end it." Mr. Nixon must not have liked my idea about sending all our country's garbage into space on a rocket because he never wrote me back. Or if he did it must have been a form letter because I don't remember it.

I'm not always happy about Dad's campaign. "August 11, 1970. Dear Diary, Daddy is running for Gov. I don't ever hardly get to talk to him." Still, I am his only daughter and I support him. "November 5, 1970. Dear Diary, The election is over. My father did not win but I'm still proud of him." Wallace won by a landslide.

Daddy chose to focus on the positive. On a shoestring budget, he convinced 125,000 people to vote for him and the NDPA, nearly 15 percent of the total. Over the years, in his retelling, this will be the election in which the NDPA "swept four counties" and his vote tally will rise to 175,000 votes. This is close enough to the truth. Dad and the NDPA did outpoll Wallace in four Black Belt counties, beginning a revolution that brought blacks back into the state legislature for the first time in nearly a century, although decades will pass before I understand the real meaning of this. Through the NDPA, my father fulfilled a promise he made to his father, aunts, and uncles about what he would do with his life.

In the meantime, when I am still seven, Election Day is hard to endure at school because everybody seems to think that my father lost badly. All eyes are on me, one of only two black kids in the class. The other black student, Jennifer, lives in one of the poor neighborhoods across California Street, far from the all-white (except for us) neighborhood where we live. She smells bad and has a lot of wax in her ears. The teacher sits her next to me. I bring Kleenex to school with Mama's perfume on it and sniff it every now and then to get over Jennifer's funk. I defend her, though, when the other kids look funny at the lunch she brings to school. Nasty-looking cold cuts and cheese with crackers instead of bread. In the last year or so I have begun to internalize my parents' creed of caring deeply, especially about black people who have a lot less than we do, and I act on it now at the lunch table. I answer my classmates' stares at Jennifer's food. "It's a sandwich!" I declare, telling them with my eyes to stop making her feel different. I don't even like Jennifer really. "She thinks she's so tough," I write in my diary. But like Mama and Daddy, I am supposed to fight injustice where I find it and I try to now. What I don't yet realize is where this family value comes from or why my parents live it so intensely. I also do not yet appreciate the lengths to which my father will go for something or someone he believes in, or the very high price he will pay for being an agitator.

The Lore

Aconfident man tends to talk about himself, and Daddy is more confident than most. His confidence was my good fortune, though. In talking he shared, and that was how I learned the family lore. He received his emotional inheritance at about the same age that I received mine. Dr. John Logan Cashin Jr., my father, was born in Huntsville, Alabama, in 1928—the second son of Dr. John Logan Cashin Sr. and Grace Brandon Cashin. Daddy was bestowed with the honor of junior even though he was the second son because John Sr. named his first son after his own father, Herschel. That given name would reverberate for four generations. The name John had an even longer etymology in the family.

I don't remember Daddy's father. My cousins, who came into this world a few years before me, would recall a sweet, jovial man they called Grandpoppy. When Daddy spoke of his father, he called him Dad. When he spoke of his father's father, he called him Grandpa Herschel. He never knew this man who became his personal hero because he died before my father was born. One wouldn't know that from listening to my father talk about him. Grandpa Herschel was three-dimensional in Daddy's memories because he heard so much about him from the elders. As an uncompromising "race man" who dedicated much of his adult life to uplifting his people, Herschel left a legacy that my father tried his best to live up to. He was determined, he always said, to "finish Grandpa Herschel's work," and Herschel became a mythic figure for me as well. In the one head shot we have of him, he stares back at us from a sepia-toned past. His white hair and mustache accentuate handsome features, neither Caucasian nor Negroid. His dress equals any dandy's. Dignity is his essence. He exudes strength, with slightly squinted eyes that convey a healthy skepticism of the world he inhabits.

Grandpa Herschel—Herschel Vivian Cashin—fathered seven children, four sons and three daughters. A son named Herschel Brewster died before his second birthday. The six remaining Cashin siblings—Vivian, Newlyn, Lillian, John, Pat, and James—all lived to see their hair turn silver, or, in the case of Aunt Vivi, an angelic white. Daddy's father, John Logan Sr., was the middle son and the twin brother of Aunt Pat.

The elders were all raised in Decatur, Alabama, and by the time my father was born, they were established in careers or marriages from Decatur to Chicago. They would reunite on Christmas and Thanksgiving, and it was at these annual family gatherings that my father absorbed the lore that shaped him indelibly. These stories, in turn, would be passed on to me. I heard fragments as a child. I heard more as a teenager. In my twenties, I stopped listening as I bore down and did my very best to escape the consequences of my father's activism. By then our family had experienced a great reversal of economic fortune, and the indignities of that reversal culminated in my father's depositing the Social Security and pension checks of his deceased mother for several years—a "protest" of the Social Security system, he said, for which he was imprisoned. At that point all of his political activism, from the legitimate to the questionable, seemed to carry too high a cost. I would visit my father at the minimum security prison on Maxwell Air Force Base in Montgomery, a "camp for wayward boys," he called it—the place where Nixon's attorney general John Mitchell and other former luminaries were sent when they fell from grace. And I blamed Daddy for everything. For violating the law when he had to know that, were he caught, his adjudicators were not likely to be merciful. For our impecuniosity and the loss of our wealth, family heirlooms, and our beautiful home. For the indignities he inflicted on Mama and for not being the father he should have been to his sons. He had always put his causes before his family, I thought. "Sometimes I become so angry with Dad that I can't stop the tears," I wrote in my diary in 1979 of our "family situation," which "could best be described as tragic," I surmised.

My brothers and I each found separate paths to survival, but the friendship we shared in youth did not survive. The lore was a complicated inheritance, and the children of each generation had to choose whether or not to accept the expectations and burdens of social duty that came with it. My father made that choice and, though I was ambivalent about the consequences, ultimately so did I. I suppressed my anger and channeled the fear that came with the shredding of my safety net into school, which led to scholarships and the ability to make my own way. I acquired degrees from Vanderbilt University, Oxford University, and Harvard Law School, and I traveled the world. I worked as a law clerk for Justice Thurgood Marshall at the Supreme Court. I worked for Bill Clinton and Al Gore at the White House. I tried returning home to Alabama in order to run for office and learned that my father's vision for me—becoming a U.S. senator—was his dream and not mine. I needed to find ways to contribute other than elective politics and became a law profes-sor. I write about race relations and inequality, and I advocate for the change I'd like to see.

As an adult I decided that the lore held the key to understanding my father's obsessions. In my thirty-seventh year, as Daddy journeyed into old-ness, I extracted a tape recorder from the detritus in my writing desk and began to interview him about the family and his life. For more than two decades, he had been threatening to write a book and I was tired of his inaction. I had heard most of his stories so many times I could repeat them verbatim. I was sick of some of them, sick of the egotism that animated them, sick of the excuses they offered for some of his choices. Still they were his, and mine. I needed to record them so that when he was no longer here I could listen to them and always be with the father I love desperately. I also needed to preserve my inheritance for myself and my children—a rich oral history that reminded me on tough days that I came from a people who per-severed and excelled in the face of anything America brought them.

Daddy explained his introduction to the lore this way:

> At the holiday gatherings Dad would always get to talkin' about the
> doggone family history. He'd bring out these things from his daddy's
> box—letters and so forth. It was an ebony box decorated with a silver
> inlay of an eagle on the top. Grandpa Herschel was like the secretary of

his family. There were letters in there that he wrote to his wife when he was a railway mail clerk. There were letters from his brothers. Dad used to read the letters aloud. He'd pull out the accounting book showing the monies that were sent to Grandpa Herschel's mother and the children in Philadelphia.

And that's where I got the story from generally, from my dad and Uncle Newlyn. Dad was proud of his father. He would talk about him all the time. The story was that Grandpa Herschel's father was a white Irishman named John Cashin. Grandpa's mother was a half-breed who had been in slavery. I guess I was supposed to hate the fact that there was slavery in the family. John Cashin and his mixed-race wife lived in an area in Georgia between the Ogeechee and Savannah rivers where interracial couples could live in reasonable peace. He saw his brothers hobnobbing with the secessionists and slaveholders and he sent his wife and children to Philadelphia because he felt surely that his brothers would sell them into slavery if something happened to him.

Whenever the subject of Grandpa Herschel came up, the conversation would always turn to politics. Grandpa Herschel went to a Quaker school in Philadelphia that is now Cheyney State. He became active in radical Republican politics and was sent to Alabama shortly after the Civil War. He went to Montgomery first. He apprenticed as a lawyer and was elected to the state legislature from Montgomery. He was the receiver of public lands for the Madison Territory, the area north of the Tennessee River. He ran the federal land bank out of an office in Huntsville, and he saw to it that black people got their due. He was the chief architect of Reconstruction in the state. As a result of his activities, in the 1890s we had three black congressmen in Alabama! Blacks had real political influence, about 43 percent of the vote. After the Alabama Constitution of 1901 our vote was less than 1 percent!

In attributing most of the political success of blacks in post-Emancipation Alabama to the grandfather he never met, my father carried a young boy's blind hero worship, formed during these family gatherings, into adulthood. In his mind, Grandpa Herschel was the person most responsible for Reconstruction in Alabama; hence he viewed the undoing of that epoch as a personal affront to his grandfather. When white supremacists grew tired of suppressing black voters in the state through violence, they held a constitutional convention to use law rather than terror to remove blacks from the voter rolls. The resulting Constitution of 1901 included poll taxes, literacy tests, and other subterfuges that achieved their intended purpose. Dad talked often of the impact of that document on black people and on the elders:

> *The old folks would tell us about how Grandpa Herschel had a fit over that Alabama Constitution of 1901. Uncle Newlyn is the one who named it the "Cashin Castration Constitution" because that law undid everything Grandpa worked for. As a no-nonsense doctor, Newlyn would use the castration metaphor. He said it in jest, but it affected Dad more than any of them. The first time I remember hearing that term was when I was about seven or eight years old at one of these holiday gatherings. I remember Dad gritting his teeth. It made him angry. He felt helpless. Over the years we had many conversations with Dad like that. Your Uncle Herschel and I knew our daddy and uncles and all the adults in the family were mad about it. We knew blacks had been disenfranchised. We made a pact with each other that we were going to finish Grandpa Herschel's work.*
>
> *Herschel was the one saying "we are going to do this." He was the eldest. If he made a decision, I supported him. We were extremely close. We were born only thirteen months apart. And we were taught you had to work together. In the schoolyard if you attacked one of us, you had to whip both of us, and that became very difficult. Whenever the subject of Grandpa Herschel would come up, we would reaffirm that we were going to do something about [blacks being disenfranchised] to carry through for Grandpa. We made a formal pledge to the family at one of the holiday gatherings.*
>
> *It was at Aunt Pat's house on Church Street in Decatur, the house that you now own. I was eleven and Herschel was twelve. We had gotten involved with the Boy Scouts. This was the first organization I was exposed to outside of the family. I started understanding the power of organizations.*

Herschel did the talking. We stood side by side. He repeated the historical knowledge that we had picked up from the adults' conversations and then said that we were going to finish the job. The entire family applauded and patted us on the back: "Yeah," "Atta boy." They were proud of us. They were playin' but we weren't playin'. We would talk about it at night before bed. We reaffirmed it in high school and college.

I remember when we were at Fisk [University] and we were pledging Omega. It was a ritual. Each pledgee was speaking about what he planned to do with his life for Omega Psi Phi. And Herschel unwrapped 'em all with his plans for the State of Alabama. And I remember these sons of bitches laughing like mad, saying, "Oh, this nigger don't know what the hell he's talking about, he's just full of steam." But they didn't know that they were messing with the real thing. 'Cause it wasn't just Herschel. It was me, too. He was serious, and if he was serious, I was serious.

So it was that family lore—truths and conjectures, anguish and loyalty—cemented the central commitment of my father's life. Here was the source of his passion. It motivated him to spend his fortune on his causes. In my twenties and thirties, I struggled with anger and resentment over some of his choices. That has given way, in my forties, to a simple need to know and understand the genetic origin of an altruism that has not diminished with time. Dad's fervor for black political emancipation, his role as an agitator, and my own social justice passions are rooted in the life and choices of his grandfather, Herschel V. Cashin.

Miscegenation

Every family has its lore, an oral history that is passed down and re-peated as truth. Our lore shaped not just Dad but all the descen-dants who heard it, although my father internalized it to such a degree that it became the central imperative of his life. Herschel V. Cashin was the first black lawyer in Alabama, Dad said. He was the chief architect of Reconstruction. He was the son of a John Cashin who emigrated from Ireland in the 1830s with two brothers. In Ireland they were the O'Cashins. Once in America, they dropped the "O." None of this, it turns out, is true. Like that childhood game where a whispered secret is repeated from ear to ear, only to be transmuted into something different, as one generation passed Grandpa Herschel's story on to the next, the lore became a semblance of the factual. Yet Herschel V. Cashin did live an inspired life that was deserving of the adulation of his children and grandchildren. He and his ancestors came alive for me in parallel universes of time that I entered through the documentary traces they left while here. Those documentary fragments told a story that jibed with the lore and introduced me to a great-grandfather who met and exceeded my expectations.

Grandpa Herschel's mother, a nameless mythic figure, was an extremely beautiful woman of color, part French, Cherokee, and African, according to Daddy. A black-Seminole-mestizo woman whom John Cashin bought from an illegal slave market and married, according to my brother John. A Creole beauty from New Orleans, said Daddy's first cousin, Betty-V, Uncle Jimmy's daughter.

I was the first person in the family to go digging for the truth. Grandpa Herschel's death certificate revealed his mother's name and other clues. Herschel Vivian Cashin, living at 509 Madison Street, resident of Decatur for forty years, died on March 25, 1924. His birthplace: Augusta, Georgia. His father's name: John Cashin. His mother's maiden name: Lucenda Boudre. Aunt Jack—my grandfather's older sister, Lillian Emmett Cashin—was the informant. She was a dutiful daughter to Herschel, a spinster who would become chair of the Fisk University English Department. Of all the people in the family, she must have known what she was talking about. Precision with language was her hallmark.

The United States Federal Census of 1860 shows a Lucinda "Cashen" living in Philadelphia, age forty, the head of a household that included a gaggle of minors named "Cashen" who were all born in Georgia, including one "Hershall." Whatever their status may have been in Georgia, in Philadelphia they were enumerated as "Free Inhabitants." According to this record, Lucinda was also born in Georgia, about 1819. She could neither read nor write. She was a seamstress. She and the children were listed as black; mulatto and white were the alternatives. Later in life, when Herschel returned south, he was identified on other censuses as a mulatto. Perhaps Lucinda told the census taker she was black. Or, because she lived among blacks, the census taker assumed she too was of African descent. Or perhaps Philadelphians, the census taker included, dispensed with gradations like mulatto. If she was a little bit colored, then she was black in his view.

Lucinda's will, found in the orderly archives of Philadelphia City Hall, was the only documentary evidence of her voice:

> Lucinda Bowdre, alias Cashin, lately of Augusta, Georgia, now residing at 615 Clifton St., Philadelphia.

> 1st: I direct all my just debts and funeral expenses to be paid as soon as practicable after my decease. I owe three hundred dollars to John P. King of Augusta, Georgia. If this sum is not paid to him during my lifetime I direct my executor to pay it after my decease.

> 2nd: All the residue and remainder of my estate, real, personal and mixed, of whatever kind and wherever situate I direct to be equally

divided between my seven children viz: Virginia Dorsey, wife of
William Dorsey, Emma Jackson, wife of James Jackson, John Thomas
Cashin, Laura Cashin, Eveline Cashin, Herschel and James Cashin,
their heirs and assigns, share and share alike . . .

. . . Her
Witness, 8 November 1865, Lucinda "X" Bowdre
Mark

The executor dutifully filed an inventory of Lucinda's estate. Cash in the
amount of $142.60, fifteen yards of carpet, one cookstove, one "chamber
do," one bedstead, feather bed, bedding, bureau, and washstand, for a total
value of $190.85. Her debts clearly exceeded her resources and yet she
undertook the formality. She was here. She lived. She bore seven children.
She got them through.

Her scrawled mark shows how weak she was at the end. It is more like a
cross than an X. She drew a strong vertical line and then a thin horizontal
scratch, her hand appearing to give way. She died twenty days later, on November 28, 1865, of "phthisis"—a disease causing the wasting of the body,
most commonly tuberculosis. No one seemed certain of her age. The death
certificate said forty-eight years, only the "eight" was heavily drawn over several initial attempts; it looks like she went from being forty-four, to forty-seven,
and then, a decisive, thickly scrawled conclusion that she was forty-eight. Either Lucinda didn't know her actual age when she spoke to the census taker
in 1860 or the people surrounding her at death didn't know it, or both.

The death certificate and the obituary printed in the *Philadelphia
Inquirer* suggest how she presented herself to the world. She was Lucinda
Cashin and a widow, although her will suggests she was never formally married. There are few other details. Her occupation at death: housekeeper.
Her place of birth: Augusta, Georgia. Through the obituary, her daughter
Virginia invited friends and family to attend her funeral on a Friday afternoon at No. 615 Clifton Street—a small house on a narrow cobblestoned
street in a working-class neighborhood that had become home to Lucinda's
brood. She must have been most resourceful and courageous, managing in
the 1860s as an illiterate woman of color to raise seven children.

Lucinda died owing $300 to one of the captains of finance and industry in Augusta, John P. King. Among other things, King, the president of the Georgia Railroad and Bank Company for thirty-seven years, financed the building of water and rail links that made Augusta's prosperity possible. He was a Democrat, lawyer, judge, U.S. senator, and industrialist who also participated in Reconstruction in Georgia by attending its state constitutional convention in 1865. The fact that Lucinda procured a personal loan from him suggests she enjoyed elevated social connections in Augusta, or maybe she knew King, who owned a textile mill, through her work as a seamstress. Her (common law) husband may also have been her entrée to a local titan.

Herschel's parents appear to have been quite intentional in forming a family together. Lucinda Bowdre of Augusta, Georgia, held herself out as the wife or widow of a man named Cashin. She gave all of her children his surname. And they all appear to have been born or raised in Augusta. Herschel's death certificate indicates as much for him. Virginia's marriage announcement in the *Philadelphia Public Ledger* identifies her as "Miss Virginia E. Cashin, of Augusta, Geo.—[Georgia papers please copy.]" Then there is Laura Francis Cashin's Freedman's Bank Record, a form completed when she opened an account on June 30, 1873. It reveals that she was born in Augusta to parents named John and Lucinda Cashin. Her "Complexion" is something other than the definitive "Brown" and "White" that appear on records of other depositors; but the single word used to denote her skin color, written with the flourishes of nineteenth-century script, is indecipherable.

Herschel's death certificate and the family lore also had it that his father's name was John. Additionally, the story was that John had two brothers, one named James. The name of the third brother varied. But there was always a James and he was always the villain—the slaveholder who might sell John's wife and children into slavery. John was painted in pastel tones. He was never thought of as a slave owner. He married the mixed-breed mother of his children and they lived together on a farm in relative peace until secessionist sentiments began to percolate. He sent his family north to protect them from the peculiar institution, and saw to it that his children were educated. Betty-V's version was slightly different.

Herschel's mother was the one who took the initiative. She and the children had to leave quickly, and they may have relied on the Underground Railroad.

There is only one John Cashin from nineteenth-century Augusta, Georgia, whose life and circumstances align with Lucinda's and the lore. Born circa 1811, by the time of his father's death in 1822, he was the second of three surviving sons. His older brother, who was named James, *was* both a farmer and a slaveholder. Inconveniently, this John Cashin, Herschel's apparent father, also owned slaves for a time. He inherited several from his father's considerable estate.

The father was also named John Cashin. John Cashin Sr., an educated Irishman born in 1780, arrived in Augusta circa 1804. He may have been part of a wave of Irish nationalists who came to Augusta in the wake of the Irish Rebellion of 1798. Herschel's death certificate stated that his father was born in Wexford County, Ireland—the county whose fighting rebels were the most successful in the 1798 uprising against the British. Aunt Jack may have had the right county but the wrong generation; Wexford may have been the birthplace of Herschel's grandfather, rather than his father.

According to Daddy, Grandpa Herschel's ebony box included a letter from a Fisk Jubilee singer confirming that she had found the grave site of his patrilineal ancestor in Ireland. Famously, the Jubilee singers traveled the world in the 1870s to raise money for their struggling new university for the formerly enslaved. Family legend has it that Herschel had given specific instructions to a young female singer on where she might find traces of his ancestors in Ireland. The letter, and the cherished box, have disappeared into the ether of the family's confusion about who had it when, or who may have absconded with it. Only vague outlines of its contents, embodied in the lore, remain. When Aunt Jack was alive, the box was safely in the care of her father, and then her brother. She was an erudite scholar, an institution within the institution of Fisk. She would have read the Fisk Jubilee singer's letter with interest. That letter might have been her source in identifying Wexford as the Irish Cashins' "father" county.

In early nineteenth-century Augusta, John Cashin Sr. prospered as both a merchant and an attorney. Operating a store on the south side of Broad

Street, the main commercial thoroughfare, he advertised occasionally in the *Augusta Chronicle* for the sale of his wares: tobacco, candles, liquors, groceries, and all manner of dry goods, including "Elegant Straw Bonnets, of the newest fashion." In the last ten years of his life, John Sr. spent much of his time in court helping propertied families settle their estates. He appears to have been an astute businessman and a mover among the city's most prosperous and genteel class. By the time of his death, he had accumulated about thirty slaves and more than 3,000 acres of land, including several lots bought directly from veterans of the War of 1812 who had drawn theirs from land lotteries in Illinois. John Sr. may also have been a veteran of the War of 1812. As an observant Catholic and a leader in the affairs of his church, he would not have been reluctant to oppose the same British who were repressing Catholics in his birth country. A tax district in Augusta, District 121, was known as Cashin's District, an honor generally reserved for captains of the local militia. After his death, his sons were each allotted a draw in the Cherokee Land Lottery of 1827 in Georgia, a privilege accorded male orphans of veterans.

John Sr. married an Irishwoman, Catherine Matilda, née Edwards, who was born in Dublin in 1783. They raised their children, three of whom died young, on a plantation in an area known as Sand Hills, just outside the city limits. Both John Sr. and Catherine were active in The Church of the Most Holy Trinity, later known as St. Patrick's, where John Jr. and his siblings were baptized. In 1816, John Sr. made a trip to Baltimore to help secure a priest for the church. His letter of introduction to the archbishop of Baltimore described him as "one of the most considerable and liberal contributors" to the building of Holy Trinity. An influx of hundreds of French Catholics, fresh from the uprisings in Haiti, caused a rift in the church over whether the sermons should be in French or English. No one seemed to care that the mass itself was conducted in Latin. In the heat of the controversy, Catherine and her daughter, Mary Ann, the only surviving Cashin sister, withdrew to the First Presbyterian Church. John Sr. stayed with Holy Trinity. Catherine must have been rather emphatic about her conversion. Her headstone leaves her with the epitaph: "A Native of Dublin . . . Resident of Augusta for nearly forty years . . . Last ten years of her life a Presbyterian."

In addition to Sand Hills, John Sr. owned several other plantations in eastern Georgia, including one known as the Swamp Plantation. His income clearly depended on slave labor. Among his slaves were field hands, skilled carpenters, house servants, and boat hands to unload the cargo as it arrived at the wharves along the Savannah River in Augusta. Through their father's dealings, the Cashin sons would be exposed to the worlds of both plantation and commerce. James chose to become a planter. John Jr. became a dry goods merchant.

~: ❧ :~

In antebellum Georgia, Lucinda would leave few tracks, perhaps because she was deprived of liberty, perhaps out of strategic necessity. This much is clear: Lucinda was not a freeholder, she owned no land. She does not appear in the registry of free persons of color, nor is she listed by name in any census prior to 1860. She is not among the lucky few slaves manumitted by the Georgia legislature upon application of their owners. She is an enigma. A colored woman who came into being in Augusta, circa 1819, with the same surname as another prominent Augustan attorney-merchant named Hays Bowdre. Bowdre, a slaveholder, was single most of his adult life. His only wife died shortly after their marriage in 1828. Lucinda does not appear on an estate inventory of slaves Bowdre owned at the time of his death in 1856. Still, there is tantalizing evidence of a possible connection.

Hays Bowdre had a brother named Thomas Jefferson Bowdre, and a sister named Lucinda Bowdre Foster. That Herschel's mother was not the first Lucinda Bowdre in Richmond County, Georgia, seems more than coincidence. Herschel's mother could have been the offspring of a Bowdre male and a free woman of color, or of a slave. That she may have been named after one of the white Bowdres invites speculation that her origins were tender rather than violent.

John Cashin Sr. and Hays Bowdre surely knew each other. A month before John Sr. died, one J. W. Beall advertised the sale of 400 acres of prime rural farmland outside the city limits. He directed interested buyers to apply to him, "or to John Cashin, or Hays Bowdre, in Augusta." Even

more intriguing, John Jr. easily could have come into contact with Hays
Bowdre's slaves. By 1830, Catherine Matilda, now a widow, and her son
John Jr. and her third and youngest surviving son, Oswell, had moved into
Ward Three of the city. They lived only a few blocks from Hays Bowdre.
While Catherine Matilda and Bowdre both hired out their slaves, enabling
them to live elsewhere, in the 1830 census their slaves are enumerated on
the same page. This proximity, maybe signifying nothing, teases the imag-
ination. The only identity this census conferred on slaves was an age, a gender, and a master's name. One of Bowdre's slaves was a girl between the
ages of ten and twenty-four. It is possible, but not proven, that this slave
girl was Lucinda. In 1830, she would have been as young as eleven or as
mature as seventeen. John Jr. would have been nineteen. Could two
teenagers on opposite sides of a frequently violated color line have found
love, or something else, in 1830, or thereafter? Lucinda's first child, Virginia, was born in 1837.

Statistically, it is more probable that Lucinda was enslaved rather than
free. Enslaved mulattoes greatly outnumbered free ones in Augusta and the
Deep South. It is also conceivable that Lucinda was never a slave. Under a
legal regime created largely by and for the elite planter class, colored children assumed the status of their mother. If Lucinda were the child of a
Bowdre and his free colored paramour, it would not have been unusual for
such a household to escape the census takers.

Whomever her progenitor, he did not, or could not, favor Lucinda
with an education. A surfeit of legal restrictions applied to both slaves
and free persons of color. State law barred them from travel without a
pass, learning to read or write, owning property, or working for a printing press. However, when it came to legal constraints designed to keep
them subordinated, black Augustans were an irreverent crowd. Among
free blacks and many slaves, the bewildering array of restrictions passed
by the Augusta City Council was usually honored by breach. The code
of the plantation did not take root in Augusta primarily because it was
more a city of merchants than farmers, although it boasted an elite cadre
of merchant-planters.

Founded in 1737 at the fall line of the Savannah River by the English
general James Oglethorpe, the city was a bulwark against the Spanish and

French. It also abutted Cherokee and Creek Indian territory and began as a place of mostly friendly relations with these tribes. Between the Revolutionary and Civil Wars, Augusta became a manufacturing center, one of a few in the south, for textiles, gunpowder, and paper. Linked by rail and river to the Mississippi Valley, the city was also a gateway to trade with Europe. With its thriving commerce, antebellum Augusta was a place to make money, and black Augustans, free and slave alike, were more intent on economic gain than complying with inane ordinances. Among other things, local laws levied heavy annual taxes on free blacks; restricted their movement, the type of work they could do, and their ability to learn; and barred them from using horses or buggies, keeping a light on after 10:00 PM, walking with a cane unless infirm, smoking a pipe or cigar in public, or having unsanctioned balls, fairs, or prayer meetings.

Because most such ordinances were ignored, in Augusta there was not much distinction between free persons of color and the many slaves who were hired out by their masters, or themselves, to work in the city. Lucinda may have been one of the free persons of color who simply disregarded a local law, adopted in 1818, that required free blacks to register with the city clerk. In 1852, only 243 free blacks were enumerated in Augusta—2 percent of a population that included about 7,800 whites and 6,000 slaves. Like virtually all of the free colored women who *were* enumerated, Lucinda's line of work concerned clothing. These ladies would eke out an income as seamstresses, laundresses, or weavers. William H. Pritchard, who conducted the 1852 census for the City of Augusta, expressed his frustration to the mayor and City Council over the challenge of finding the colored folks:

> There are so many superannuated—so many as free as the laws will allow—so many who are evading the ordinances regulating negroes living out separate and apart to themselves—so many who indirectly hire their own time—so many whose owners are in other counties, that there are many difficulties in the way of counting or enumerating them. . . . [A] number of negroes, free as well as slave, live or rent kitchens or rooms in kitchens, attached to houses occupied by white families . . . such colored persons are liable to be unnoticed and unenumerated . . .

I have had to depend upon Free Negroes themselves for their returns. Many of them have no Guardians. A large number of the Free
Blacks move so often, from house to house, from ward to ward, and
from suburb to city, that it is difficult to find all of them. Many are exceedingly reluctant to tell the full number of their families, fearful of
being caught in some "Tax Trap." Although the number and names
of 243 have been obtained, . . . I feel satisfied, that there are, at least
four hundred negroes of the half-free, & fully free—& the superan-
nuated slaves—and the very young—and the law evading class of
whom I have received no returns. . . . [T]he number of negroes, including the free negroes, who reside out to themselves, and appear, in
most cases to operate on their own account, is not less than 1200 . . .

～∗～

In 1834, John Jr. received his portion of his father's estate, including
"The Mill plantation on Spirit Creek," located in Burke and Richmond
Counties, a tract of land in Wilkinson County, Georgia, several tracts in
Hancock County, Illinois, "Lot #3 on south side of Broad Street,
Augusta," four shares in the Georgia State Bank of Augusta, certain
slaves, shares in the Savannah-Augusta Steamship Company, and sums of
money. The Cashin family store on Broad Street had at least two stories.
Goods were sold on the ground level and there were living quarters on
the second floor. Advertisements in the local *Chronicle & Gazette* imply
that John Jr. lived in these quarters.

John Jr.'s mother, Catherine Matilda, died in 1838, one year after Lucinda's
first child was born. If she knew about her probable mulatto grandchild, one
suspects she would not have been pleased. She was, after all, a slave-owning
woman who had shown little tolerance for French-speaking Catholics.

John Jr. tried his hand at several things, including a year studying medicine
and serving as the secretary and treasurer of the Central & Western Wharf
Company, in which his mother owned shares. He was elected to the "Division No. 3" committee of the Augusta Benevolent Society in 1840. Although
he tried to make his way in business, he does not appear to have been nearly
as successful as his father. Most of his property wealth appears to have come

from his participation in the Cherokee Land Lottery and from his inheritance. In 1841, he forfeited 130 acres of his land in a sheriff's sale to pay a judgment debt against him. The same year, inexplicably, the family store on Broad Street was sold, and an auctioneer arranged for the sale of all remaining merchandise. By 1849, the same year he received $5,000 from his mother's estate, John Jr. announced to the Augusta public that he was open for business as a "General Commission Merchant." Like his father before him, he began to place notices of goods he had for sale.

Periodically John Jr. left Augusta and possibly the entire state. In the 1840 and 1850 censuses, he is recorded as a single person without family. In 1840, he owns a few slaves, male and female. In 1850, he owns none. By 1852, he appears in the Augusta city census conducted by Mr. Pritchard as a single man owning nine male slaves. These urban-dwelling bondmen would have provided labor for John Jr.'s merchant business. There is no record of him having married Lucinda or anyone else. Nor is there any record of him having purchased or inherited Lucinda. His connection to her is purely circumstantial, but compelling.

Although John Jr. was never enumerated as living with a family, his numerous landholdings offered ample opportunity for him to raise a family outside the scrutiny of official Augusta. The family lore maintained that Herschel's father saw to it that his family was taken to Philadelphia in the 1850s. John Jr.'s regular advertisements for sale of goods in Augusta stopped between 1856 and 1858.

The year 1856 seems pivotal. John received the remainder of his inheritance from his mother's estate that year, and he had sold a plantation the year before. Lucinda's last child was born in 1856, in Georgia. Meanwhile Hays Bowdre died in 1856. If there was a filial connection, any support that came with it now ceased and Lucinda was not mentioned in his will. Apparently, 1856 was also the year Lucinda left Augusta. On July 15, the Augusta post office advertised in the *Daily Chronicle & Sentinel* that there was an undelivered letter for "Bowdre, Lucinda." The name appears in a long alphabetical list of other Augustans who had not collected their mail. Two words buried in a newspaper are the only concrete evocation of her life in Augusta. That she received mail in her own name suggests she was among the free, or freely moving in the city. In October, a similar "dead-letter" advertisement appeared for "Cashin, John," indicating that both of them were now away from the city at about the same time.

According to the lore, Herschel's father died before the Civil War. John Jr. died between March 1859, when he applied to administer the estate of an intestate who apparently owed him money, and May 1860, when Louis Delaigle, a wealthy Augustan and longtime friend of the Cashins, applied to administer John Jr.'s own estate. At death, all John Jr. owned was some basic household furnishings worth less than $300. Leaving no will, nor any wealth, John Jr. must have spent, or arranged for the distribution of, the substantial resources he received only a few years earlier. Aid from John may explain how Lucinda, an illiterate colored seamstress in pre–Civil War Georgia, moved her large family to Philadelphia, established a home, and provided for them.

The names of Lucinda's children and their dates of birth also suggest that John Jr. and Lucinda formed a family together. Her first son was named John, conceivably after John Jr., and her youngest was named James, possibly after John Jr.'s brother. One of her daughters, Catherine Eveline, who would be called Evelina, could have been named after John's mother, Catherine Matilda. The tax records also indicate that John Jr. left Richmond County between 1842 and 1845. Lucinda did not bear any children during this period. Above all, no other John Cashin in Augusta appears eligible to have fathered Lucinda's children, who were born between 1837 and 1856.

Then there is the DNA evidence. Fortunately, the Y chromosome doesn't change much over ten generations. A father begets a son, who in turn begets a son, and if a male line continues long enough, the DNA of a twenty-first-century Cashin could help me determine whether John Cashin Jr. of antebellum Augusta, Georgia, was my progenitor. Fortuitously, John Jr.'s younger brother Oswell did produce male offspring for four generations. Oswell's great-great-grandson didn't know me when I wrote to him, gingerly asking whether he might be willing to place a cotton swab in his cheek and risk establishing relations with a line of black Cashins. If his Y chromosome matched my father's, then it would be a virtual certainty that John Cashin Sr.

was our common ancestor. My would-be Irish American relation answered my letter with a telephone call on St. Patrick's Day, 2006, ironically enough. He was a polite South Carolinian who exuded a Southernness that was familiar to me. As an Alabamian, I could relate to him in the same way that most black and white Southerners have become comfortable with differences that are bridged by frequent proximity.

He had heard some things from his parents and grandparents about the Augusta Cashins and was open to learning more. I had sent him a memo summarizing the genealogical research I had unearthed. He knew that I was asking him to volunteer to be identified with nineteenth-century slaveholders. That history did not burden our conversation or the communications I had with several other white Cashins I had contacted. One happily told me, "I hope I am related to you." Another claimed me, ending each of her e-mails with "Cousin Joan."

The DNA evidence was also tantalizing, if not definitive. Forty-one out of forty-three of the Y chromosome markers of Daddy and Oswell's descendant were identical. The two other markers were nearly identical. This, coupled with the circumstantial genealogical and historical evidence, eliminated any doubt in my mind. I had found Grandpa Herschel's father and confirmed the outlines of the lore.

I had also made the disturbing discovery that my great-great-grandfather actively participated in the peculiar institution. It was troubling to think that slavery may have been the source of the colored Cashins' relative advantages, that is, the ability to leave the South and pursue a Northern education. Certainly slavery contributed to John Jr.'s inheritance. If he shared it with his children, he would have been similar to other white slaveholding fathers who expanded the small class of free mulatto elites when they chose to provide for their colored offspring. I took solace in the fact that, later in life, Grandpa Herschel chose to identify with and aid Negroes who were oppressed, rather than elevated, by slavery.

Herschel's engagement with politics may have had antecedents in that of his father and uncles. All three of the white Cashin sons were active in the Whig Party, which included a mostly Northern anti-slavery faction. Southern Whigs tended to be adherents of states' rights and were attracted to the party's philosophy of congressional supremacy over the executive branch. The Cashin brothers may also have been pragmatists who supported the Whig Party's advocacy of economic modernization, especially its rigorous program for "internal improvements." As legacies of Augusta's merchant class, the Cashin sons would have supported investments in railroads, bridges, and water transportation—investments that would enable Augusta to maintain and improve its position as a portal to the Deep South.

In July 1840, John and James were appointed as delegates to the state Whig Party Convention. Oswell would become an overseer of the polls for his district in Augusta. In January 1843, John and Oswell protested the state legislature's decision to change the date of Augusta's elections, arguing that those "Yankees" had disenfranchised a large sector of the city's electorate. By 1845, James was the secretary of the Whig Party of Richmond County and lost a bid to become the county receiver of tax returns. Oswell was more successful as a politician. He became the chief telegraph operator for the new Washington and New Orleans Telegraph Company in 1848. In 1852 and again in 1854, he was elected clerk of the superior and inferior court for Richmond County. By September 1853, James had become a committeeman of the Conservative Party of Richmond County. With the Whig Party being torn asunder by the question of expansion of slavery into the new territories, James, like other Southern Whigs, looked elsewhere for a political home.

Herschel Vivian Cashin was born during this period of political upheaval. According to his death certificate, his date of birth was February 10, 1854. His name may suggest something about the mindset of his father, or his mother. It was not a common moniker. The governor of Georgia between 1853 and 1857 was Herschel Vespasian Johnson, a Democrat who served briefly as a U.S. senator in the late 1840s, when he was appointed to fill a vacancy. Before then Johnson had practiced law in Jefferson County, adjacent to Richmond County. Other than this brief geographic convergence, there is no reason to think that John or Lucinda knew Herschel V. Johnson. In 1850, Johnson was a pro-slavery politician with strong secessionist leanings. While serving as governor he switched positions and became a strong unionist. Johnson's supporters claimed that he merely envisioned that slavery would be preserved along with the Union. Whatever Johnson's reasons, his change in political posture on the question of secession was of a piece with a growing sentiment throughout the country that slavery was a marked institution. John and Lucinda may have liked the resonance of "Herschel V." for a son. Or they may have hoped that Herschel V. Johnson's reversal was a harbinger of better possibilities for their unusual family.

They had good reason to be clandestine in their relations. Mulattoes in the antebellum Deep South existed in a land of blackness. The great plantations were at the center of the Southern economy; hence, so was slavery. Even in the merchant city of Augusta, free mulattoes were a tiny minority. They were tolerated to a great degree before 1850 but were viewed as a growing threat as secessionist feelings hardened. Had she been a free mulatto who "married" a scion of a prominent white Augusta family, Lucinda would have been a rare exception to the prevailing norm of black and mulatto slavery. Granted, Augusta had some of the cosmopolitan flavor of its mother city to the north, Charleston, South Carolina, where free mulattoes outnumbered enslaved ones by two to one. But Lucinda's family would not have gone unnoticed. There were precious few examples of formally sanctioned, interracial marriages in the city. In the late eighteenth century, some French refugees from Haiti, forced out by native rebellions, arrived in Augusta with their mixed-blood wives and children, creating a discombobulating but miniscule class of wealthy mulattoes who spoke French. The mid-nineteenth century was a much less hospitable era for such dangerous liaisons. Race mixing in the context of slavery was accepted, although many a white Southern woman looked askance at the light-skinned children turning up among her husband's slaves. The reasonable tolerance for miscegenation among free people in the first half of the nineteenth century gave way with the issue of secession. A desire for the clarity of a sharp distinction between master and slave, with no intermediate people muddying the hierarchy, was the impetus for an increasingly stringent series of legal prohibitions.

In 1852, the Georgia Assembly adopted a law rendering it a crime punishable by fine or incarceration, or both, for any "white man, and woman of color, of any shade of complexion whatever, free or slave, who shall live together in a state of adultery or fornication." In 1859 and 1860, in the aftermath of John Brown's raid, extremists in the Georgia legislature debated whether to support a bill that would expel or enslave all free Negroes in the state. Although interracial marriage was not banned in Georgia until 1861, by the 1850s such marriages faced considerable social opprobrium, even in the relatively cosmopolitan atmosphere of Augusta. And the state and local laws regulating free mulattoes became increasingly severe. Ultimately, the state legislature enacted a law that permitted city recorders to sell free blacks into slavery on mere suspicion of misconduct.

In the early 1850s, John and Lucinda would have sensed these changing winds. A widely read Swedish writer, Fredrika Bremer, wrote of a "slave mart" she visited in Augusta circa 1851. It was filled with light-skinned mulatto girls ranging in age from twelve to twenty, "some of them very pretty," and some indistinguishable from whites in their appearance. If the family lore was true, John would not have been unfounded in his fear that brother James, or someone else, might sell his beautiful daughters into slavery. According to Bremer, a fair, handsome girl fetched $1,500 at the slave mart at a time when a prime slave hand sold for $1,000. In an environment of increasing hostility to free mulattoes, those who could afford to move to the North did. Lucinda and her brood were part of the exodus.

CHAPTER FOUR

Philadelphia

Whether Lucinda arrived in Philadelphia circa 1856 by her own pluck or her husband's sponsorship, it was a place of destiny for young Herschel. Boasting the largest population of blacks of any Northern city, in the mid- and late nineteenth century, Philadelphia was a beacon of Afro-American urbanity. In this epoch it was also the nation's center of black intellectual and institutional life. And the Cashin clan would join one of the city's wealthiest and socially influential black families when Herschel's sister Virginia married William Henry Dorsey in February 1859.

Virginia's new father-in-law, Thomas Joshua Dorsey, rose from fugitive slave—one of a steady stream that came to the Quaker City via the Underground Railroad—to owner of one of the leading catering businesses in the city. The elder Dorsey was at the very top of a guild of black caterers who evolved from house servants, butlers, and cooks to masters of the culinary arts that dominated the social world of Philadelphia through their food. He made a fortune sufficient to live in a style commensurate with the upper classes. His home at 1231 Locust Street was a grand, multistory manor, attended by servants.

Dorsey took great pleasure in entertaining notable activists, including his good friend Frederick Douglass and John Brown, who lodged at the Locust residence in June 1859, not long before proceeding to Harper's Ferry. Most likely, Dorsey was the first exemplar of a successful race man whom Herschel would be exposed to, and emulate. The old man never forgot the horrors of slavery, and this made him a fierce ally of old-time abolitionists like Charles Sumner and William Lloyd Garrison. W.E.B. DuBois described Thomas Dorsey as "the most unique character," a man with "the sway of an imperial dictator" who once refused to serve a Democrat because "'he could not wait on a party of persons who were disloyal to the government, and Lincoln'—pointing to the picture in his reception rooms—'was the government.'"

Virginia's mother-in-law, Mrs. Thomas Dorsey—Louise Tobias, a free native of Pennsylvania—had a similar independent streak. Writing in his final autobiography, Frederick Douglass credited her as the lone person among his colored friends willing to risk the affront of being turned away at the White House on the occasion of President Abraham Lincoln's inauguration in 1865. Exhibiting the courage and dignity of pioneers demanding respect for an entire race, Douglass and Mrs. Dorsey succeeded in overcoming the hostility of obstructionist police guards to be received with warm delight by the president amid a sea of elegantly dressed visitors in the East Room. No doubt this story reverberated throughout the Dorsey and Cashin families, an early example of breaking down an unjust racial barrier—the idea that coloreds were not to be received by a president—simply by declaring through one's actions that the prohibition no longer exists.

Herschel's new brother-in-law, William Dorsey, was a race man like his father, Thomas, albeit one of a different sort. William worked briefly as a waiter, most likely in his father's business, and as a personal messenger to the law-and-order mayor, William Stokely. He worked harder at his avocations. Throughout William Dorsey's adult life, he claimed "artist" as his primary occupation. Yet he became famous in his self-appointed role as archivist of the doings of colored people. With the benefit of some inherited income, his modest earnings as a painter, and a wife who worked, he was able to spend his prime years immersed in his many intellectual interests, despite having six children of his own to raise. Painting and collecting were his passions. In his lifetime he created 388 scrapbooks and 914 biographical files, much of which concerned the life and accomplishments of the Negro. Through his collecting, Dorsey created a comprehensive portrait of the era—a labor of love that was memorialized in 1991 with the publication of the book *William Dorsey's Philadelphia & Ours*.

It is unclear how William and Virginia met. *Dorsey's Philadelphia* waxes eloquent about young William undertaking "a personally dangerous journey to the slave state of Georgia to marry Virginia Cashin" and bring her back north. Their marriage notice in the *Philadelphia Public Ledger* conflicts with this account as it implies that the nuptials took place in the city. Whatever its origin, this union would prove formative for Herschel. It placed him within the orbit of some of the nation's leading Afro-American intellectuals and activists as he was transitioning from boy to man.

In the early years of their marriage, William and Virginia lived with the Cashin clan, or it might be more correct to say that the Cashins lived with them. The 1860 census identified Lucinda as the "head of household," likely because she was the eldest, but it is more probable that William Dorsey played that role. William inherited the refinements of his father, yet he was decidedly introverted by comparison. A big man of sober bearing with the red complexion and high cheeks of a Native American, he was a loner preternaturally suited to the solitary pursuits of painting and collecting. He would be "the man of the house" as Herschel was growing up and Herschel would develop a similarly serious, dignified bearing and fascination with the accomplishments of his people.

The Dorsey-Cashin household of ten people started out at 1213 Federal Street, on the southern outskirts of the city. The neighborhoods below South Street, which had been populated by waves of Irish immigrants a generation before, were becoming the province of many blacks, fugitive slave and free, who were pouring into the city in search of opportunity. Industrial jobs were reserved mainly for European immigrants. Blacks struggled to make their way, often undertaking the most menial labor. As in Augusta, Lucinda continued to work as a seamstress, apparently out of the home, as was the practice of many colored women in the city, and now Virginia also took up the trade of dressmaking. William worked as a waiter. Together the three of them would provide for a house full of minors.

By 1864, they moved closer to the town center, to 615 Clifton Street, located just below South Street and near the heart of the black community. To this day, the street is lined with the small, three-story row houses built by the first wave of Irish immigrants. To my amazement, the house my great-great-grandmother lived in is still standing. It looked timeless on the day I visited it, and improbably small for her extended family. The only hint that Lucinda might have been there was a well-worn marble front step. I sat down on it and ran my hand over its smooth concave surface, metaphorically touching her and hopefully receiving some of her power. There was a distinct possibility that it was the original front step, according to a neighbor who happened to be a local historian. Between the houses was a narrow lane just wide enough for horse-drawn carts. It was laid with unique cobblestones known as "Belgian block"; the ballast components that had steadied the ships that brought huddled masses from Europe were put to sensible use.

The Irish called the houses "Trinities" because they consisted of three open rooms, one to a floor. Each floor was connected by a ladder or narrow spiral staircase. The ground floor featured a fireplace, a kitchen toward the front, and a living area toward the back. Here families would spend their days, as it was the only level heated by a fire. They would ascend to higher floors only to go to bed. Built to accommodate poor workers, the Trinities were made with the mismatched handmade brick available at the time, and because taxes were based on the width of the house, they were only 12 $^1/_2$ feet wide, but 31 feet long. A privy shared by several households was in the alley behind the row houses, where any animals or carts were also kept. Before modern methods and concerns with sanitation prevailed, the kitchens had been in the alley, competing with the stench of the privy and animals. When they weren't negotiating these challenges, doing whatever was necessary to keep the many young mouths fed, Lucinda and Virginia would have spent most of their time before the fire, sewing.

William Dorsey appears to have cultivated his interest in art while a student at the Institute for Colored Youth (ICY), a Quaker institution that evolved from a trade school to a provider of a free classical education for talented Negro children. The institute, now Cheyney University of Pennsylvania, was founded in 1837 with $10,000 bequeathed from the estate of Richard Humphreys, a successful white Quaker philanthropist who emigrated from the British Virgin Islands. After a race riot in 1829, one of several conflagrations that erupted in the city in the nineteenth century, Humphreys empathized with the plight of blacks who were competing with an immigrant influx to find work. In his will he charged thirteen fellow Quakers to design an institution to instruct descendants of the African race in academics, mechanic arts, trades, and agriculture, "in order to prepare and fit and qualify them to act as teachers." Humphreys' bequest became Herschel's good fortune, affording him both an education and an instinct for social contribution that, like his given name, would also reverberate for generations.

In 1864, Herschel and his sister Evelina entered the institute's Preparatory Department—a precursor to the school's rigorous high school curriculum. The Dorsey family must have had some influence. William was a graduate and Mary Louise Dorsey, his younger sister, was also enrolled in the preliminary program. The institute operated, physically and metaphorically, at the vortex of Philadelphia's black community. Lombard Street, east of Broad, was the center. At the corner of Seventh and Lombard, the institute was a stone's throw from "Mother Bethel," founded in 1794 as the first black church in the city and the progenitor of the nation's first black denomination, African Methodist Episcopal. The *Christian Recorder* newspaper, an abolitionist organ of the AME church, was published a few blocks away.

The Institute for Colored Youth was a source of great race pride for the community. Its annual oral examinations in Latin, Greek, mathematics, and other disciplines were open to the public and avidly covered by the *Christian Recorder*. The school also sought to edify the black masses in its midst. It threw open the doors of its library to the colored public and expressed gratification in its 1864 annual report that "[t]hree thousand nine hundred and thirty-five volumes" were loaned that school year. It also offered a series of public lectures delivered by eminent colored men. Frederick Douglass was the leading light among eight speakers who appeared in 1863–1864. His topic, "The Mission of the War," ultimately accommodated even the pacifist Quakers. He argued that "the mission of the war was the liberation of the slaves as well as the salvation of the Union" and reproached the North "that the Union cause would never prosper until the war assumed an anti-slavery attitude and the Negro was enlisted on the side of the Union."

By the time Herschel and Evelina enrolled, the institute had reformed its mission to focus exclusively on producing learned Negro graduates, themselves trained by black teachers, who would become teachers to the race.

Especially after the Civil War, ICY students were encouraged, even before graduating, to move south to fill the great need for instructors. In the exhilarating days following the close of the war and Emancipation, the institute sent more teachers to the South than any school in the nation. The institute was also singular in that it was the only school in the city effectively run by blacks. Believing sincerely in its mission, the Quaker board allowed Afro-Americans to serve as principal, heads of departments, and teachers. With job opportunities scarce for educated blacks, the institute was able to hire the most erudite of men and women to fill these roles.

The principal, Professor E. D. Bassett, was one of the best-known black scholars in the nation. The head of the boys' department, Octavius Valentine Catto, was a man of outsized talents and ambitions for his people. Catto, the valedictorian of the institute's class of 1858, was promptly hired as a teacher upon graduation. It is quite probable that Herschel's passion for Republican politics and the education and social uplift of Afro-Americans was incubated during his five years under Catto's wing.

Octavius Catto was a dynamic example, a handsome bachelor possessed of athletic prowess, social conscience, and oratorical skill. When tapped by the institute to deliver a commencement address in May 1864—"Our Alma Mater," delivered in the classical style—Catto expounded a personal philosophy that he must have inculcated in his young charges: "It is the duty of every man, to the extent of his interest and means to provide for the immediate improvement of the four or five millions of ignorant and previously dependent laborers who will be thrown upon society by the reorganization of the Union." Catto taught English literature, higher mathematics, and classical languages and had a habit of founding and leading black organizations in Philadelphia. He created the Banneker Literary Institute, the Union League Association, and the Pythian Baseball Club. As captain, player-coach, and mean shortstop for the Pythians, Catto led them to become the first recorded all-black team in the country to play and beat an all-white club—the City Items.

Catto would also be the first civil rights giant Herschel would know personally. He was a voracious intellectual who constantly strove to improve the Negro's lot and was not above involving the institute in his causes. He once marched a group of ICY graduates to the state capital in Harrisburg in a vain attempt to break the logjam against black enlistment in the Union army. He worked closely with Frederick Douglass to recruit young black soldiers and was the main force behind the eleven colored regiments from the region that were raised, trained, and ultimately sent to the battlefront. He became increasingly enamored of political agitation and was the moving force behind the Equal Rights League. Like its civil rights successors in the South a century later, the league would succeed in protesting segregation of Philadelphia's streetcars and in advocating for black voting rights. Catto and other league militants orchestrated a nonviolent campaign in which men and women blocked streetcars with their bodies and filled them up with Christian ministers, sick children, pregnant women, and wounded war veterans. When police and conductors ejected these sympathetic riders from the cars, the ensuing publicity converted many hearts to their cause. It took a successful court battle in 1867 to clinch victory.

In 1866, the Institute for Colored Youth moved to a beautiful, three-story building on Shippen Street, later known as Bainbridge, west of Ninth. These commodious environs offered divided space for the male and female departments, a reading room and lyceum, and a science laboratory. The audience for the commencement exercises that year swelled to 3,000, for a class with only four graduates. With an average annual attendance of about 100 for all grades, the lucky few who passed through the halls of the ICY would necessarily be steeped in a sense of social responsibility.

Herschel and Evelina were apparently affected. They were the only Cashin siblings to attend the institute and the only ones lured south by Reconstruction. Among Lucinda's seven offspring, ultimately only Herschel would make the South his permanent home. He left the institute before graduating in 1869—the same year Catto was passed over as principal in favor of Fanny Jackson, a formidable Oberlin College graduate who had been his counterpart in the girls' department. Jackson, who later married Levi Coppin, the minister at Bethel AME church, would lead the institute for more than three decades.

It may have been an act of loyalty for Herschel to withdraw from the school. More likely, he answered the siren call of opportunity and contribution that the

Reconstruction South now offered educated men and women of color. Ironically, with the adoption of Reconstruction constitutions throughout the states of the former Confederacy, blacks in the South had greater voting rights than those in Philadelphia, who would await the final ratification of the Fifteenth Amendment in 1870. And there were many more possibilities in the Reconstruction states for the most ambitious and skilled Afro-Americans. The toppling of the Confederacy had created a power void, and many a colored elite rushed to fill it.

Black Philadelphians would lose their chief civil rights advocate in 1871. On the day of the first city election in which black men exercised their new voting rights, Octavius Catto was shot in the back by a Democratic Party operative, as Irish immigrant gangs, rioting to prevent a Republican takeover of city government, raged against black voters. By then Herschel was sowing the seeds of a career in radical Republican politics.

CHAPTER FIVE

Reconstruction

Reconstruction presented choices both geographic and psychic. It marked the beginning of a diaspora for Herschel and his siblings. Virginia, the oldest, remained in Philadelphia. After Lucinda died, she and husband William continued to reside at Clifton Street for a year before moving, appropriately, to Locust Street, near the elder Dorseys and the family catering business. They cared for the younger Cashins until each was ready to enter the world and raised six children of their own. When their thirty-year marriage collapsed in 1890, Virginia moved into her own abode, continued to work as a dressmaker, and, euphemistically, claimed to be a widow for the remainder of her days.

John, the oldest Cashin son, moved west to become a prospector. In 1880 he was living in the town of Rico in Ouray County, Colorado. Rico, Spanish for rich, was the locus of a mining rush that began in 1878. The fabled ebony box included correspondence between Herschel and John about his fortunes, or misfortunes, in silver mining.

Emma, the second-oldest daughter, who married a man named James Jackson before Lucinda died, must have met an early death. Laura Francis did not list her as a sibling in her Freedman's Bank application in 1873.

Laura Francis, the third daughter, worked at an oyster bar cum saloon in Westchester County, New York, before settling down at the ripe age of twenty-six. She married a mulatto barber named John D. Jackson on April 18, 1877, in Philadelphia and they began their life together in Salem, New Jersey, the groom's hometown. Marrying a barber was a solid choice, as this trade afforded independent means to an enterprising colored man and conferred on Laura Francis the relative luxury of "keeping house," as the 1880 census characterized her occupation.

By 1870, Evelina, the youngest girl, had returned to Georgia; she lived in Savannah with her husband, Charles Henry Taylor, a mulatto physician from the West Indies. By 1880, she had moved to New York and was married to Eugene Williams, a mulatto railroad conductor. In both men she found providers who enabled her to be a homemaker.

James, the youngest, and Herschel's closest sibling both in age and affinity, had moved from Philadelphia to New York City by 1880; he lived with Evelina and Eugene and plied his trade as a bartender.

Although Herschel's precise path is unclear, after he concluded his studies at the Institute for Colored Youth, he moved back to Georgia, where he must have had an entrée to work. The 1870 census finds him living in an Augusta boarding house, age eighteen, working as a bookkeeper in a store. Like everyone else in the house, he is listed as a mulatto. Emma Hall is the proprietor of this establishment. With the exception of Herschel and a family of four headed by a fish peddler, Miss Emma's boarders were mostly single men working as barbers. Despite his job as a bookkeeper, Herschel did not pay any taxes that year, suggesting that his stay in Augusta was brief. A few years later he was living in Alabama.

And here again, the family lore varies, depending on the narrator. Per Dad, Herschel was sent to Alabama by the Quakers. Per my brother, John, he fled the hostilities of his father's brothers, jumping the first train out of state, which happened to be headed due west to Alabama. Somehow I grew up believing that Grandpa Herschel came to Alabama to work for the Freedman's Bureau.

However Herschel made his way to the heart of Dixie, his psychic passage is clear. The so-called mulatto elite began to disappear as a separate class apart from the black masses in the decades after Emancipation and, unlike at least one of his siblings, Herschel became thoroughly black. Reconstruction was most radical in the Deep South, and it was there that the bonds between educated mulattoes and blacks were most strongly formed. Herschel chose to enter this milieu, minting the racial inheritance of future generations of colored Cashins.

Often the elite movers were sponsored by benevolent societies. They went to work as teachers or missionaries or under the auspices of the Union army to provide relief to Negro refugees of war. The most ambitious colored professionals were especially intent on moving to Black Belt communities thick with would-be parishioners, students, clients, customers, and most important in the Cashin family legacy, voters. The antebellum plantation economy created the Black Belt. The largest planters monopolized broad swaths of the most fecund land and brought slaves by the thousands to these regions, creating counties in central Georgia, mid-Alabama, the lower Mississippi flood plain, and beyond, where as much as 90 percent of the population was black. Herschel settled in Montgomery, Alabama, the seat of a Black Belt county.

It was a courageous choice. Unlike South Carolina, Mississippi, or Louisiana, Alabama's black population, while large, was not sizable enough to exert definitive influence over state government. Reconstruction got a late start in the state, largely because Republicans were fractured and disorganized. The interracial alliances among newly emancipated Negroes, recently arrived Northern "carpetbaggers," and moderate Southern "scalawags" that animated successful radical Republican politics in other Southern states were slow in coming and short-lived in Alabama. After an initial defeat, in 1868 a majority of Alabama voters, most of whom were black, ratified a progressive state constitution guaranteeing universal male suffrage. The state's first Reconstruction legislature convened the same year. It included twenty-seven proud colored men. With the help of Negro votes, this legislature made some valiant strides toward a vision of human equality. In 1869, it adopted a system of free, albeit segregated, public education and ratified the Fifteenth Amendment.

By the time Herschel arrived in the state, this brief interlude of inclusive, interracial politics had come to an end. Racial battle lines had been drawn, or redrawn. The Ku Klux Klan, the Knights of the White Camelia, and other secret societies were now the terrorist wing of the Democratic Party. Many a young new Klansman who had missed out on the action in the war now relished the opportunity to kill Negroes or their white allies. Between the terror of the secret societies and the machinations of Democratic politicians, resistance to black participation in politics and lawmaking was now systemic, organized, and concrete. The threat of murder or mayhem was constant for Republican activists and ordinary black voters, as were economic reprisals. The planters would tell their hired hands to vote the Democratic ticket or be dismissed. Blacklists of colored men who voted for the radical Republicans were common.

In 1870, the Alabama Democratic Party adopted the slogan of "white supremacy"—its official clarion call for a near century until 1966, when my father and his reform-minded friends demanded a less offensive motto. Alabama Republicans responded to the white supremacy movement by relegating blacks to the lowest positions in their party and suppressing their demands for participation in government. Phillip Joseph, Negro publisher of the Mobile *Watchman,* complained bitterly in August 1874 that despite blacks' fealty to the radical Republicans, "there is not one colored holding any state office; neither is there one in any of the departments of the State as a clerk."

Against these considerable odds, Herschel entered the state's political fray. He ran for the state legislature in the fall of 1874 as a radical Republican—an election in which Democrats would succeed in retaking control of all branches of state government, using every legal and extralegal method at their disposal. A month after the election, one black Republican expressed his dismay in a letter to President Ulysses S. Grant and Congress:

> [F]or three or four months past, especially, our lives and the lives of nearly all Republicans in this state have had no protection . . . hundreds of the active and earnest Republicans of this state . . . have been assassinated and many of our race were shot down and killed at the polls on the 3rd day of November last only because they chose to exercise their right to vote.

The violence did not deter Herschel. In Montgomery, he was among five Republican compatriots elected to the legislature; four were colored. Negro candidates succeeded mainly in Black Belt counties in which the sheer numbers of black voters overwhelmed any armed insurgents. There were 80,000 newly registered black voters in the state, and many of these former bondsmen were determined to exercise the signature right of citizenship, even at the risk of death or loss of livelihood. Initially, the *Montgomery Daily Advertiser* would identify Montgomery's newly elected representatives only as "Five Radicals." A week later, the paper grudgingly identified its new representatives by name and made a point of publicly marking the colored among them: "Elias Cooke, negro, Captain Gilmer, negro, —— Fagan, negro, E. R. Mitchell, H. V. Cashen, negro."

In a legislature dominated by "white supremacy" Democrats, Herschel made an earnest effort to champion the cause of education. His bill "for relief of teachers of free public schools" was tabled. His bill to "fix the salary of the Superintendent of Public Instruction" never made it out of the committee for fees and salaries. Two of his bills did pass—an act authorizing the transfer of cases from city court to circuit court (perhaps affording colored people a fairer forum) and an act to prevent sales of liquors within three miles of Dublin, Montgomery County.

~: ❀ :~

Dad grew up believing that his grandfather sponsored the first public education bill in Alabama. He must have gotten that from his father. In an interview with a local historian a few months before his death, my grandfather claimed that his father had sponsored the first "compulsory school law" while serving in the legislature. This, too, does not appear to be true. Grandpa Herschel's greatest strides for public education would come decades later in Decatur. Yet he was there. He participated, at the tender age of twenty-two, or younger, in Reconstruction's grand, imperfect experiment—America's first genuine lurch toward political equality for all of her people. He was one of 700 blacks who served in legislatures of the former Confederacy in the late nineteenth century. This great stream of history; the fact that blacks wielded power commensurate to their numbers; that nineteenth-century Alabama boasted three—three!—black congressmen—imbued my father with a sense of the promise of his people. And Grandpa Herschel's trajectory became fused in his mind with the successes of Reconstruction. As a man prone to exaggeration, consciously or unconsciously Dad would mix kernels of truth with fiction. But this lore *was* his truth and his personal religion.

I remember watching my father speak literally from a pulpit about it. In a February in the late 1970s, during Black History Month, he was the featured speaker at the First Baptist Church in Huntsville. By then he had made the transition from Unitarian to Baptist, mostly for utilitarian reasons. "Intellectually I'm a Unitarian, but politically I'm a Baptist," he always said, smilingly acknowledging the great organizational power of the black church. As he spoke at First Baptist, Dad reminded his audience of what blacks had achieved in Reconstruction and connected that to our collective obligation to organize and vote in the twentieth century. "Get ready," he said, he had a plan for the next election cycle, even though the NDPA had folded. His goal was audacious. Blacks were capable of wielding a majority in the state legislature, he argued, and we needed to respect ourselves enough to organize and live up to our potential. *Homo sapiens Africanus Alabamus*—a phrase he coined to denote the gene pool that survived the Middle Passage, slavery, and Jim Crow in Alabama—had to be a superior people who could do anything they set their minds to, he lectured. Forever and always he dreamed of restoring *Africanus Alabamus* to his or her rightful place of influence and respect in the political sphere.

～· ✂ ·～

Despite the disappointments of his first term, Herschel ran again in 1876 and succeeded in retaining his seat. The Montgomery delegation now included Samuel Farrow Rice, a senior member of an influential Montgomery law firm who would later become the chief justice of the Alabama Supreme Court and a possible entrée for Herschel into the legal profession. The numbers of blacks in the legislature had dwindled. Serving in a weak political minority, Herschel did not have much room to maneuver and was thus less ambitious in his second term.

He sponsored three bills. The first attempted to reform Alabama election law, to no avail. His other bills also appear to have failed. He sought to amend a law prohibiting public vulgarity, although it is unclear whether he was attempting to strengthen or weaken the law. Maybe an act "to prevent the use of abusive, insulting or vulgar language in the presence of families and females" was a clever means of protecting colored women and children from the debasements of racial hostility. Or the act may have been the source of unfair prosecutions for Negro men. His final bill was an effort to repeal a law abolishing the fencing of animals in portions of Montgomery County—perhaps on account of local Negroes who drew sustenance and livelihood from raising livestock.

During his second term it became clear that Reconstruction was essentially dead in Alabama and the South. With the Hayes-Tilden Compromise in January 1877, the weary Republican Congress agreed to remove federal troops from the last of the occupied Southern states in exchange for Democrats' accepting Rutherford Hayes as the electoral winner in a disputed presidential election. Through violence, fraud, economic reprisals, and gerrymandering, Alabama Democrats tightened their hold on power. After 1878, Negro lawmakers all but disappeared from the Alabama legislature, and most of what was left of Republican politics in the state concerned who would hold federal patronage jobs during Republican administrations and which faction would represent Alabama at the national Republican conventions. Throughout the South, the Republican Party would fracture into what was known as the "black and tan" and "lily-white" wings. In Alabama, there were even competing black factions as gerrymandering pitted black candidates against each other, in what amounted mostly to black political powerlessness.

Herschel allied himself with the Republican Party's most progressive elements, those most responsive and fair to the colored man. It took much intestinal fortitude, or faith in a brighter future over a horizon not then visible, to continue with politics at all. With black votes prohibited, discounted, or stolen, and a party of Lincoln that now deserted or even sought to exclude them, most Negro politicians simply gave up.

While he stayed active in political affairs, Herschel wisely prepared himself to make a living apart from politics. He began studying law while serving in the state legislature. In the waning years of Reconstruction, a new breed of black political leader began to emerge—professionals who trained at the new black colleges or apprenticed in law. Herschel's proximity to leading lawyers in the state certainly presented the opportunity for training, and he must have had a willing member of the bar take him on as a protégé. One C. Max Manning wrote a letter to the *Christian*

Recorder in Philadelphia, proudly extolling Herschel's admittance to the bar in a Montgomery courtroom in 1878:

MR. EDITOR: It affords me a vast deal of pleasure to acquaint you with a very signal catastrophe which transpired in this city, on Wednesday the 16th of January 1878. Some time in the year 1869 there was a young man who left the Institute for Colored Youths in your city . . . having left the South to attend that School he returned to the South where his services was [sic] most needed, and where he could best serve his people. . . . He therefore took an active part in the political struggle that was going on. Being sensible of his significance, and being imbued with the right spirit he soon gained eminence as a politician and filled several lucrative, and honorable positions; such as State Legislature, tax collector, clerk in the house of representatives &c. During all this time he failed not to apply himself to the study of law. As you well remember, the republican party of which he is now a member was completely routed during the last campaign and this young man together with many others, was thrown out of office. But being determined to service his people, as well as to make an honest living, he saw brighter prospect ahead and applied himself more closely to the study of the law.

His success gives rise to the writing of this letter for it was our privilege on the above date to see him pass the most rigid yet brilliant examination imaginable. Many were present for no other purpose than to laugh at him in derision in case of failure, as was expected by many, but in stead of deriding him at the conclusion of his examination many of the legal profession congratulated him with a hearty shake of the hand. Even the Judge (who was presiding over the court which was then sitting and which suspended on account of the examination;) spoke complimentary of the great success of the applicant. This young man, Mr. Editor, is none other than Hershel V. Cashin, who is now admitted to the bar in the State of Alabama,— Another Star in the crowns of Prof. O. V. Catto and Miss Fannie M. Jackson. Is not this sufficient inducement for the Graduates who may be counted by score in the neighborhood of 11th and Pine Sts. Philadelphia?

I grew up believing, because Dad always said it, that Grandpa Herschel was "the first black lawyer in the State of Alabama." That mantra shaped my identity as much as Herschel's political heritage shaped my father. I was enormously proud to be the descendant of a man who managed to pursue a profession I longed to enter, and I marveled that he did it at a time when most blacks seemed to be oppressed by the law. In our family, becoming a lawyer in Alabama was revered both as a near-sacred feat and a means to advance our people. Although the first black lawyer in the state would be admitted a few years before Herschel, a Negro lawyer in Alabama was a rare commodity, intentionally so, well into the middle of the twentieth century. A license to practice law was a source of respect and power in the Negro community that Herschel would wield quietly for the benefit of others for the rest of his life. Yet in the difficult years after the collapse of Reconstruction, his Republican connections, and the patronage jobs they afforded, were what put food on the table for his growing, happy family.

CHAPTER SIX

Uplift the Race

I n the years following Reconstruction, the divergence between Herschel's path and those of his siblings, especially his younger brother, would become wider. Herschel was next in age to James and they were close. Like the Irish American brothers John and James a generation before—who chose the way of the plantation or not, to fraternize with the colored race or not—Herschel and James faced the color line and made quite different choices. According to family lore, James slipped into whiteness—a move likely made easier in the relative anonymity of New York City. Herschel embraced his lineage and the challenge of uplifting the race into which he was cast. His skin color may have left him little choice. In the precious few photos we have of him, a hint of pecan is unmistakable. For him, passing was simply not an option.

For James, passing may have been inadvertent, a silence borne of necessity rather than considered intent. Post-Reconstruction life was quite hard for the American Negro. Reconstruction's brief window of expanded opportunity had closed, most Republicans had exhausted their interest in colored people, and racial oppression now escalated. James's choice to move to New York, where, supposedly, he became a successful lapidary, and elder brother John's choice to move west to become a prospector were of a piece with the choices of many a light-skinned person in the era. As someone who was more Irish than African, James could pass by day, telling his employer he was white to secure a job he deserved just as much as anyone else. According to my family, Herschel never judged him nor spoke of it. And James didn't mind being "colored" when he came south to visit his brother in Alabama, or when the census takers called.

In his actions and deeds, Herschel continued to bind himself to people of color. He was a leader in the Prince Hall (colored) Freemasons in Montgomery, serving as the lodge's grand secretary and its delegate to a national meeting of colored masons held in Wilmington, Delaware, in May 1878. That year at both the national level and in Alabama, disparate colored lodges felt the need, as the *Christian Recorder* reported, "to heal the breach" caused by the existence of two separate black Masonic organizations. Noting "our conditions as a race required the abolition of all dissension in our ranks," the national convention consolidated into one unified national Grand Lodge, and Herschel was a leader in the successful effort to combine the colored lodges in the state into one "Sovereign Grand Lodge of Alabama." In so doing he was participating in a century-old tradition of free black men who struggled to become self-sufficient socially and economically through the work of fraternal orders and benevolent societies. Future generations of Cashin men would take similar steps toward black kinship, joining the black Freemasons, the Boulé, Omega Psi Phi, and the Improved Benevolent and Protective Order of Elks of the World—organizations that modeled black manhood and citizenship and inculcated a collective Afro-American identity in their members.

In the midst of politics, civic duty, and attempting to work as a lawyer, Herschel managed to meet and marry Minnie V. Brewster, a petite colored beauty of eighteen. They wed in Montgomery in a Presbyterian church on July 2, 1879, the beginning of a marriage that would endure nearly five decades until they both died mere months apart. With a smile, Daddy told me of the tender love letters the two exchanged when Herschel's work took him away from Minnie—more family memorabilia infuriatingly lost with its ebony container. According to Dad, Herschel wrote rather ardent letters to his wife. There was no lack of conjugal relations between Herschel and Minnie. In the census of 1900, she would be listed as the mother of ten children, six of whom lived.

In my parents' attic I discovered a charcoal drawing of young Minnie that suggests her pre-marital innocence. Her features are rendered with photographic realism. Eyes: direct, open, and trusting. Hair and skin: a fine silk betraying a mixed heritage not unlike her husband's. Her noble forehead, high cheekbones and calm dignity hint of Indian-ness. Cousin Betty-V—Elizabeth Cashin McMillen, Uncle Jimmy's daughter—claims that Minnie was the daughter of a full-blooded Cherokee chief who sent her and her younger sister, Lillian, to normal school to be "de-Indianed." Betty-V's brother, Blinny—James Blaine Cashin Jr.—shared a similar story, only it was Minnie's mother who was the Indian princess; they lived in a wooded area among Muscogee-Creek Indians. I found nothing to substantiate these colorful tales. But the paper trail does not directly refute them.

Minnie was the oldest of three children born to Henry and Courtney Brewster of Montgomery. Courtney appears to have been the backbone of this struggling mulatto family. The 1870 census lists Courtney as a domestic servant who could read but not write. She and Minnie, who at the age of ten also worked as a domestic, were the breadwinners. Henry had "no occupation" and could neither read nor write. He may have been disabled in some way. He died of consumption in 1874, at the age of thirty-seven.

Courtney was clearly possessed with determination to succeed. She rose from domestic to dressmaker to trained nurse, working privately for Montgomery families that could afford such personal care. She saw to it that both her daughters married well. Lillian wed Alfred Coleman Dungee, a Howard University College of Medicine graduate who became a licensed physician in Alabama in 1891. Dungee was a close associate of Booker T. Washington, headed the Health Department at Tuskegee Institute, and operated a pharmacy in Montgomery. Herschel likely came to know Mr. Washington through his brother-in-law. In later years, he and Washington would have political differences, yet their mutual admiration and friendship endured.

As William Dorsey had done for him a generation earlier, Herschel assumed the head of a household that included his wife's mother, sister, and brother, Robert. In 1880, the Cashins and Brewsters lived together at McDonough Street between South and Line streets in Montgomery. The city directory and census listed Herschel's occupation as "lawyer," although the odds were stacked heavily against a colored man earning a living as an attorney. There was the ever-present problem of accumulating enough paying clients. One historian of black officeholders in Alabama's Reconstruction reports that Herschel V. Cashin operated a barroom in Montgomery—a claim that seems at odds with his legislative efforts to ban liquor sales in certain parts, and family lore that renders him a teetotaler. If he did engage in such extracurricular commerce, he wouldn't do so much longer, as he soon received a patronage appointment that would bring his family a steady income.

On July 1, 1881, Herschel was appointed as a railway mail clerk for the U.S. Postal Service, with a princely annual salary of $900. The job was a benefit of President James Garfield's narrow Republican popular victory over Winfield Hancock, the overwhelming favorite in the Democrat-controlled South. Frederick Douglass, or rather his writings, taught me the significance of this position. Reflecting on his awe at having been entrusted to deliver electors' votes in the 1872 presidential election from New York to Washington, D.C., Douglass exclaimed in *Life and Times* that "[o]nly a few years before this any colored man was forbidden by law to carry a United States mail bag from one post office to another" and he "was not allowed to touch the sacred leather, though locked in 'triple steel.'"

Railway mail clerk was quite a step above postman. It was a job that placed a gun in the hands of a colored man. He rode in the mail car, ensuring the safe passage of the U.S. Post. In the Deep South in the 1880s, the federal government was still a source of bitterness to broken-hearted Confederates. The U.S. mail car was a symbol of the villains in Washington and an easy target. Herschel's first route was between Macon, Georgia, and Montgomery. Dad recalls reading one of Herschel's letters to Minnie, in which he recounted the mail car being shot at by "rebels" in Uniontown, Alabama.

The appointment enabled Herschel to purchase his first plot of land. In December 1881, he paid $250 for a half lot at the corner of Lafayette and Madison Streets in Decatur, Alabama, presumably land that would become 509 Madison, where he would reside for more than forty years. Gradually, he would expand the homestead, buying two more lots in the vicinity, and Minnie would purchase a property on Church Street in her own right in 1898.

Built on the banks of the Tennessee River, Decatur was at the crossroads of the expansive Louisville & Nashville Railroad, on which one could ride nonstop from Montgomery to Louisville, Kentucky, and the

Decatur-Tuscumbia, the first U.S. railroad built east of the Appalachian Mountains. Herschel may have chosen Decatur out of convenience. In July 1883, his salary was raised to $1,000 and his route now ran between Montgomery and Decatur. Or he may have chosen north Alabama over Montgomery because it offered better race relations and Republicans were still making inroads in local elections.

Herschel soon emerged as a leading force for blacks in the city. Reportedly, he was Decatur's first colored attorney. In November 1883, he presented a petition of colored citizens to the city for the creation of a free colored school. It would be more than a decade before his advocacy would bear fruit. When the city finally opened a school for Negroes in 1893, Herschel and four other prominent colored men were appointed as trustees of the "Cherry Street School." Until then, colored children had to make do with a private school that operated in a makeshift building on Lafayette and Well Streets before it moved to a Methodist church that Herschel regularly attended.

One of his fellow school trustees was Matthew Banks. The collective memory of black Decatur elders is that Mr. Banks became the first colored city councilman when he was elected to that post in 1884. Mr. Banks had a granddaughter, Athelyne, who perpetuated his memory by living to age ninety-eight and becoming the female sage of Decatur. By the time it occurred to me to inquire about Grandpa Herschel, she was the only living soul I could talk to who had actually laid eyes on him. Athelyne was a protégé of Herschel's daughter Patty (known to us as Aunt Pat, my grandfather's twin sister). Athelyne lived two blocks away from Aunt Pat, in a small house on Sycamore Street that she occupied from birth to death. When I visited her she was ebullient and sharp; her home was immaculate and ordered, just as she demanded of students in her forty-two years in public education. She first encountered Herschel and Minnie as a small girl and remembered them as "more outstanding" than others in the colored community:

> *He was a very good lawyer. The town people would go to him to get things done. He was a real black leader for the city of Decatur. He stuck with them and helped them open doors. Minnie was tiny, no more than 4 feet 6 inches. He was stout, well built and much taller than her. Both*

of them were nice dressers and dignified. They looked like a very loving couple; they were very affectionate with each other. She supported him; she was less of a public figure than he was.

Of course, Athelyne was speaking of a seasoned Herschel, in the 1910s and 1920s. But her memories made the younger Herschel, whose paper trail I was following, more palpable. In 1885, he continued his professional ascent on the railways when he was assigned the coveted route between Montgomery and Nashville. However, his tenure as railway mail clerk would end after his final reappointment in 1887. He appears to have been a victim of race politics within his own party. When President Benjamin Harrison took office in 1889, he adopted a strategy that played to the Southern segregationists in his party, the "Lily-White" Republicans. In Alabama, Harrison recognized a newly organized party, which excluded colored men, as the official Republican organ and appointed only ranking white men to patronage positions throughout the state. When "Black and Tan" Republicans protested, a few colored men were appointed to offices, but Herschel was not one of them.

Herschel would have had to look elsewhere for income. Apparently he only relied on his legal practice intermittently. Available records suggest his appearances in the Decatur courts were exceedingly rare. He seems to have spent more time on business and political endeavors. An account of H. V. Cashin's life published in 1905 in both the *Morning Mercury* and the *Hunstville Weekly Democrat* stated that he was "the owner of considerable property" in Decatur and its twin city, Albany, and was "largely identified with the progress of those places, having been an original stock holder and among the organizers of the Decatur Land Company." More intriguing is the bipartisan support he commanded: "He was for several years a member of the City Council of Decatur, having been elected by the votes of democrats and republicans and was appointed by a democratic mayor as Chairman of the Committee on Education of that body."

Such cordial race relations and ecumenical politics prevailed in certain north Alabama counties in the 1880s and 1890s. In adjacent Madison County, Republicans, Independents, and Greenbacks formed a coalition that brought blacks into office in the early 1880s. Huntsville, the county seat, was lauded by the black editor of the *Huntsville Gazette* as a cultured place that was a decade or more ahead of the rest of the state in its inclination toward racial fairness. There blacks served on the City Council, on the police force, and on juries, and many were employed by city businesses. One black city councilman in Huntsville, Daniel Brandon, operated a highly successful contracting business with his father, Henderson. They and generations of Brandons, from whom my Grandma Grace descended, would build several of the edifices that stand today in historic Huntsville, including the old U.S. Post Office, built in 1880. In an era when black voter registration in Huntsville effectively equaled that of whites in the city, Brandon may have begun to feel a little too equal for some of the white establishment. Legend has it that when Dan Brandon began building himself a house as fine as that of the richest white man in the city, suddenly his company was no longer favored with building contracts and his business began to suffer.

Herschel, too, would learn firsthand to appreciate the limits of racial tolerance in ostensibly enlightened north Alabama. On October 20, 1894, he bought a ticket to return to Decatur from Huntsville as a regular-class passenger on a train operated by the Memphis & Charleston Railroad. He must have taken this route often, and as a former railway mail clerk, he was used to commanding the rails. Likely he had ignored a state law passed in 1891, which required the segregation of black and white rail passengers, and sat where he pleased. The day became exceptional when, about five miles outside of Huntsville, two railroad employees assaulted, beat, and then ejected Herschel from the train.

I didn't hear this story from family. Instead, I discovered it because Herschel did what any lawyer so violated would do: He filed a lawsuit in Morgan County Circuit Court seeking $1,000 in damages for the violence and indignity he suffered. He must have been aware of the fate that befell William Hooper Councill, the eminent founder and first president of Colored State Normal, now Alabama Agricultural and Mechanical University, north of Huntsville. When Councill was forcibly removed from a first-class section of a train he boarded in Georgia in 1887, he filed a suit that resulted not in damages but in a rule that accommodations for Negroes had to be equal to those of whites. Councill also complained to the Interstate Commerce Commission. For his impertinence, he was removed from the presidency of A&M for one year. One historian surmised that the experience contributed to an "unctuous sycophancy" on Councill's part; henceforth, he advocated that Negroes accommodate to and accept second-class citizenship. Another viewed Councill more charitably as "an adroit and shrewd student of the foibles and prejudices of his white contemporaries," who exploited their "susceptibilities" to the best advantage of his beloved university.

In choosing to sue, Herschel clearly was in no mood to accommodate. Wisely, he did not attempt to represent himself. His lawyer was Osceola Kyle, a white gentleman who was a well-known Democrat and former Alabama legislator. As the son of a grocer who grew up in heavily black Tuskegee, Kyle was not unlike many a white Southerner who could maintain intimate, friendly relations with the coloreds he knew while participating in a political party ostensibly committed to white supremacy. Kyle did not mention race in the complaint. Their legal theory was mere breach of a contractual "duty to transport him safely and in a respectful manner." Herschel claimed that the conductor commanded two lackeys to beat and eject him.

The case does not appear to have been successful, as there is no record of its disposition. Herschel may have decided not to impart this story to his children because the object lesson and end result were bitter. What hope could it give them if the rule of law did not vindicate his position? His case was filed in June 1895, a few months before Booker T. Washington gave his legendary "Atlanta Compromise" speech, in which he chastised "the wisest among my race" to "understand that the agitation of questions of social equality is the extremest folly." It was one year before the Supreme Court notoriously decided in *Plessy v. Ferguson*—another case in which an "octoroon" was denied passage alongside whites on a train— that "separate but equal" would suffice under the U.S. Constitution. The regime of Jim Crow was now officially sanctioned by the federal government; in Alabama, it had already taken root with a vengeance.

In this dispiriting epoch, Herschel hewed even closer to the progressive elements of his party. After the demise of Reconstruction, Republicanism in the state had been marked mostly by periods of intense intraparty factionalism with ever so brief interludes of unity. At one point there were four different factions—one lily-white, one lily-black, and two mixed, black-and-tan—competing to be recognized by the national Republicans, holding separate state conventions to select national convention delegates, or fielding different slates of candidates. The race question dogged the party as Republicans struggled to be competitive in a state where "white supremacy" was an easy organizing principle for Democrats. But even Democrats competed for black votes, as did Lily-Whites, Greenbacks, and Populists, or Kolbites. Outside of the all-black and Black and Tan Republican organizations, every political party of every hue and ideology seemed to want the black vote but not the obligation of equality and fairness that blacks thought they were owed for their loyalties.

When Lily-White Republicans sought to attract black votes by deception, creating a Black Republican League, authentic black Republicans, including Herschel, took matters into their own hands by holding their own Black and Tan state convention in Montgomery in April 1892. The *Atlanta Constitution* reported that the meeting was composed of about 150 men, twenty-five of whom where white. The session started off orderly, but by the afternoon, the *Constitution* alleged derisively, it descended into an uproar in which "it was hard for the chair or anyone else to be heard above the din of forty or fifty howling Negroes, trying to talk at once." They had good reason to shout. Ultimately, the convention condemned the Lily-Whites, petitioned the Civil Service Commission to investigate their practices, and sent their own delegation to the National Republican Convention in Minneapolis, including Herschel V. Cashin. At Minneapolis the Lily-Whites' delegation, which included a token Negro, would be seated as the official representatives of Alabama Republicans.

Ironically, Dad and the NDPA would fight similar battles a century later. The Black and Tans, like the NDPA, were a black-led, biracial independent party struggling to be recognized by a national party ostensibly committed to racial equality as the authentic voice of the people and *real* democracy in the state. Most of all, these parties were asserting Negroes' right to represent themselves, to be thoroughly actualized citizens, in politics and in life. In Dad's lore, Grandpa Herschel was the principled stalwart, the one who would not compromise or step-and-fetch for any white faction that was not a true friend to Afro-Americans. Some historical threads support his impression. A few Negro leaders, including William Hooper Councill, switched from Republican to Democrat. In an effort to exert influence within

the party that wielded decisive power in the state, Councill delivered black
votes to his new party, helping to defeat black Republican candidates. Councill's rival, Booker T. Washington, would exhort Negroes to stay out of politics. Both Washington and Councill later found themselves in the position of
imploring the Democrats not to cut the Negro out of the franchise altogether.

As long as Democrats and Populists made inroads with black voters,
national Republicans had a vested interest in retaining black Alabamians.
In 1896, Alabama's Black and Tans offered a delegation that was recognized at the National Republican Convention. Again Herschel was selected
by his party to serve as an at-large delegate. At these national meetings he
met and befriended George A. Myers, a well-known Negro barber and
political activist in Cleveland, Ohio. Myers operated his barber business
out of the famed Hollenden House, Cleveland's finest hotel. His shop was
a mecca for black politicians, who would hash out the prevailing theory for
Negro advancement. The two began a correspondence that would result in
a precious gift: four letters, written and signed by Grandpa Herschel, in
elegant, gracious prose, preserved for posterity in Mr. Myers's archives.

Herschel's letters were hammered out on what appears to have been a
serviceable if imperfect typewriter. He signed his name, "H.V. Cashin," in
a handsome script that would be considered calligraphy today. He wrote
fondly of "the acquaintance begun when we were both advocates of the
matchless McKinley at Minneapolis, and whom we were happy to crown
at St. Louis in 1896." Among other topics, he made inquiries about a property he was considering purchasing for cash across the street from Myers's
establishment in Cleveland. He wrote of his plans to accept an invitation to
participate in a speaking campaign for Republican candidates in Ohio and
applauded "the glorious record you Buckeye Republicans have been making." And he entreated his enterprising friend that should he ever "desire
to visit this State with its wondrous fertility and inexhaustible mineral
resources, the best wife and children in the world, except your own, will
welcome you at my home in Decatur."

As Herschel and fellow Afro-American Republican leaders grew more
astute in demanding and receiving a larger share of patronage appointments,
their eager support of President William McKinley paid handsome dividends.
In virtually every state with sizable black populations, McKinley named Negro

men and a rare woman to federal positions that secured their position in the middle or even upper classes: collector of internal revenue, postmaster, recorder of deeds, minister or consul, typically to a dark-hued nation. Herschel was part of the phenomenon. In 1897, McKinley appointed him receiver of public monies at the U.S. Land Office in Huntsville, a position of considerable importance that would draw on his legal skills.

The land office was the federal government's vehicle for the homesteading of publicly held lands, many of which were wrested from Indian tribes. For a modest fee, a homesteader could secure title to a plot of public land upon residing on or cultivating it for five years. The Huntsville Land Office was the oldest in the United States. It opened in 1810, nearly a decade before the Alabama territory became a state, in an effort to hasten the development of the Tennessee Valley.

When Herschel assumed the position of receiver, there were 322,000 acres of land in his district subject to the Homestead Act. Over the next eight years, he and the register of the Huntsville Land Office, Judge John A. Steele, would oversee the initial distribution of 247,000 of those acres to some 3,700 persons, about 2,800 of whom ultimately gained title. In north Alabama, this meant that any colored person interested in acquiring virtually free land went to H. V. Cashin at the Huntsville Land Office. Family legend has it that he taught them what to do and how to succeed in acquiring the thing that was most enduring to any striver.

Herschel developed a healthy respect for the power of ownership and inculcated this in his children, especially his sons. Land, like personal principle, was something to stand on. Both were to be defended to the utmost, never sacrificed or sold. Generations of black families in north Alabama benefited from his tutelage in the rudiments of property ownership. In the vicinity of Huntsville especially, a class of black owners rose up in neighborhoods like Brandontown—the province of Grandma Grace's ancestors—and Spring Hills and Mullin Flats, rural dominions that would later be bought back by the U.S. government to build Redstone Arsenal. By the time the arsenal became the early testing ground for the rocket boosters that would first put man on the moon, the black families that once lived there would be erased from memory. Yet through the worst of Jim Crow, the Depression, and beyond, families in these environs survived on the land they owned. Their gardens and animals gave them sustenance in the warm months, and they prepared for winter by canning their food. They formed benevolent societies. In the 1890s, a No. 3 lodge in Brandontown was a dues-paying organization that would bestow a $50 bereavement benefit on any member whose family met tragedy. Their churches, social clubs, and fraternities together created the only safety net these communities would know. So it was in the black neighborhoods of Huntsville, so it was wherever colored people claimed a stake in the nation.

By the turn of the century, Herschel's evolution to "race man" was complete. He began to claim and extol the achievements of his people decades before the Harlem Renaissance and its New Negro cemented a proud, collective Afro-American identity for the race. He co-wrote a book designed to ensure that the black "Buffalo Soldiers" of the Tenth U.S. Cavalry received proper recognition for their heroics in the Spanish American War, in particular the famous battle at San Juan Hill. Created by Congress at the close of the Civil War, the Tenth Cavalry was one of several black military units that distinguished themselves in campaigns against Indian tribes in the West and in the campaign in Cuba. After America's "splendid little war" concluded in victory in a matter of months in the spring and summer of 1898, regiments of the Tenth were sent to Huntsville, where they would remain stationed through 1901.

When discussing the war, most black Republicans sidestepped the charge of imperialism and focused on the benefits of the war to the Negro race. Before it commenced, there were only five Negro officers and about 4,000 privates in the U.S. military. For a war begun on impulse, an off-guard U.S. government had to turn to volunteers. They gladly accepted thousands of blacks into the ranks of the military and put them on the front line alongside white Rough Riders in Cuba. In short order, black units swelled to 266 officers and 15,000 privates.

Initially the Tenth received its due in the victory celebrations. In the opinion pages of the *Washington Post,* one white Southerner offered an unequivocal validation:

> If it had not been for the Negro cavalry, the Rough Riders would have been exterminated. I am not a Negro lover. My father fought with

Mosby's Rangers and I was born in the south, but the Negroes saved
the fight, and the day will come when General Shafter will give them
credit for their bravery.

Theodore Roosevelt himself called the black cavalry "an excellent
breed of Yankees" and the Tenth marched in review before President
McKinley in Washington. The accolades would not last. The brotherhood
and mutual respect of the white soldier for his black comrade in the heat
of battle gave way to a normalcy of racial hierarchy, or loathing.

Whether out of concern that their important contributions in the war
were being obscured by celebrations of Teddy Roosevelt's Rough Riders,
or a simple desire to capitalize on a rage of race pride that blacks everywhere felt for their beloved Buffalo Soldiers, Herschel organized an effort
to collect and corroborate the testimony of soldiers and their commanders
regarding the black soldiers' definitive role. In a letter to General Joseph
Wheeler—a former Confederate general, member of Congress, and the
commander of all volunteer cavalry in Cuba—he requested that the general lend credence to his manuscript by writing an introduction. "[M]y
associates unite with me in most earnestly requesting that you favor us with
an expression . . . of your opinion as to the courage, discipline and sol-
dierly qualities generally of the colored troops who served under you in
Cuba." His intent was clear: to "[fix] the status in future History of the Colored soldier." Wheeler was happy to oblige, writing back in three days of
his "great pleasure" in favoring the book with an introduction.

The book itself, *Under Fire with the Tenth U.S. Cavalry*, was first published in 1899 with Herschel V. Cashin billed as the lead author among
five contributors, including a chaplain, assistant surgeon, and sergeant who
served in the campaign. It received little attention when it first appeared
but has emerged as a minor classic of U.S. military history in that it offers
rare testimony of black soldiers themselves. In one account, a soldier con-
curred that the Tenth Cavalry had saved the Rough Riders from certain
extermination. He described the Rough Riders' march into a narrow valley, only to be flanked by the Spaniards at both front and rear, with shots
raining down upon them. The Tenth, adopting methods its soldiers had
used fighting Indians, turned the battle and repulsed the Spaniards.

The book prefaced the valiant Cuban campaign with a précis of the contributions of black revolutionary patriots and the Buffalo Soldiers of the Indian campaigns, in a language eerily suggestive of a chauvinistic pride of race that I have heard all my life—from Dad.

Of the revolutionary patriots: "[T]he Negro accepted [his] situation, and, with an intense religious fervor, displayed a love for freedom, a willingness to fight and make sacrifice for the common cause of liberty, a valor and intrepidity, even when his own prospect of sharing in it was not promising, that have not been paralleled by any race, under similar conditions, in the history of the world."

Of the Tenth Cavalry at Santiago de Cuba: "[T]he Negro proved himself a soldier—that he appreciated the danger of the situation, the peril of both the geographical position and the treachery of the Spaniards; but he went to perform a duty which no element could furnish power enough to hinder, and he clearly demonstrated a heroism that is not common in any race."

It is unclear which co-author wrote such prideful prose. As the leader in this effort, surely Herschel would have put his imprimatur on the book's tone. A valedictory conclusion is especially glowing in its racial boosterism. Negro soldiers were "the sable sons of silent, wronged and magnificent Africa." At "the memorable siege of Santiago and the never to be forgotten charge up San Juan Hill . . . he challenged the admiration of the American people and solicited tumultuous applause of every liberty loving nation throughout the civilized world!" I read this and it becomes clear to me that my father's avowed black supremacism, his belief in the greatness of black people, was inherited.

The imperatives of racial solidarity must have grown stronger for Herschel as racial oppression and sentiments toward total disenfranchisement grew. In political circles, white leaders in opposing parties began to coalesce around the idea that Negroes were to blame for creating so much discord in Alabama. It was much easier to contemplate eliminating the black man's right to vote than to continue competing with fellow white men for his allegiance, or to steal his vote. White leaders and industrialists in north Alabama especially had grown weary of watching the elite planter class of the Black Belt dominate the state by fraudulently producing thousands of black "votes" that would consistently provide the margin of victory in state elections. In the Black Belt, wealthy planters used violence, intimidation, and outright doctoring of ballots to produce an absurdity: blacks "voting" in overwhelming numbers for the party of white supremacy. Both the white working man and his industrialist bosses in other parts of the state were tired of being disempowered by such fakery.

There was a simple remedy to this state of affairs as nothing, not even the Fifteenth Amendment, stood in the way of cutting most blacks out of the vote. With the collapse of the Populist Party in 1898 and a Republican camp badly weakened by multiple fissures, by 1900 Democrats were completely dominant. Following the lead of Mississippi, South Carolina, and other Deep South states, in January 1901, Alabama Democrats issued a call for a state constitutional convention, with the chief aim of removing the Negro forever from the political life of the state. Booker T. Washington, in a futile effort to retain a measure of voting rights for the Negro, publicly agreed that some restrictions should be placed on the franchise. This prompted a direct response from H. V. Cashin. From his experience as a legislator, when Democrats retook the state in an election victory orchestrated by violence, "the white vote was the menace, since the Black vote had been controlled since 1874," and "a convention based on race prejudice would limit the franchise to white men and depress Negro voters." The historian who attributed this rejoinder to my great-grandfather did not identify his source, although he suggests that Herschel used a Black and Tan publication, the *Huntsville Republican,* as his platform for contradicting Mr. Washington.

The legislature put the issue of whether to hold a constitutional convention to a statewide voter referendum. While the Black and Tans, the black press, and blacks themselves tried mightily to defeat the proposal at the polls, as had become standard, the returns in Black Belt counties were warped in favor of a measure that was directly against black interests. One hundred fifty-five white men, most of whom were Democrats, were sent to the constitutional convention in Montgomery to decide the fate of black and poor white voters. The president of the convention, John B. Knox, was pointed in his opening keynote address as to the task at hand, "to establish white supremacy in this State . . . by law—not by force or fraud." He canvassed some of the race-neutral innovations that had been deployed in other Southern states to elude the Fifteenth Amendment, arguing that such provisions were justified "in law and morals" because of the purported intellectual and moral inferiority of the Negro.

The convention was a key test for black leadership in the state. The constant refrain in speeches, the white press, and political meetings in favor of disenfranchisement was this notion of white intellectual superiority and the horrors of Radical Reconstruction—the specter of black rule reasserting itself in the state as coloreds swelled in numbers and education. A group of twenty-four accomplished blacks, led by Booker T. Washington, filed a petition with the convention, seeking to assure them that the "Negro is not seeking to rule the white man"; he merely asked "that he should have some humble share in choosing those who rule over him." Their language alternated from obsequious entreaties to moral warnings. They apologized for Reconstruction: "Immediately after the war, we made mistakes . . . but we have learned our lesson." But they rightly presaged "that nothing that is not absolutely just and fair, will be permanently successful." Of course, six decades would elapse before this prophesy came to pass.

As independent black editors wrote at the time, ultimately the petition was a beggar's errand. Even the petitioners acknowledged that the convention delegates' power was unrestricted by the federal government or any external force and that the Negro's future rested largely with their moral conscience. On the seventh day of the convention, the delegates allowed the five-page petition to be read aloud, then tabled it.

Herschel was not among its signatories, which included his brother-in-law, Dr. Alfred Dungee, and William Hooper Councill. Dad developed an apocryphal story about this painful episode that I grew up hearing repeatedly. In his version of events, William Hooper Councill and other black Democrats came running to Grandpa Herschel for his advice on what to do about the constitutional convention, to which he replied dryly, "Why don't you ask your Democratic friends?" If such a meeting did occur, I suspect Grandpa Herschel was more tactful. The evidence suggests he weathered an extraordinary transformation of the political fortunes of black Alabamians by continuing, as a Black and Tan stalwart, to assert the rights of the Negro with tenacity and dignity.

The odds against making any inroads for the benefit of colored Alabamians were now even greater than at the close of Reconstruction. The convention delegates produced a proposed constitution that deployed several subterfuges to disenfranchise black voters, chief among them poll taxes and literacy tests. The "Cashin Castration Constitution," as Uncle Newlyn dubbed it, was ratified in November 1901 in another tightly contested state election in which the margin of victory was provided by Negroes in the Black Belt who "voted" overwhelmingly to disenfranchise themselves.

Initially, it seemed that poor white voters would be saved by liberal discretion afforded local registrars or by grandfather clauses that automatically qualified men or their ancestors who fought in previous wars. Yet the effectiveness of the grandfather clause waned with time, and the constitution's permanent provisions had an effect that was intended by white elites to protect their wealth and political power. Within a few years of ratification, poor whites were being disenfranchised by the thousands.

The effect of the 1901 Constitution on black voting strength was devastatingly swift. In 1900, there were 181,000 eligible black voters in Alabama. By 1903, their numbers had been slashed to fewer than 3,000. To this day, this transformation looms large in Dad's psyche. Like many black elders who carry the hurts of past centuries with them, Dad remains as outraged by this turn of events as if it happened yesterday. The family lore imbued him with a mythology he carried with him throughout life. It did not assuage his anger—indeed, it amplified it. But the mythology did clarify his purpose.

CHAPTER SEVEN

The Talented Tenth

Although Herschel would not play the sycophant to the constitutional convention of 1901, he did maintain good relations with Booker T. Washington, whose speech in Atlanta had launched him to the stratospheric height of America's most influential Negro. When Theodore Roosevelt unexpectedly became president after William McKinley's assassination, he sought Washington's advice on whether to retain Herschel as receiver for north Alabama. Washington wrote enthusiastically: "Mr. Cashin has a very fine reputation among the colored and white people in Alabama." And Roosevelt swiftly reappointed Herschel. In another letter, Washington commented to a colleague that Roosevelt's reappointment of Mr. Cashin, even as he removed another black appointee, was a premier example of the Roosevelt administration's willingness to advance qualified colored men. He testified again to his esteem for Herschel in a letter he wrote to William H. Taft, then secretary of war, recommending that in addition to consulting Alabama's congressional delegation, H. V. Cashin's opinion should also be sought regarding an important judicial post in Panama that they proposed to fill with a well-known Alabamian.

Mr. Washington also showed his regard when he attended the wedding of Herschel's oldest child. On an inevitably warm July day in Decatur in 1906, Vivian (known to the family as Vivi) wed a third-generation Oberlin graduate named Carroll Napier Langston. The two celebrated their nuptials at St. Paul's, the family church. Afterward, Herschel and Minnie held a luncheon for the wedding party at their home on Madison Street. They would have gazed approvingly at their finely attired offspring. Vivi, New-lyn, Lillian, John, Pat, and James were becoming the sturdy young citizens their parents had worked so hard to cultivate. They would have been prouder still to bind Vivi to one of America's leading colored families, the Langstons. Aunt Pat would later marry into one of Decatur's most promi-nent Negro families, the Sykeses. A family friend would say wryly that the Sykeses communed with the Cashins, and the Cashins communed with the Langstons, and the Langstons communed with God.

Carroll Langston, who went by the nickname Tode, was a grandson of John Mercer Langston—the founder of Howard Law School, a late-nineteenth-century congressman from Virginia, and a consul to Haiti. Tode was a few years into an auspicious career as a banker at the One Cent Savings Bank in Nashville. The "Penny Bank" would become Citizens, the oldest continuous black-owned bank in America. It was founded by Tode's formidable uncle, James Carroll Napier, who was affectionately known as Nashville's "first Negro."

Uncle Tode must have spied Aunt Vivi while she was attending Fisk in Nashville, or perhaps they met through family connections, as both could claim activist Republican partisans among their people. He wore dapper clothes and a serious countenance and, like Vivi, was white in appearance but a Negro in his heart. A story passed through the generations was that once, when Tode and Vivi were courting and he made the pilgrimage to Decatur, Vivi was anxious that he be suitably impressed with her charis-matic family. Her adored little brother, John, my grandfather, greeted the scion of Negro royalty adorned with more whitewash than the clapboards he was supposed to be painting. His full name was John Henry Logan Vas-sar Cashin, and although he was named augustly, after Jonathan Logan, a Civil War general, he was mischievous by nature.[1] Covered in wet paint, he extended his hand to Tode, testing whether his would-be brother-in-law thought too much of himself or his clothes. His jest did not deter Tode from proposing in the classical style of a gentleman, on his knee, before Vivi's family.

Mr. Washington's wedding gifts to Vivi and Tode were exquisite; they hang in a place of honor in my home, above my bed, blessing my own mar-riage. Three framed photographs of statues of lovers, one pair nude; the male worships at the feet of his beloved, gently caressing and kissing her shin while she sits literally on a pedestal, breasts full and erect, receiving his adoration. The image is surprisingly erotic for that Victorian age, and from such a paragon of rectitude. The baroque frames he chose, and the tenderness the figures show each other, suggest that there was a roundness, playfulness even, to Booker T.

Despite his good relations with Mr. Washington, Grandpa Herschel's direct, aggressive engagement with politics and his success in raising six refined college or professional graduates suggest that he was a DuBois man by philosophy. By 1903, W.E.B. DuBois had begun his intellectual assault on Washington's industrial pragmatism, offering his conception of the "Talented Tenth": Black freedom would come from the work of exceptional men dedicated to serving the race; and such men would be formed only in an educational system that offered the Negro the highest learning and culture. As Octavius Catto and the Institute for Colored Youth had done for him, Herschel modeled this philosophy for his sons *and* daughters. All of his children attended Fisk University, DuBois' first alma mater.

Betty-V and Blinny, brother and sister, grew up hearing stories of their grandfather, Herschel, from their father, James. They also learned much about Herschel from Aunt Vivi, James's oldest sister. Vivi lived to a very old age, surviving all but one of her siblings. She was especially solicitous of Betty-V and Blinny, as they lost their father far too early and she lost her only son in World War II. The sensitive aunt passed much on to her sensitive niece and nephew. It is a strain of the lore that comes closest to rendering Grandpa Herschel in three dimensions.

Grandpa Herschel and his progeny were small in stature. He stood no more than 5 feet 7 inches and probably appeared somewhat tall and stout to little Athelyne Banks only in relation to his miniscule wife. He was a giant to his children. According to his grandson Blinny: "He was absolutely fierce, respected by everyone. When he placed a mandate on the boys it was taken seriously." A common parable that Uncle Jimmy would share with his son was that Grandpa Herschel would give a licking on Sunday that would last all week, just in case he did something wrong. Although Blinny is an advocate for people with developmental disabilities, his everyday speech mirrors not his formal education but the language of the home he grew up in. In his erudite vernacular, this fable "was hyperbole to joust the jocundity of the soul of a little boy."

Actually, Grandpa Herschel used the whip sparingly. He didn't need to. Once he spoke to his children, whatever he called for was done. The other character trait burnished in Blinny's memory was Grandpa Herschel's tenacious work ethic. Blinny received this wisdom in the form of a slogan that his father repeated often: "A Cashin never gives up." He likened Grandpa Herschel to a honey badger, an African mammal that will bite down on its prey and never let go. Uncle Jimmy would affirm this value he learned from his father through repetition: "A Cashin never gives up. You never quit and you never get tired. You just work, work, work and if you are tired you never admit it to yourself."

Dad's received impression was of Herschel's conservatism: "He never drank. He was a man of principle, a real gentleman. Reserved. Kind of stiff. A straight arrow. Very honest." Dad's brother Herschel inherited many of these traits while Dad, the extrovert, did not.

From this oral history and the few pictures we have of Grandpa Herschel—taken in his golden years—he emerges as an aristocratic figure who commanded great respect. From my writing desk at home, I turn to look at his sepia portrait in moments of weariness. As he did with his children, he tells me with his steady gaze to buck up and get on with it, and I do. Minnie's companion head shot conveys her sweetness and maternity. Her lined face, rounded with age, also exudes dignity.

Uncle Jimmy's stories of his childhood explain how Herschel and Minnie contributed to the atavism of later generations, descendants whose speech and deportment evoke an earlier age. Precise use of language was insisted upon and language was learned through recitation. Their parliament of enunciating youth was required to master excerpts from the Bible and from poetry—the Rubaiyat, Edgar Allen Poe, even Latin verse. It was family recreation. In the evenings, each child would recite something that would sound unintelligible coming out of most young mouths. They became constant readers and reciters and a family replete with "good talkers" because communication was the arena in which they learned to compete.

The family ethic also demanded preciseness in physical appearance. Cashin men were taught to keep their shoes well shined. The care of shoes, they learned, said a great deal about a man. Through daily attention to detail, a man signaled gentlemanliness and self-respect. Herschel would line his sons up for inspection. Consequently, in youth and manhood, they would walk on small, neat feet.

In addition, they were raised to be tough and fearless fighters. The learned value was: Nothing worth achieving will be handed to you; you have to go out and earn it, and never be afraid to try. Uncle Jimmy learned to swim by being hoisted into a swimming hole, either by his father or older brothers. Like the young gazelle that must learn to walk, then run, in minutes before any predator may arrive, he was instructed to kick and strike out with his arms, to pull the water behind him with all his strength—a quick baptism into life.

Above all, the Cashin children learned that they were never to think of themselves as separated from that whole that was the American Negro. The family inhabited and thrived in the black world, even as Herschel moved constantly back and forth across the color line as he traveled between home and work. He would expose his children to every sphere, taking one or two of them with him on his business or political trips out of the state. When he attended the National Republican Convention in Philadelphia in 1900 as a McKinley delegate, he brought along Vivi and Jimmy, explaining in a letter to George Myers that he wanted to give "my youngest boy . . . an outing for the summer." At the time Uncle Jimmy was seven; he was named after another of Herschel's heroes, James G. Blaine, who died six months before baby Jimmy was born.[2] It was an act of hope to name a colored son born in Alabama in 1893 after the author of the constitutional guarantee of equal protection under law. In theory, the law was enforceable against any recalcitrant state by the full power of the U.S. government; with rare exception, in practice it would be Herschel's grandchildren who would see the law come to life in the state.

At the Philadelphia convention of 1900, Herschel and Jimmy were photographed with Theodore Roosevelt and one of Roosevelt's daughters. Then the governor of New York, Roosevelt was the reluctant, newly named vice presidential nominee for the Grand Old Party. Betty-V remembers the photo vividly. Her father had on his "Lord Fauntleroy clothes," his hair was "fairish and long with finger curls much nicer than mine, and his face had been blackened in the picture." In life, Jimmy's fair skin was not discernibly different from that of Roosevelt's daughter. It was altered by the newspaper that published the photo in order to clarify that he was in fact a little colored boy. The copy attending the picture made much of Roosevelt appearing with a Negro Republican. In the eyes of the young girl Betty-V when she saw the picture, Roosevelt and Herschel were equals, their elevated social stature confirmed for her by their prominent handlebar mustaches.

Herschel attended his fourth and final National Republican Convention in Chicago in 1904. He was seated once again because the Alabama Black and Tans prevailed over a competing Lily-White-plus-token-black delegation. Although he was pledged to his vigorous federal patron, President Roosevelt, his tenure as receiver of public monies would come to an end six months later, in February 1905. This time he was not a victim of political machinations but of his own success, along with that of the land office register, Judge Steele. Federal law required that the Huntsville Land Office be consolidated with that of Montgomery because the publicly held acreage in north Alabama was now too small to justify keeping the office open. Herschel used the occasion to announce that he would resume his law practice in Decatur. Under the bold headline "Receiver H.V. Cashin Retires from Office," the Huntsville papers covered the story in a long article chronicling his life. Their compliments speak volumes about his stature in the community *and* whites' magnanimous view of themselves in Southern race relations:

> Receiver Cashin retires from the office with the good will and respect of this community in which he has lived during the past eight years, and in this connection, if he were typical of the race in general, there would be no prejudice against the negro [*sic*]. The cultured South has never hesitated to acknowledge any evidence of meritorious service on the part of any member of the colored race. The life of Receiver Cashin proves this; after four years of service as Receiver in the land office he was endorsed for reappointment by many of the most prominent citizens as well as by every probate judge and clerk of the circuit courts in the land district—all of whom were democrats; all testifying to his good

character and prompt and accurate transaction of business submitted to him by their offices. He is a man of extended education and fine business capacity; has borne himself with becoming dignity and good sense and although an aggressive republican, enjoys the confidence and respect of all classes of Huntsville citizens, without reference to party.

Herschel was in his early fifties. Seven years hence, his beloved Black and Tans would cease to exist in Alabama. With so few registered black voters available to cultivate, they struggled to establish a firm political base in the state and to be recognized nationally. The Black and Tans would not be welcome in Teddy Roosevelt's Bull Moose Party. By 1912, Roosevelt had adapted to the political realities in the South; there, he emphasized, the Lily-Whites would form the basis of his party. By 1916, the national Republicans followed suit, turning, once again, to the Lily-Whites for succor. In the meantime Herschel focused on his law practice, his business ventures, and most of all his family. If, in this time and place, politics was no longer a successful means for Negro advancement, he would ensure that the next generation be prepared to contribute in other realms.

Herschel took great care to cultivate independence in his sons. The boys would work their way through school, even though their father could clearly afford to sponsor them. For his daughters, who were raised to be proper young ladies, he was the ultimate provider; their education was paid for without question. The sons rose to their father's expectations. John, my grandfather, worked as a short order cook on the railroad to put himself through Fisk. Jimmy attended Fisk on his wages as a waiter and busboy. Perhaps because he never sired any children, the lore is silent on the financial means Newlyn deployed to attend Phillips Exeter and Howard University.

When Jimmy was admitted to the University of Michigan School of Law circa 1914, he declared to his father that he would pay his own tuition, just as he had as an undergraduate. Herschel's other sons had turned to medicine as a profession. Now Herschel's youngest was entering his profession of law, via a predominately white school in which there would be few if any other Negroes. Herschel demurred, insisting that he wanted Jimmy to think very carefully about what he was saying. Having taken up the law as an apprentice, without the benefit of a law degree, Herschel must have been enormously proud of the leap his son was taking one generation later. He would have wanted him to be unencumbered, free to devote himself completely to his law studies, to demonstrate that he could compete head to head with the brightest minds in the country of whatever race.

Jimmy did not relent. While at law school he insisted on working part-time as a Fuller Brush salesman. The learned ingenuity and persistence required for such a job would suit him well in law practice, at which he became fabulously successful in Chicago. As with all his siblings, Jimmy's respect for his father was genuine. Each child would excel in the world because, above all else, they wanted to prove themselves to the patriarch, who was skilled at signaling his desires to his progeny.

Jimmy had a favorite story that conveyed the enormity of his father's influence. He had recently entered college. He and his father were standing at an elevator, waiting for the door to open. Wanting to demonstrate to his father the man of the world he had become, and the accoutrements of men of the world, he lit a cigarette. The patriarch expressed his disapproval with a piercing stare. The look informed his son that this was not a habit he was going to form. Jimmy understood his meaning. Reduced in seconds from man of the world to son of H. V. Cashin, he put the cigarette out. No words were exchanged; the elevator door opened and they stepped in. In adulthood Jimmy would allow himself no more than one cigarette a day, feeling his father's admonition from the grave. Of course, my grandfather, John, had a contrarian streak and became a heavy smoker—one of a few habits he acquired that his father would not have approved of.

A snapshot I have of Herschel suggests how he and Uncle Jimmy would have appeared that day before the elevator. They are dressed immaculately in three-piece suits, stiff white collars, ties, and hats. Herschel sports a bowler, Jimmy a fedora. Jimmy, then the tallest Cashin man, stands about an inch over his father. They look at each other with mutual admiration, Herschel lightly touching his son's back. By appearance the patriarch is unmistakably a Negro, while his son is not. Herschel's gaze at his son says, "I am proud of the young man you have become." Jimmy stands with his hands behind his back, with an erect confidence, brashness even, and a smile that conveys his delight in his father's approval.

None of Herschel's children disappointed him. He and Minnie lived to see their offspring established in careers or marriages that mirrored their own happiness. All three of their daughters became educators upon graduating from college, although under the laws and mores of the time, Vivi stopped teaching public school once she married. Lillian Emmett, called "Aunt Jack" by Dad, became a university professor after obtaining master's degrees from both Fisk and the University of Chicago. According to Dad, Aunt Jack "*was* the Fisk English Department." "Miss Cashin" stood only about 4 feet 10 inches tall, but as chair of her department she loomed large. Dad speaks of her with the utmost reverence, always emphasizing the same point: "She never raised her voice above a normal speaking tone. Whenever she spoke, it was with eloquence and all who heard her listened." As she learned from her parents, Lillian stood on principle. She was engaged to be married to a man named Poe, who may have been a faculty member at Wilberforce, until a tragic accident altered her course. She fell down a flight of stairs, breaking her hip, and was told she would not be able to bear children. Knowing that her fiancé wanted to have a family, she gave up the man she loved, insisting that they break off the engagement. Henceforth, she poured all her energies into Fisk. She taught generations of students and faculty to study and deploy language and literature with the same care that she did. To this day the "Little Theatre," one of the oldest buildings on the campus, is dedicated to her.

Aunt Pat, my grandfather's twin sister, had a distinguished career as a schoolteacher in Decatur while she took care of her husband, Leo Sykes, who was blinded in World War I. According to Athelyne Banks, she was admired in the community for giving needy colored children money to continue their education. As with her father, the townspeople knew they could talk with Pat about what they needed and she would deliver.

Aunt Pat named her only child Lillian, after her sister, and sent her to live with her namesake as a teenager. Aunt Jack would mold Lillian Estelle Sykes to be an independent, resourceful woman who could burn water with her words. She graduated from Fisk, received a master's from Smith College, and lived a bohemian life in Paris before settling in New York City's Greenwich Village, where her vocation was social work but her avocation was art, jazz, and never suffering fools. Like Aunt Jack, she also never married.

Cousin Lil's lore was mostly of Aunt Jack and the Sykes family. She had no stories of Herschel and Minnie to tell, probably because her communication with her mother, Pat, was so poor. In Lil's unvarnished language, "I couldn't stand her." No one, not even Athelyne, who was close to both mother and child, could explain their tension. Once Pat placed Lil under Aunt Jack's wing, the preoccupations of the emancipated teenager apparently did not give rise to conversations with her aunt about the ancestors. Aunt Jack's influence resonated through Lil, though. She cultivated a love of the arts and a streak of independence in her niece, and Lil, in turn, did the same for me.

⌒: ⚘ :⌒

After Newlyn, the oldest son, finished Howard University College of Medicine in 1908, he set up his practice next door to his father's law office on Railroad Street in Decatur. Early city directories list Herschel, the attorney, at number 411 and Newlyn, the physician, at number 413—two pillars of the community and, presumably, great friends. Newlyn married Countess Harris, the daughter of another Afro-American Reconstruction legislator, Charles O. Harris of Montgomery, and the future sister-in-law of Dr. Ralph Bunche, the Nobel Peace laureate and UN undersecretary.

Like his sisters, Newlyn was diminutive; on a good day he was no more than 5 feet 4 inches tall. Yet he was fearless, and jovial. Blinny remembered stories of Uncle Newlyn going deep into the backwoods of north Alabama and southern Tennessee to treat colored patients. They were Negroes who had mixed with Creek or Muscogee Indians and were so sequestered, the story improbably goes, that some were not even aware that the Civil War had ended. The yarn gets richer. Newlyn reportedly earned his reputation as a backwoods doctor by riding his horse in these roadless environs, bringing along a mule for portage of medical supplies and equipment. He would ride in as far as possible; then he would continue on foot, carrying whatever he could. Once, a man's leg was injured so badly that Uncle Newlyn had to amputate it right where he found his patient or he would have died. Then Uncle Newlyn carried the one-legged man out on his shoulder for a mile to one of those little plots of land where people enclaved.

The story makes me smile. I find it more than a bit incredible, although I suspect there is some shred of undiscoverable truth in it. Likely, he drove a fine car to a distant rural colored hamlet to treat patients for free and thus his legend began.

My father always bragged about Uncle Newlyn playing a role in the Scottsboro boys' trial, testifying on their behalf that the white girls in question were not raped. I was quite skeptical that a colored doctor, even a light-skinned one, would have been allowed to examine the accusers to test their veracity. To my amazement when I researched the issue, I did find that Newlyn testified at the trial, to great effect for the defense, but not for the reasons Daddy claimed.

When the Scottsboro boys were enduring their second trial-cum-fight-for-their-lives in Decatur in 1933, Uncle Newlyn and Leo Sykes's brothers, Drs. Newman and Frank Sykes, were among the supremely educated Negroes the defense attorney paraded before the court to demonstrate the patent discrimination of a criminal justice system in which blacks never served as jurors. With the International Labor Defense, an adjunct of the Communist Party, supporting the defense, the trial became a national preoccupation and a constitutional test of the jury system throughout the South. Uncle Newlyn and Frank Sykes created something of a show on the witness stand. They were among the handful of registered Negro voters in the county; the defense attorney, Samuel Leibowitz, made much of the fact that this feat required them to demonstrate their ability to interpret the federal Constitution. The *Birmingham News* noted that the Negro witnesses were "unusually intelligent in appearance and employed good English." Thomas Knight, the attorney general for the state of Alabama, conducted the cross-examination. Frank Sykes replied to Knight's aggressive questions with polite but immodest self-confidence, an indignation that spurred the Ku Klux Klan to burn a cross on his front lawn as warning for violating a Southern code that depended for its efficacy on Negro submissiveness.

Newlyn was even more "uppity" than Dr. Sykes. Under direct examination he calmly attested to his educational credentials and his life as a practicing doctor for twenty-four years; he vouched for a list of some 200 Negroes he and others must have assembled for Leibowitz. The list included doctors, businessmen, educators, and ministers. Decatur was not short on educated Negroes. Or men of honesty, intelligence, integrity, and sound judgment—the litany of character traits demanded of a juror. Newlyn also stated that in his lifetime he was not aware of a single instance of a Negro being called to serve on a state court jury in Decatur or anywhere else in the state.

The Morgan County Jury Commission was responsible for assembling the roster of potential jurors. In a county with 8,000 Negroes among its 46,000 residents, the state government itself also could not produce evidence of a single Negro ever having been called to serve on a jury. The state attorney general pounced on Newlyn in his cross-examination: "Do you know that this county has a jury commission?" he demanded. As historian Dan T. Carter put it, "Cashin looked Knight squarely in the eye and with a tone of unmistakable disgust replied, 'I know it is supposed to have one.'"

The townspeople were quite angry at Leibowitz for attacking their way of life; he frequently demanded in open court that Knight address the Negro witnesses as "Mister" or "Doctor." Fortunately for the veritable blue book of Negro society that had been called to the witness stand, the militant elements of Decatur had a focal point for their anger—the "outsider, agitating Communists." Only a cross burning ensued, rather than a lynching. Still, I marvel that Newlyn, that tough little man, escaped the wrath of the Klan. The stories that don't come to light are of the blacks who pushed back, who organized security details in their neighborhoods and were ready, with force and arms if necessary, when racial conflagrations threatened to destroy all they had worked for. I don't know whether Uncle Newlyn and the Sykes brothers undertook such protective measures, but I do believe that they would rather have died than cower or retreat from this particular fight for equality.

In the end, Newlyn and his fellow "men of intelligence," as the U.S. Supreme Court described them, were successful in destroying the credibility of the state. In *Norris v. Alabama*, the Court ruled unanimously that the record of many qualified Negroes in the county demonstrated their systematic exclusion from jury service on account of their race and held this to be a violation of the Fourteenth Amendment—an unexpected assault in 1935 on one plank of the Jim Crow regime, from a case mired in racial hysteria.

‿: ❦ :‿

John chose to study dentistry at Meharry Medical College in Nashville, most likely so that he would not be in direct competition with Newlyn for clients or glory. As a young boy, he was forever getting into trouble. The quintessential story was of his fool's gamble with his transportation money. Grandpa Herschel gave his boys two nickels each for the trolley fare to and from school. John, Jimmy, and their best pal, Bo Ferguson, would ride together. One day after school, John spied a piece of pie in a shop window that would cost him all of his remaining five cents were he to savor it. He flipped his nickel to allow fate to choose whether he should go home with Jimmy and Bo or have his pie, but fate chose a third course. The nickel rolled down a street grate, leaving him with no ride and no pie.

Despite the long walk home, John continued to live life on his terms. He fell in love with a chubby, vivacious girl named Grace Brandon who was nineteen to his thirty-three when they married. He set up a practice in Huntsville rather than Decatur, perhaps perceiving that the neighboring cotton-mill town was ascendant. His Brandon in-laws, with their multi-generations of business success and acumen, would be useful. Mostly, he built his practice on Negroes and poor whites who had few other options but to go to "Doc Cashin" for $1.00 fillings.

❦

Herschel marveled at his first grandchild, Carroll Napier Langston Jr. In a picture apparently taken the day of the infant's christening, he lifts the child, clad in a crisp white lace dress for the occasion, so that he may contemplate him, eye to eye, as new mother Vivian smiles approvingly. Vivi and Tode cherished their baby, born in late September 1917, a year in which race riots broke out in four American cities as rampant inflation, unemployment, and newly assertive Negro soldiers vying for jobs and dignity fueled white resentments. The riots spread to twenty cities two years later in the "Red Summer" of 1919. Yet the Talented Tenth continued to advance.

In the 1920s, Tode moved his wife and son to Chicago in order to take a job with the Binga State Bank, the first black-owned bank in Chicago and a financial engine of Chicago's "Black Metropolis"—that city within the city on the South Side where colored people built businesses, social institutions, and a night life to envy, with scarce assistance or attention from the outside world. Being at the center of what would become Chicago's "Black Wall Street," Tode was careful to cultivate a race consciousness in his son, who was even whiter than he in appearance. He also relished black culture. He was an early member of Sigma Pi Phi, better known as the Boulé—a fraternal organization founded in 1904 in Philadelphia by six colored men, mostly doctors and dentists, for the mutual support and cultivation of high-achieving Negro professionals. The exclusive secret society, akin to a black Skull and Bones, was a tight brotherhood of men of like attainments and tastes who met regularly to inspire each other.

In 1927, Tode was elected as the Boulé's seventh national leader, its "Grand Sire Archon," and would serve two terms. In his world, and even more so in his family, color equated with excellence. He was a lifelong student of Negro history, perhaps because he grew up hearing stories about the exploits of his grandfather, John Mercer Langston. Like William Dorsey in Philadelphia, Tode and Vivi kept clippings of all things Negro. Their archives of family and race history landed in our attic, planting the seeds for the amateur family historian I would become. Among their treasures is a nineteenth-century portrait of John Mercer Langston, taken by Washington, D.C., photographer C. M. Bell, and a letter written by Langston to his wife in February 1869, from Washington, D.C., on Freedman's Bureau stationery. Although struggling with the agonies of acute dyspepsia, Langston eagerly anticipates his wife's impending visit to Washington; he intends to get better so that he may take her by boat down the Potomac to Mount Vernon, to see "the resting place of George Washington whose remains all true sons of America love to look upon."

Vivi, the lightest of all her siblings, lived with the challenge of being a white-skinned colored person. In Decatur, she once accepted an invitation to tea and arrived at a well-appointed home full of Southern white women. With no other Negroes discernible, she exited the party, not because she did not feel she belonged but because she did not wish to associate with people whom she believed would only accept her as the white person she was not. Blinny jokingly shares his suspicion that the group simply did not rise to Vivi's level of cultivation.

Vivi was regal, but she taught Blinny and Betty-V, her nephew and niece, to be kind to everyone, never to think they were better than others, *and* to understand what it meant to be colored. She, Tode, and their cohorts in Chicago exuded a pride tinged with a hint of racial superiority, meaning a confidence in their abilities and that of all Negroes. As Blinny said of them: "They were elitist to the degree that they thought they were special in the face of a great force that opposed them and they knew that they were as good or better. And better by definition of their effort, dignity, and honor and in the training that they obtained. That was the way this generation perceived themselves."

When the Binga State Bank collapsed during the Depression, Tode, who had become president of the bank, lost his job. He adjusted, entering law school at Chicago-Kent College of Law, shortly before his own son, the fourth-generation Langston to graduate from Oberlin, would enter the University of Michigan School of Law. Both father and son would practice for a period with Uncle Jimmy in the law offices of Morris and Cashin, until Tode opened his own law offices.

Ultimately, Tode and Vivi's son, Carroll Langston Jr., met a tragic fate. Despite being a quiet soul without a hint of warrior in him, Carroll was eager to join the colored regiments being sent to battle in World War II. Initially, he was rejected; the albumin levels in his urine were such that he could not pass the military's screen for infantrymen, or so the story, passed on by Blinny, claimed. Carroll was undeterred. Airmen, he learned, were exempt from the albumin test. He returned to the recruitment line another day, standing behind a Negro man who was gruffly rebuffed when he declared his desire to be a fighter pilot. The scene brought out a rare ire in Carroll. At his turn, he laid down a challenge, "I want to be a flyer and what would you say if I told you I was colored?"

No one would suspect as much upon looking at him. He was a tall, lanky, disarmingly handsome man with straight dark hair and a movie-star smile. The recruiting officer relented. Carroll was sent to Tuskegee for flight training, where he became one of the revered Tuskegee Airmen. Uncle Jimmy was furious. He was quite close to his nephew and did not believe Carroll was cut out for war. He was amazed that Carroll enlisted without telling him or Tode, who was on the draft board and might have been able to pull strings, if needed, to help Carroll avoid service.

They had done too good a job in cultivating another fearless young man in the family. Shortly after marrying a gorgeous woman named Marguerite, whose blonde hair and blue eyes belied her race, Carroll departed with his unit for Europe. Uncle Jimmy tried to give him a .45 pistol for personal protection, but Carroll would not take it, saying, "I'm not going to use that on anybody, you keep it."

As a pilot, Carroll participated in some of the decisive battles of the Italian campaign. His unit ran forays hitting trains, and gas and oil depots. His plane was shot down over the Adriatic; his wingman saw him eject. The *Chicago Defender* reported that his body and parachute were riddled with bullets; the paper railed against Germany, as the shooting of an ejected pilot was against the rules of war. According to Blinny, the news created a furor, rallying the entire city to the Allied cause. Among the treasures in our attic were Carroll's Purple Heart and his eloquent war diary. Mama would read the journal aloud to me and my brothers, pausing occasionally to comment on its timeless wisdom. He was a philosophical soldier, reading Plato's *Republic* and law books in his spare time, reflecting on whether and how a universal language might be achieved to unite humanity, copying his wife's love-struck letters into the book. In his careless enthusiasm, Dad gave the beautifully written, sensitive diary to someone who was supposed to help get it published, or so Mom claimed with evident frustration—another piece of our personal history that I have no choice but to accept as lost.

Grandpa Herschel died on March 25, 1924, after an illness of three and a half months. Reportedly, he was seventy, but more likely his actual age at death was seventy-two. According to the death certificate, he suffered from multiple ailments including "malaria" and "dementia." Minnie also succumbed to malaria three months later, although one suspects her grief at the loss of her dearest husband simply overtook her will to live. The *Albany-Decatur Daily* printed a brief obituary of the patriarch; funeral services were held on a Thursday afternoon at the family residence on Madison Street, with a Reverend Turrentine officiating: "The deceased was one of the best known negroes in North Alabama . . . having served in charge of the federal land office in Huntsville." The obit seems to confirm that his studies at the Institute for Colored Youth in Philadelphia were his only formal education: "He was educated in the north, studied law and was admitted to the bar." It concludes by acknowledging his twenty years of practice "at the local bar" and as "a leader among the negroes of the Twin Cities."

My father was born four years later. His grandfather's influence would be felt through exposure to family lore and the example of his father, aunts, and uncles, especially Uncle Jimmy, who came closest to picking up Herschel's mantle of political, social, and economic engagement on behalf of "the race." Uncle Jimmy transferred from Michigan to Chicago-Kent College of Law because a prominent Negro lawyer in the city, "Mr. Benjamin," as Blinny remembered him, could not wait for him to finish his studies. Benjamin put Jimmy to work while he was still a student. Upon graduation he became a "doughboy" in World War I, but saw no combat action. He married a woman from a leading black family in South Bend, Indiana. Hortense Fears, who was salutatorian of her class at Oberlin, was eerily similar to Newlyn's wife, Countess, in her Negro society pedigree, light skin, and reserved personality.

Uncle Jimmy became known in Chicago as "Attorney James B. Cashin," and later as "Commissioner Cashin" after he was named to the Cook County Civil Service Commission. He was active in local Republican politics, although he began to sour on the Grand Old Party during the Hoover administration. He was part of a cadre of black Chicago Republicans who thought they had an understanding with Hoover that they would deliver black votes to the 1928 Republican presidential ticket, and Hoover, in turn, would open up new categories of government jobs to the Negro, especially the waves of Southern migrants pouring into the city. Oscar DePriest, then America's sole black congressman, was their leader. Ultimately, the group felt betrayed. Uncle Jimmy's only other overt foray into politics was a failed bid to become a state court judge in Cook County.

Instead, he became something of a legend as a lawyer. He built a client roster composed of many of the major black-owned businesses in the city, including the venerable *Chicago Defender*, the Metropolitan Mutual Assurance Company, and Metropolitan Funeral Home. He would count members of the Rosenwald family—part owners and leading executives of Sears Roebuck—among his many Jewish clients. Blinny also recalls a connection with Post Cereals. Uncle Jimmy must have represented the company in some capacity, as the house was always filled with more Post Toasties than Blinny's young stomach could accommodate—a "lagniappe" for his father's good work, Blinny said, with a common parlance that sends me, once again, to the dictionary.

An oft-told tale of Uncle Jimmy's courtroom prowess concerned a witness in a homicide case in which he represented the defendant. The case turned on the testimony of a white woman who was the prosecutor's sole witness. She claimed the victim's assailant was a Negro and positively identified Uncle Jimmy's client. He began an unusual line of questioning into the vagaries of race, which the judge allowed.

"How do you know the killer was a Negro? Is the judge a Negro?"

"No."

"Is the prosecutor a Negro?"

"No."

"Am I a Negro?"

"No," the witness demurred for the third time.

The courtroom broke into laughter because "Attorney Cashin" was a well-known race man, even if his skin color didn't match his ardor for his people. The witness was flummoxed and her credibility undermined; he won that case. He also once won a $1-million judgment against the U.S. government on behalf of an Indian tribe. Betty-V still remembers the $100,000 check her father showed her; the zeros of his fee made her young eyes pop at what amounted to a king's ransom in the late 1940s.

Jimmy's legend was burnished, however, when he was named as a special prosecutor to bring a case against fourteen corrupt Chicago policemen who had been on the payroll of Al Capone and Frank "the Enforcer" Nitty, Capone's successor. Among other things, the defendants had been paid by Capone and later Nitty to murder their rivals, rendering Uncle Jimmy's job inherently dangerous. Police guards were assigned to a twenty-four-hour detail at his home. One evening when he was out of town, after the children were put to bed, his wife, Hortense, heard footsteps on the stairs. She called out, "Is that you, Holly?" thinking it was Uncle Jimmy's trusted driver and family friend, but no one answered. A mid-stair landing created a right turn, obscuring her view of the ground floor. Her silhouette on the wall revealed to whomever was approaching from below that she was armed with a pistol. The ascender stopped, the house went quiet. Thirty minutes later, Holly returned from an errand. All the guards had disappeared. A subsequent investigation revealed that no Chicago policeman had been sent to the house that evening; the men who were there initially were posing as such. Investigators surmised that this was an aborted attempt to kidnap Blinny and Betty-V. The plan foiled, Attorney Cashin persevered, winning the corruption case and placing fourteen former officers in prison.

Uncle Jimmy was sufficiently respected in both white and black legal circles to be elected chairman of the Chicago Bar Association. He also provided a valuable assist in *Hansberry v. Lee*, the case famous to all students of civil procedure, in which the parents of future playwright Lorraine Hansberry succeeded on a technicality with the U.S. Supreme Court in defeating a racially restrictive covenant that would have denied them the right to live "out south," the term negroes used to describe the predominately white neighborhoods south of Sixty-third Street in Chicago. Although James B. Cashin was not an attorney of record, he helped his dear friend Earl Dickerson prepare his brief and argument for the case.

Uncle Jimmy's own residential infiltration of mostly white environs was much quieter than that of the Hansberrys. As a bachelor and in the early years of his marriage, Uncle Jimmy had lived in a three-apartment building he owned at 4900 Washington Park Court, a very desirable address on the South Side. Vivi and Tode lived in one of the apartments, forming a small but happy Cashin-Langston commune. Uncle Jimmy and Hortense had begun to contemplate buying a single family home, but housing options were not easy to come by in a world of tightly orchestrated racial covenants.

Their move was serendipitous. Hortense, returning from a downtown lunch with her husband, observed a woman on Drexel Avenue who looked burdened, emotionally and physically. She offered her a ride to her home, which turned out to be a brick mansion located on South Greenwood Avenue, a few blocks from Washington Park Court. The ride led to tea and pleasant afternoon conversation. The distressed matron was Jewish, recently widowed, related by marriage to the Rosenwald family, and feeling that the large home was more than she could now manage. She was relieved to sell it to the Cashins in a private sale and was completely indifferent, or unaware, of the race of her purchasers. The neighborhood was predominantly Jewish and welcoming. Almost immediately other well-to-do black families began moving in, resulting not in white flight but residential integration.

The Greenwood Avenue home was but one of Uncle Jimmy's extensive real estate holdings. Following his father's example, he invested heavily in land, acquiring many commercial and rental properties throughout the South Side. He and his Chicago cohorts believed that business was essential to black society. To be self-sufficient, to generate as much business as possible was their aim. They worked to build a black "gold coast" that ran from the South Side to the similarly organized business and residential strips developed by Jewish business leaders on the North Side. They had a vision for their community, and Attorney Cashin was a prime mover in that society from the 1940s until he died unexpectedly of a heart attack in 1952. For many years he served as chairman of the board of the *Chicago Defender*. The *Defender*, black America's most widely read newspaper, was synonymous with the kind of racial boosterism and advocacy Jimmy had observed in his father and learned to emulate. He embodied that spirit as chairman of the board of trustees of Tuskegee Institute, as a longtime trustee of Fisk University, and as the thirteenth grand sire archon of the Boulé in 1948–1950. His racial advocacy would extend to colonial Africa, as a result of an appointment by President Harry S. Truman. In 1946, Uncle Jimmy was one of twelve Americans sent to Ghana, then the Gold Coast; the delegation produced a paper that was part prediction and part road map for the country's independence within twelve years. In fact, Ghana became independent within ten years, the first crack in British colonialism in Africa.

Uncle Jimmy's most enduring legacy would be the values he imparted to his children and favorite nephew. Like Aunt Pat, he continued a family tradition of helping those who needed it to gain an education. "Sponsorship," as the family called it, was the means by which many Negroes paid for college or professional school. Uncle Jimmy sponsored Uncle Tode, his nephew Carroll Langston, and his niece Lillian Sykes in their professional education, and numerous others to whom he was not related. My father continued that tradition, and on more than one occasion, Blinny has encountered men who delightedly informed him that John Cashin "put me through school." Uncle Jimmy also imparted a sense of connection to the Negro community and its most conservative mores. The former Fuller Brush salesman surrounded himself with "Fuller Brush" people, men and women who were persistent in the face of tough odds and confident in their abilities—character traits and relationships that transcended class. Jimmy related to and respected the barber, the shoe shiner, and the gandy dancer just as much as the colored doctors and lawyers in his midst. He taught his children to respect and relate to pride of effort, wherever they found it. Blinny especially was privy to this attitude in his walks with his father down Fifty-first Street in Chicago and in his observance of the men who would come to the back door at South Greenwood for food. He learned to recognize absolute dignity, even among those who were broke. He could see in their faces that they believed, despite their condition, that they were second to nothing on earth. Here was a class of people that had to battle to stay alive, by doing the most menial work, and had to endure the worst insults, both physical and mental. The men on the street and the men at the back door did not have any laxity of spirit, nor did they harbor any expectation of accommodation by society. They simply persevered. In the next generation, my father would identify utterly with such deserving colored folk, only his battleground was Alabama.

CHAPTER EIGHT

Man-Child

My father was born in April 1928, thirteen months after his older brother, Herschel. Uncle Herschel received the name of the patriarch and Dad got to be John Logan Jr. It seemed like a fair arrangement, although the ladies in the neighborhood made it clear to Dad that the gene pool had not been distributed equally. "Oh, what a pretty boy," they would exclaim, fawning over Herschel and marveling at what God had done for Grace and John Sr. in creating such a perfect cherub. "Oh, he's cute," they would say less enthusiastically of my father.

That was another story told and retold by my grandfather to my father, who repeated it ad nauseam to me. Through its repetition my father was made to feel that his brother was lighter of skin and silkier of hair. In pictures and in life, they both looked "high yellow" to me. I could not decipher any gradations between them, but apparently some of the adults that inhabited Dad's childhood could. Decades would pass before most Negroes ceased to be color struck or concerned about "good hair." In the meantime, my father thought of himself as the dark one in the family and competed vigorously with his brother in realms he could control.

Each boy exceeded ten pounds at birth. John Sr. cried like a baby himself with the worry of waiting for his very large sons to arrive. Both sons were born at the home of Grace's parents. Claude and Idella Brandon lived at 210 Church Street in Huntsville in an imposing two-story house made friendly by a front porch that was two steps up from the sidewalk. Like his Brandon forebearers, Grandpa Claude was a successful building contractor and had built the house himself. He and Idella slept in a spacious bedroom on the first floor that was warmed by its own fireplace, the room where my father and uncle were born. On the second floor, a long hallway ran the length of the house, presenting an avenue of closed doors that sparked the curiosity of the boy my father would become. Behind each door was a bedroom for the boarders Claude and Idella took on, usually for love rather than money during the Depression. As John and Herschel grew, the porch became their playground, which later extended to the sidewalk, the yard, and anywhere Idella could see them from the porch. The action was on the porch, though. A neighbor whom the Cashin boys were taught to call "Miss Dora," or her husband, Lee Lowery, would cross the street to greet Claude and Idella. Then a stranger walking by would overhear the conversation, offer an opinion, and quickly become a friend. The five rockers on the porch would soon be filled, and the adults' conversation would flutter above John and Herschel's heads, as they all watched the doings on Church Street.

Dad frequently referred to his grandparents' street as "Nigger Main." For him, it was a term of affection, arising from the same black culture that created the dozens—a game of repartee in which insult becomes art form. To this day he utters the N-word without concerns about political correctness, although he never says it in the presence of someone outside his tribe. Every town in the segregated South with a critical mass of colored people had its black main street. In Huntsville, the intersection of Church Street and Holmes Avenue was the heart of the colored business district, the core of which ran about two blocks along Holmes. Grandpa Claude owned Brandon's Grocery and a building in which he rented space to other Negro-owned establishments, including his son-in-law's dental practice. This black economy also included Citizens Drugstore, Bailey's Cleaners, Royal Funeral Home, Ross' Barber Shop, Parker's Shoe Repair, a beloved restaurant called The Sweet Shop, a gas station, and two pool halls owned by Lee Lowery. His son Joe, who became the Reverend Joseph Lowery, civil rights activist par excellence, was like an older brother to John and Herschel. The elder Lowery was an astute businessman who watched his money carefully and knew how to squeeze revenue out of the habits, both high and low, of his people. He may have owned pool halls, but according to my father, he was also one of the largest stockholders of the Supreme Liberty Life Insurance Company in Chicago.

The Lowerys lived across the street from Claude and Idella and three doors down from Bailey's Cleaners. In the back room at Bailey's, there was a twenty-four-hour poker game that ran for decades and reportedly continues in a different location to this day. John Sr. religiously attended the game on Wednesday afternoons, his time off from his dental practice. He was an expert poker player but not an expert drinker. If he had no more than one drink, he came home a winner. Decades later, when my father was practicing side by side with my grandfather, he learned to collect the old man from his Wednesday forays while he was still ahead.

When their boys were toddlers, John Sr. and Grace moved into an impressive house on Oak Street that Grandpa Claude built for them. It was the only two-story brick house in the neighborhood. It had huge back and side yards, lush pecan and magnolia trees, and a covered front porch that provided a cool expanse of shade. The front rail supported a row of columns that ran the width of the house and featured Claude's masterful, dancing brick patterns. Years later, Oak Street would be renamed Gallatin Street. The home of my father's youth, 509 Gallatin, was what I came to know as "Grandma's house." The neighborhood was known as "the Grove," a name derived from a grove of pecan trees on its edge that shaded and fed generations of Negro children. Like countless Negro neighborhoods throughout the South, the Grove was immediately adjacent to an upper-crust white neighborhood and to downtown. The black serving classes could walk to the elite houses in which they worked and to downtown.

Grace and John Sr. raised their boys essentially as twins. John was the precocious one with something to prove; Herschel was a quiet leader. They attended Miss Annie's nursery school, where John became a favorite pupil and Miss Annie a second mother. He was a quick learner. Miss Annie taught him the alphabet on a Ouija board. He was reading by age three. All the black upper classes of this epoch expected their children to be prodigies, and Grace and John Sr. were no exception. They started John in elementary school at age five, placing him in the third grade with his brother, who had also been skipped ahead by a grade. After three weeks they relented, allowing John to be placed with the second-graders. Eventually Herschel was returned to the age-appropriate grade and the boys rose through school together.

John was always the youngest in his class by a few years, a situation that propelled him academically. He was competitive by nature and did not like losing to anyone. Being younger and smaller than all of his classmates meant that he could not excel at any sport. He could win only at academics and occasionally at romance. In a contest with Lucian Damien for the affections of Hazel Battle, "a pretty little skinny brown-skinned girl," she came to appreciate the benefits of being John's habitué on the schoolyard. He won her over with trinkets he would extract from his mother's box of discarded costume jewelry. In another realm, John would lose badly if he did not have an assist from Herschel. He was an easy target for the class bully, both because of his size and his long silky hair. Grace hated to cut her sons' curls, and this was a source of derision at school. The bully, who was nicknamed "Ip," would grab John by his hair, and if a teacher or Herschel, his protector, was not around, John would take a beating. If Herschel showed up, together the Cashin brothers would beat Ip. In this way my father became dependent on his older brother and learned to follow his lead.

He was also motivated by his parents' expectations. Grace and John Sr. instilled in their sons that they were supposed to be the best at what they did, especially in school. "In elementary school, my classmates would receive gifts like bicycles for a report card with three or four A's on it; if I didn't get *all* A's, I got my ass whipped," Dad would joke. It was a frequent mantra he inflicted on his own children when he became a father. There was a kernel of truth to this story in that both my father and uncle knew that their parents expected straight A's and they usually delivered. As a young girl I felt the same pressure; if I came home with a 95 on a test, Dad would ask, "What happened to the other five?" I learned early on that I was capable of 100 percent and became a straight-A performer simply because I had internalized the lesson, from Daddy's countless stories of his own learned academic discipline, that that was what a Cashin was supposed to do.

As a child, my father quickly figured out that Grandma Grace was the true boss in the household. She was the strong one, the backbone of the family. If a disagreement arose between her and her husband, she always had the last word, and she made the major decisions for the family. John Sr. was content to bask in his wife's competence. She was a strict disciplinarian, the enforcer at home and at work. As a schoolteacher and later a school principal, she was a respected taskmaster. Three decades after her death, I still encounter elderly men and women who speak fondly of their former teacher or superior. One told me:

> *She was tough. . . . But she could accomplish more with just a look. She would look at the child, stern, with her head to the side, and say, "Did you do it?" We would never have any trouble out of that child again.*

Such skills were especially useful when she served as principal at West Clinton Junior High; virtually all of its pupils were residents of Binford Court, a housing project adjacent to the school. She was just as effective and caring with her poor charges as she was with her own children.

At home if her sons needed a whipping, she was the one who administered it. Dad was in trouble more often than his brother; his immense curiosity led him to do things like taking apart clocks, even valued ones, in hopes of learning how they worked. The whipping ritual involved a salutary degree of mental torture, ensuring that such episodes would be rare. The accused would be required to go out into the yard to select the instrument that would be applied to his backside. Grace had strict standards; "Bring me a peach limb or a hedgerow," she would command. The instrument had to be at least two feet long. She knew from experience that peach limbs rarely broke. If the accused did not bring an instrument to her liking and she had to select one instead, the whipping would be much worse.

The situation necessitated careful calculation. How to choose a switch that met Grace's standards, yet would not hurt too much? My father's first mastery of a law of physics occurred when he correctly intuited that if he selected a hedgerow and did not strip it of its leaves, the sting would be less intense because the leaves inhibited the velocity of his mother's swing. When he shared this insight with me, I was in my forties and aggrieved that he hadn't let me in on the secret earlier because I was subjected to the same ritual. When my bad behavior tested the limits of her tolerance, Grandma would intone, "Go in the yard and bring me a switch."

Yet she was sweet. She laughed easily and sang beautifully. A former Fisk Jubilee singer and a coloratura soprano, she was often asked to perform at community events, and she never declined. At her church's annual harvest celebration, she sang "City of Heaven." She walked slowly down the aisle of Lakeside United Methodist, moving the congregation from sadness to joy:

> I am a poor pilgrim of sorrow,
> I'm tossed in this wide world alone,
>
> . . .
>
> I've heard of a city called Heaven,
> I've started to make it my home.

As part of the performance a man dressed as the devil followed her, a red menace with a pitchfork. Dad was five years old then and perceived a threat. He ran down the aisle and tackled the devil because he was about to attack his mama, to uproarious laughter.

Around the house Grandma Grace always sang her favorite gospel, "[H]is eye is on the sparrow, and I know He watches me." She taught my father her love of singing; he was a boy soprano in the choir at Lakeside, until his voice cracked and he evolved into a fine tenor. She wore Jean Naté perfume and liked elegant things, yet she had an earthy side. The same dignified persona, the public Grace, would come home, take off her shoes, and work in her garden. Uncle Jimmy and Uncle Newlyn found her a delightful sister-in-law. On trips to Chicago, Newlyn, John Sr., and James would take their wives to the racetrack, where Grace would put the men to shame with her knowledge of horses. She would outbet the men and win. She was buxom, beautiful, and could give tit for tat in the family jousts.

She was also a classic grandmother, the person from whom I learned that there were appropriate and inappropriate ways of doing things: how to set a table, to hold a fork, to butter and eat one's bread. The dinner roll should always be divided into four pieces, each piece delicately placed into the mouth, not chomped on like you were starving. You were required to say "Yes, thank you," and "No, thank you" when asked if you wanted something. You were also required to read in the summers when your parents parked you, sometimes for weeks, in her care. The answer to professed boredom was always a trip to the public library, one short block from her house.

She paid me a nickel for each "plus" I received on my report card. She taught me to play checkers, both the American and Chinese versions, and delighted on the rare occasions that I managed to beat her. She brooked no nonsense but always found ways to indulge her baby-grands. Despite being a diabetic, she would place a nest of peanut M&M's in front of us, followed by ice cream, while we watched Ed Sullivan. Her food, like her many hugs, conveyed pure love.

While my father got his discipline from his mother, he learned much about empathy from his father. John Sr. could relate to all manner of people and John Jr. followed suit. His best playmates, "Bass" and "Salmonhead," lived in shotgun houses with no indoor plumbing, while he lived just two blocks away in one of the nicest houses occupied by a Negro family. They grew up during the worst of the Depression, and my father found it difficult to watch his friends' deprivation. He followed his parents' example of being generous to the needy in their midst, only he was more aggressive about it. He would smuggle food from the pantry to his friends, sometimes sacrificing his own dinner so that they might eat. An elder I recently met who was an elementary school classmate said of him, "John always played with the poor kids." Herschel, the introvert, was more aloof.

My father's first experience with unvarnished racism was literally a baptism by immersion. He was eight or nine and a frequent customer of the (white) YMCA's model airplane shop. From the first time he saw a picture of an airplane in a magazine, he became hooked and he was spending all of his earnings as a newsboy on "funny books" and model airplanes. He had graduated from airplane kits and would cut gliders of his own design from the loose balsa wood that only the YMCA stocked. He bought his prized supplies through a basement window from Paul Taylor, a friendly white teenager whom he knew well because Paul's father owned a grocery store he frequented. One day, leaning through the window, waiting expectantly for Paul to fill one of his orders, a cascade of water came down on his head. He looked up, thinking it was an accident, then exclaimed, "Hey, you better watch what you're doing with this water, you might get somebody wet." "Yeah, little nigger, and if you stay there much longer I'm gonna drown your black ass!" responded the manager of the Y, a sinister grin spread across his face. My father realized that the head of this "Christian" establishment had intentionally poured a bucket of mop water on him, and enjoyed the sport of it. He ran home, crying. His parents' stoic response was, "Stay away from there." He never returned, the first of several accommodations to Jim Crow he would have to make. Before this incident he had been well aware of segregation, but not the ugly meanness that could animate it. His parents had tried to shelter him, but he was adventurous, and he had a bicycle. He could ride out of the Grove and into whatever awaited him.

And so the race lessons continued, especially once childhood gave way to adolescence. At about age thirteen, two white boys who were part of the neighborhood gang, Dick and "Squirt," announced that they were now young white men and, because John and Herschel were colored, they would have to call them "Mister." The Cashin brothers laughed at the irony of the request. They had played with these boys, the sons of two different grocery proprietors, for years. Race distinctions had never been an issue when the gang occupied their fortress, a large abandoned barn on the old McAnally estate. Nor in the fourth and fifth grades, when the boys who were now demanding a title came to John and Herschel for help with their homework. They were dumb as far as my father was concerned, and from that moment on they were no longer worthy of his friendship. The Cashins also stopped trading at the stores owned by the families of these newly minted segregationists.

This was their usual response to racism, to withdraw to the comfort of the black world, its institutions and reliable friends. When such incidents would arise, my grandparents would instruct their sons simply to leave white people alone. Try to understand them, but keep your distance. At the dinner table, whenever the conversation turned to "the race problem" the elders would make a joke about it. The notion of white supremacy was amusing to them because they knew they were better educated and more cultured than most of the whites in their midst. At least that was the message Dad received. He knew he was Dr. Cashin's boy, and this invested him with a self-esteem that made the occasional insults of Jim Crow bearable. Although they sometimes laughed at the ironies of segregation, the elders also conveyed that white supremacists could be dangerous. Rather than teach John and Herschel to be subservient, they taught them to be smart. The best strategy, they advised, was avoidance.

The message seemed inconsistent to my father, knowing that his father made much of his money from his poor white patients. Dad thought his father was too lenient in his attitudes toward whites. He knew his father was frustrated by racism and, as a boy, he thought his father was too accommodating. As an adult he would better understand his father's inaction, although he believed that Jim Crow would have lasted another 100 years had subsequent generations displayed his father's lack of ferocity or resignation. John Sr. may not have had the mettle of his brother Newlyn, or the freedom from intimidation that James enjoyed by living in Chicago rather than the Deep South. John Sr.'s only outlet was to cuss the white folks, which he did only after having a few drinks. In the context of a violence-backed Southern racial regime, the only system he had ever known, my grandfather seemed to believe that there was little that could be done about the situation and, like many other Negro men of his time and place, was not inclined to fight. Instead he enjoyed his life—his family and practice, his weekly poker game—and he gave his sons everything he had, including the tools to maneuver successfully within a racial caste system ostensibly set against them.

Grace was more resolute, at least in the eyes of the son who worshipped her. She lived long enough to see him become an agitator, a role she had never anticipated for either of her sons. Yet she supported him and was immensely proud of him. In 1964, when the president of First National Bank, one of the oldest banks in the state, called her to request that she instruct her son to stop stirring things up in his role as member of the Alabama Advisory Committee to the U.S. Commission on Civil Rights, she politely ended the conversation. As a woman who saw no limits for her son, she was indignant and insulted that anyone should ask her to impose any restraints on him. "John, I know there are going to be some tough times coming, but I want you to know that I am with you all the way. You do what you think is right," she told him.

She had prepared him well for flight from her nest. Dad and Uncle Herschel attended the only school available to Negro children in Huntsville. William Hooper Councill High School was named after the prominent north Alabama educator and protégé of H. V. Cashin. All its teachers were Negro and very caring. Most had some college training, typically from Alabama A&M, where Grace had completed her undergraduate education. But Councill High was not accredited. It lacked science labs and other

facilities that were standard at the all-white high schools. It also came with
certain aesthetic disadvantages. On a hot day the teachers would open the
windows to let in some air. Unfortunately, the air was not always fresh. My
father can still recall the stench of the city dump wafting in. Or worse, the
stink of the honey pots. Most of the homes in the Grove lacked indoor toi-
lets. When a certain fetid odor invaded the classrooms of Councill High,
my father knew that Bud Moore, the driver of a horse-drawn sanitation
wagon, was in town. Blocks away, Mr. Moore was dutifully emptying the
honey pots and re-hanging them in the outhouses of the Grove.

A Negro child in Alabama in 1942 who wished to attend an accredited
high school had only three options in the entire state, one of which was
Alabama A&M High School, located on the campus of A&M in Normal,
Alabama. Although it meant her young sons would have to live on a college
campus, thirty minutes away from her, Grace saw to it that they enrolled at
this school in the tenth grade because she wanted them to have the very
best education available. At A&M her sons' teachers were thoroughly
educated college instructors. Her offspring also received music instruction
and Dad took up the trumpet. In addition, they were ensured access to the
college's science laboratories, as well as a distinct extracurricular education that Grace would not have approved of.

They lived on campus in Grayson Hall among collegians from across
the state. At fourteen, my father grew up fast in this environment. Among
other skills, he learned from his hall-mates how to cheat at blackjack. Herschel remained his roommate, best friend, and primary example. He was
very principled, "so principled it would make you sick," Dad would say.
There was no hustle or guile about Uncle Herschel. He did everything by
the book. My father was inclined to find the shortcut to any result he
desired; Herschel was the dedicated plodder. He was extremely conscien-
tious in his studies, and Dad was determined to best his brother's effort.
The sibling rivalry propelled the brothers to the top of their class. They tied
for valedictorian with Ethel Harris, who became Dr. Ethel Hall, a pioneering educator.

Alabama A&M also reaffirmed the brothers' sense of history and their
place in it. Mr. Elmore, their history teacher, would speak of the black leaders of prior generations, including H. V. Cashin. At night, in the dormitory,

they would discuss their future and recommit to "finishing Grandpa Herschel's job," which for Dad meant rendering the U.S. Constitution effective for black people in Alabama. They intended to do whatever was necessary to return blacks to their rightful place as citizens vested with equal rights and real political representation. Their future activism, they concluded, would require preparation and a foundation for independence. Like their father and uncles, they planned to be self-employed professionals who could not be fired by the white segregationist establishment they hoped to topple. Seeking further education fit with their parents' plans for them, which of course meant going to Fisk University.

Manhood

It made sense for a second generation of Cashins to attend Fisk University. As my father and uncle were approaching their college years, most of the adults in their lives considered Fisk to be first among historically black colleges, excepting those who went to Morehouse, Tuskegee, Howard, or wherever educated Negroes had vested their bragging rights. Fisk *was* the first historically black college to gain approval of national and Southern accreditors, and it attracted and cultivated the very best that Negro America had to offer. Sociologist Charles S. Johnson, author Arna Bontemps, poet James Weldon Johnson, and artist Aaron Douglas were among its elite faculty. And Fisk students and alumni were necessarily all strivers—a cultural milieu the Cashin boys may have taken for granted given the dictates of their upbringing.

The school's culture was certainly not foremost on my father's mind when he arrived on the Fisk campus in Nashville in the fall of 1944, at age sixteen. His immediate impression was, "I never saw so many pretty women in my life; I thought I had died and gone to heaven." Grace had advised her sons with a wistful playfulness that they might meet their wives during their first week as freshmen. With much of the male competition eliminated by the draft, it was a happy hunting ground. Uncle Herschel was more successful than Dad with the ladies. Endowed with high cheekbones, a smooth olive complexion that betrayed his mother's Indian heritage, jet-black silky curls, and a quiet demeanor that suggested choirboy goodness, he was the epitome of the "pretty Negro." When he walked into a room every woman's head would turn. "He had his *choice*," Dad exclaimed sixty years later. Other men on campus shared my father's envy and crowned Herschel with the moniker "Sir Maidenswoon."

The Cashin brothers could not get into too much trouble in their freshman year because they were carefully situated. Again they were roommates, and they were assigned to live in Richardson House, which shared a driveway with Aunt Jack's home. Her proximity compelled rectitude. The privilege of being Miss Cashin's nephews brought with it the burden that they were expected to be as correct as she was. Every Fisk administrator, faculty member, or night watchman knew exactly who they were. They behaved largely as expected. Both brothers enrolled in a pre-med curriculum and continued to excel academically.

The spring semester brought an important rite of passage. It was pledge season for the fraternities and sororities on campus. All such organizations, most of which came into being in the first or second decades of the twentieth century, were oriented toward character building and social cohesion among those Negroes fortunate to enter collegiate life. Once Herschel announced, "We are going Omega," Dad deferred to his older brother, as he did in all things, despite their sibling competition. They were both attracted to the four cardinal principles of Omega Psi Phi: manhood, scholarship, uplift, and perseverance—ideals commensurate with the values that had been passed on from the patriarch, to their uncles and father, to them.

They would be molded from "dogs," the lowest form of animal life, into Omega men only if they could survive the eight-week pledge period. Dad, the shortest, was Dog No. 1 and Herschel was Dog No. 7 on a line of fifteen brothers. They were required to attend weekly pledge meetings on Friday or Saturday evening, at which time they would be inculcated in the history, rituals, and principles of Omega. At the end of each meeting, Omegas from Tennessee Agricultural and Industrial, Meharry, and the graduate chapter in Nashville would stop by to sample the fresh meat. "You were obligated to turn your ass up for that paddle," Dad recalled, the physical pain still resonating. The entire pledge experience was formative. "It built character. You had to decide you were going to persevere through it." Fisk's Omega chapter, Eta Psi, was mild compared to the mighty Rho Psi of Tennessee A&I, now Tennessee State. At A&I, half the football team were Omegas and strong with the paddle. Charles Brandon of Rho Psi especially enjoyed stopping by the Fisk campus to haze his first cousins.

The pledge rituals were mental as much as physical. The dogs on the line had to maintain their grade-point averages or be expelled from the fraternity, and demonstrate proper deference to the big brothers, which meant doing everything they were told to do. The most challenging hurdle was Hell Week, in which the dogs had to dress alike in dark suits, march together, and each carry a kerosene lamp, signifying the quest for light, wherever they went. For one week they ate all meals together and were not allowed to break from the line except to attend class. The big brothers also intended that they not sleep for the entire week. Each dog knew better than to lay his head at his normal residence, as a big brother would rouse him in the middle of the night with an assignment, the worst of which was a scavenger hunt at a nearby cemetery. By sunrise the dogs had to prove they had located the headstones of a list of persons buried at the multi-acre graveyard. Dad did sleep intermittently during Hell Week because he had the perfect hiding place, the attic in Ballantine Hall, which he knew about because Aunt Jack had lived in the building. It had a trapdoor that rendered the space invisible to unsuspecting eyes. He was happy to share it with his buddy Morton Rogers, Dog No. 14. Uncle Herschel's refuge was more comfortable; the Deltas, sister sorority to the Omegas, took care of him.

Hell Week concluded on April 16, 1945, when Dad happily "crossed the burning sands" to Omega-dom on his seventeenth birthday. From that point on, if he needed anything that his own extended family could not provide—an entrée to an important opportunity, a place to stay in a strange town, a discreet political favor—he turned first to the fraternity of Omega brothers, and typically they would deliver. The brotherhood was especially dominant in Nashville, and in his college and professional school years, anyone who became an important mentor to my father seemed to be an Omega.

Without the leavening influence of Aunt Jack as a neighbor and Herschel as a roommate, Dad found his way to mischief in his sophomore year. Uncle Herschel was drafted in the summer of 1945; while he trained to become a paratrooper and then an officer, line-brother Morton Rogers would be Dad's roommate. They lived in Burroughs Hall, a new dormitory with four apartments and eight male Fiskites to each apartment. Dad and Morton shared a bedroom that had been converted from a kitchen.

The mischief arrived in the spring, on my father's eighteenth birthday. He was a bold sort who figured, with his Uncle Jimmy on the Fisk trustee board, he could get away with breaking the rigid codes of Fisk conduct—*if* he got caught. He decided to celebrate his passage to manhood with a co-ed party in the proper, adult style. On Jefferson Street, the main drag between Fisk and Tennessee State, it was easy to purchase liquor as a minor; the only requirement was adequate cash—an errand made all the easier by a frat brother who managed a package store.

Dad had put on a few soirees in his apartment before, but this party would prove exceptional. Each man in the apartment invited a date and the gathering quickly swelled to about ten couples. It was a cardinal sin to invite members of the opposite sex into the dorm, and even worse to serve them alcohol. The taboo added to the revelry. "We were partying like mad until there was a loud knock at the door," Dad recounted.

Boom, boom, boom, boom.

"Who is it?"

"President Jones."

"Piss on the floor and swim under," they laughed, thinking it was a classmate who wanted in.

Jones kept knocking. "Oh, shit," my father realized, "it *is* President Jones." He launched into action, instructing everybody to go down the back stairs. He would stay behind and take the fall if necessary. The revelers tiptoed down the stairs while Dad changed into his pajamas and stalled as long as he could. He put on a good act, opening the door to greet Thomas Elsa Jones, the last white president of Fisk, and the night watchman.

"What's going on here?" Jones demanded.

"I don't know, I was asleep," Dad said, feigning grogginess.

The record player was still turning, the last 78 scratching in an endless loop. They had been swaying to an Erskine Hawkins number, "After Hours," then the national anthem of colored youth intent on assuaging their libidos with a close slow dance.

The night watchman, a Negro universally nicknamed "Willshoot" because he had a "trigger hand" when it came to reporting student violations, was the one who had alerted the president. President Jones and Willshoot searched the empty apartment. Glasses with lipstick were everywhere. The chances of Dad's plan of evasion working were slim and finally dashed by a sole reveler, Thomasera Payton, who had locked herself in the bathroom. Willshoot entered the bathroom through a window that opened onto a hall landing, to find Thomasera hiding in a linen closet under the shelves. Determined to ferret out all culprits, President Jones took my father and Thomasera, who were not romantically linked, to his office.

At the interrogation, Jones was incensed that neither defendant would confess to anything or name names. He ordered Willshoot to corral every single man on the campus. Willshoot cleaned out the library, every dormitory, and the co-op, a venue where students tended to congregate around a jukebox. He then paraded scores of men through the president's office, while Jones scrutinized the reactions of both defendants as each man entered.

Dad and Thomasera maintained poker faces, refusing to identify any co-conspirator, which incensed the president even more. The interrogation continued for two hours; my father kept up his act of professed ignorance even as several of the young men who had been at the party passed by in the lineup. Later, one of the revelers, Frank Lanier, would marvel to him, "Cashin, man, you're the coolest SOB I ever saw, I was about to piss in my pants." The next day the dean of students threatened my father with expulsion, berating him as immoral scum who would never amount to anything, and hurling any invective he could think of to get him to name his co-conspirators. He refused and the university expelled him, sending him home with Tubby Johnson, the football coach, athletic director, and a former Fisk all-star. Morton rode home with his roommate as a gesture of emotional support. When they pulled into the yard on Gallatin Street, John Sr. came out cursing at his close friend. "Tubby, dammit, if you had been doing your job the boy wouldn't have gotten in this trouble." To his son he said only, "That was a stupid thing to do." "Maybe it was stupid but I got away with it before," my father said of his earlier parties and his logic.

My grandfather must have seen some of himself in his son. In a sense, Dad was continuing a family tradition. John Sr. never received a degree from Fisk because a religion professor smelled cigarette smoke on his sweater and, for the sin of violating a strict code of conduct, flunked him in

Bible, a required course. He was able to enter Meharry Medical College and graduate with a dental degree in 1920, but he was forever embittered by the experience. According to Dad, whenever my grandfather had a drink or two he would rage against organized religion and the "damned unctuous hypocrite" who flunked him in Bible. John Sr. could empathize with a son who was being penalized for enjoying a few vices and reserved his ire for Fisk and Tubby, whom he cursed for leaving a hole in his son's schedule that was big enough to encourage deviance.

Grace was quiet. She was disappointed, but now that Fisk had expelled him, she received the news with equanimity, in part because she knew instinctively that this was not the end of her son's education. Perhaps in telling me the story, Dad conveniently forgot, or glossed over, his mother's devastation. When I questioned him about it, he only recalled that "she wasn't all that upset, I was still her baby." I imagined that the taskmaster I knew as a grandmother would have given him a tongue-lashing, at least, for failing to live up to the standards she had set for him. But I could also imagine that she was inclined to support her youngest when external forces were conspiring against him, even if he had brought the trouble upon himself.

Whatever her attitude, Grace used the opportunity of her son's expulsion to take a monthlong trip to see her sister, Marguerite Brandon Fletcher, in Houston. For Dad, serving as his mother's chauffeur was a joyful punishment. Her 1939 Cadillac sport sedan was a sweet ride that enhanced the attention he received from the young ladies of Houston.

Tennessee A&I proved an excellent alternative, although Herschel teasingly told his brother that it was "a cow college" and that A&I stood for "Athletic and Instrumental." The public, historically black college down the road did not have the reputation of Fisk but it was academically sound and Dad used his fraternity connections to gain entrance. Dr. J. D. "Chick" Chavis—Nashville's answer to Erskine Hawkins and conveniently an Omega—was forming a marching band at A&I. Like Hawkins had done with his 'Bama State Collegians a generation before, Dr. Chavis was looking for the best musicians he could find to form the "Tennessee State Collegians," who would perform both as a marching and swing band.

Dad paid a visit to Dr. Chavis, taking the trumpet he had learned to play at Alabama A&M with him, and talked his way into a music scholarship.

According to Dad, Dr. Chavis recognized that the assertive young man standing before him was not an excellent musician. He must have seen potential beyond the realm of music in my father and decided to do him a favor. Playing with the Tennessee State Collegians became one of the greatest experiences of my father's life; he became fifth chair to some fabulous trumpet players—the fifth being the weakest player in the line of horns—and began taking courses in the summer session. Perhaps because he excelled at other pursuits, he was humble about his lack of musical talent. "I was the sorriest member of the horn section, my only strength was I could play loud," Dad told me. "I was not a real musician but the guys were so nice to me. They let me have a solo on 'Bear Mash Blues,' the only solo I could manage; otherwise I was only drafted to play solos when a band member got drunk."

The Tennessee State Collegians garnered much fame for innovations like marching with flashlights tied to their shoelaces. At halftime at the Tennessee State football games, once the lights were dimmed, the crowd would roar in anticipation. For Dad it was a time of sheer happiness, and a source of characteristic bravado: "We were the best black collegiate band in the country and had a football team to match. We were kicking everybody's ass." Among his band-mates who went on to some fame as professional musicians were Phineas Newborn, a pianist with an exceptionally fast hand, and Jimmy Cleveland, the finest trombone player Dad ever encountered.

As fifth-chair trumpeter, my father's primary contribution to the Collegians was as a budding political organizer. The *Pittsburgh Courier* had begun its annual band poll, inviting its readers to vote for the best black collegiate marching band in the country. The pink-papered rag bought by more than 200,000 Negroes each week was a source of enlightenment on the main streets of black America, where it was distributed by newsboys and in the barbershops, drugstores, and other Negro establishments that sold it. Just in case the *Courier*'s readership did not see things his way, Dad stacked the deck in his new school's favor. He had learned printing in high school at A&M and understood instinctively what it would take for the Collegians to mount an effective "campaign" in three weeks.

When he explained his strategy to Sonny Hemphill, a frat brother who owned Hemphill Press in Nashville, Hemphill allowed him unlimited use of a print shop for two days. The project took about twelve hours. Dad printed 35,000 precise facsimiles of the *Courier* ballot. Then he built an impromptu, nationwide network, relying on frat brothers, band members, classmates, and anyone else who would volunteer to hand out ballots and instruct recipients to vote for the Collegians. In cities across the South and beyond, his volunteers collected ballots wherever the *Courier* was sold and turned them in for supporters of the Collegians. He took the self-assigned job of campaign manager quite seriously, the same kind of focus he would bring to bear on civil rights and NDPA campaigns in the future.

His "organization" bent the rules by printing their own ballots and canvassing would-be voters. They did not falsify any ballot, but they did their job too well. In the final count, the Collegians garnered about 15,000 of the 20,000 votes cast. Florida State's marching band polled at second place with a few thousand votes. As the "winners" of the contest, the Collegians were invited to play at Carnegie Hall in a double bill with the Buddy Johnson Orchestra, featuring Arthur Prysock, then one of the most popular R&B bands in the country. The Collegians were eternally grateful to my father. This was his second successful political campaign. His first had involved getting Goldie Gibson elected as Miss Fisk. She was not a classic beauty; she was, however, a Delta and that was enough incentive for her Omega brother to marshal his fraternity to her cause.

In addition to playing in the band he loved, Tennessee A&I enabled Dad to pursue his lifelong fascination with airplanes. The school had initiated a new Department of Aeronautics, and he was able to demonstrate that he was a worthy candidate for an aviation scholarship by donating five model planes he had built from kits and his own designs. He was ready to move from playing with radio-controlled models to flying real airplanes. A&I rewarded him with two forty-hour flight instruction scholarships. In the summer of 1946, he learned to fly in an Ercoupe, a single-engine tricycle of an aircraft that traveled slowly and low to the ground. His flying idol was Daniel "Chappy" James, a World War II bomber squadron leader who would later become the nation's first black four-star general. James was training at Godman Field in Kentucky at the time and had extended his legend when he reportedly buzzed the Fisk campus in a B–25 bomber and threw an apple into the bell tower of iconic Jubilee Hall. In an Ercoupe, any form of acrobatics was impossible, and for the time being Dad had to content himself with acquiring a pilot's license and an instrument rating, and occasionally lowering the window to wave at an earthbound creature he wished to impress.

~: ⚘ :~

In the fall of 1946, my father entered his third year of college as a full-time student at A&I. He was doing well academically, and he began to consider his future. Herschel had declared that, upon return from active duty, he wanted to pursue law rather than medicine. From the beginning, whenever John Sr. had introduced his boys to anyone, he had always concluded by saying, "and one is going to be a doctor and the other a lawyer." Having heard this edict his entire life, Dad accepted it as a given. Once Herschel decided to pursue law, it never occurred to Dad to be other than a dutiful son and brother, and follow the course that had been predetermined for him, which meant joining his father's dental practice. Decades later, when he was fighting political battles in Alabama, he would begin to think that he should have been the lawyer and his brother the dentist. But as a scientifi-cally inclined collegian, it had made sense to him to pursue medicine.

When the spring semester arrived, he approached Fisk about eliminat-ing the "incompletes" on his transcript, the result of his expulsion the year before. He intended to apply to Meharry Medical College for dental school and wanted to remove those blemishes from his record. At the time, Meharry, John Sr.'s alma mater, and Howard University's College of Med-icine, Uncle Newlyn's alma mater, were practically the only schools avail-able to Negroes who wished to study medicine or dentistry. The competition for entrance was fierce. The Fisk brass relented, readmitting him for the limited purpose of extinguishing his incompletes. He cemented his reputation as a genius among his classmates when he began to carry a full load of classes simultaneously at A&I and Fisk.

Those who perceived Dad as the brilliant one who rarely studied were not privy to his strategic manipulations. He finessed carrying a full load at both schools by taking essentially the same classes at A&I that he was com-pleting at Fisk. A Jefferson Street bus that ran every five minutes facilitated the feat. Fisk was at the intersection of Jefferson and Eighteenth Street, A&I at Jefferson and Twenty-eighth. Between the two institutions of higher learning were the haunts where my father completed much of his extracurricular education. At the Waikiki, a soul food restaurant favored by Fiskites and Meharry men, his favorite table was in the back, near a door where he could leave undetected when he had a "hot date." At the Del Morocco, a blues club, restaurant, and bar, there was a regular crap game in the rear of the second floor and if he had 50 cents he didn't need, on a lucky night he could run it up to five or ten dollars. The Omega House was behind the Del Morocco and the fraternity brothers would often proceed from orderly meetings to it or another beloved nightclub, the Revilot—the owner's name Toliver, spelled backward. Both clubs were venues on the "chitlin' circuit" where some of the best jazz and R&B artists in the country would play, including one who would eventually become Dad's patient. As part of his burgeoning outrageous act, Little Richard would pick up a cocktail table with his teeth. When he became born again in 1957 and moved to Huntsville to study religion for a year at Oakwood College, my father would be the person who dealt with the consequences of Richard's "table eater" routine.

But in the meantime my father was busy with school. Dad would travel back and forth between Fisk and A&I, sometimes as many as four times in a day. The bus ride cost only a nickel and took no more than five minutes. Upon arriving at one end of Jefferson Street or the other, he would jump off and run as fast as he could. Because he was an excellent student, his teachers usually forgave him for committing the indecorous infraction of entering their classrooms after they had begun to lecture.

Neither institution was aware that he was enrolled at the other, and he used the situation to his advantage. Physics was his most challenging course. He surmised that as long as neither of his professors knew he was taking the same class at a rival institution, he could go to one professor when he had trouble with the homework assigned by the other. It was a singular rarity in the 1940s for a young man to have two Negro professors, each with a Ph.D. in physics, at his disposal. Dr. L. R. Posey at A&I and Dr. Jim Lawson at Fisk both took great personal interest in the student with seemingly independent queries about the laws of physics. Dad didn't have to study as hard as he might have with his system of reliance on impromptu tutorials with alternate professors. "I was piling up hours and A's," he said of that semester. What his classmates didn't see was how he would rise well before dawn to study with intensity when, despite his stratagems, his double course load demanded it.

Eventually Posey and Lawson figured out my father's ruse, but they continued to cooperate because they were quite amused by his ingenuity. They invited him to join a group of science faculty and star students who would congregate at the Waikiki to eat and discuss the problems of the universe, both literal and figurative. "The Literati," as Dad called them, had a regular table near the front of the restaurant. Inevitably, the race question would arise, and my father's mentors would talk about the contributions that blacks were going to make to science. Their confidence in their own genius, and in the ability of their people to make revolutionary discoveries, fueled Dad's someday aspirations of bringing about radical change in Alabama. Until his time came, he would continue to lay his foundation for independence, and squeeze all that he could into his life.

When Herschel returned from active duty, the two brothers returned to being roommates, this time living rent free in south Nashville in an apartment building owned by Grace's oldest brother, Uncle Jack. Like Grandpa Herschel, Uncle Jack—Claude Jackson Brandon—had earned his way into the black upper classes as a railway mail clerk on the Louisville & Nashville line. He parlayed his secure government paycheck into a string of business ventures in Nashville, including Marge's Saratoga, a successful nightclub of questionable repute, and a stake in the black-owned Brown Belle Bottling Company, which manufactured and distributed a cola favored by black Nashvillians.

The Cashin brothers called their off-campus apartment "The Seraglio," a word that could connote either a sultan's palace or a harem, and they likely intended both meanings. With the money he received from the GI Bill, Herschel returned to his studies at Fisk with cash to spare. They furnished the apartment at a standard above college issue, and, free of the rigid codes of conduct of the university, entertained an "in-crowd" in a manner that made Dad's sophomore birthday party seem quaint. Despite his stellar grades, my father was beginning to earn a well-deserved reputation as a playboy, a social status that almost kept him out of Meharry. In an interview in 1972 with a doctoral student writing about the NDPA, he would reflect on this period of his life with evident derision. Eventually he matured, he said, and got serious about activism. The revelation of living in complete freedom in Europe, after graduating from dental school, would accelerate that process. In the meantime, he worked hard and played harder.

Dad applied to dental school in the spring of 1948. It was an unusual case for the admissions committee. What to make of a kid who had been expelled from Fisk for socially odious reasons, who did not have enough hours to receive a degree from A&I, yet had more A's than most other applicants? The committee was sharply divided. The "blue noses," as Dad called them, objected to his character. According to Dad, the dean of the Medical College, Clifton Dummett, and Dr. Carl Henry, an eminent dental professor and frat brother, were so impressed with his record that they threatened to resign if the committee did not accept him.

Dad entered the School of Dentistry in the fall of 1948, although he almost betrayed his sponsors' trust. The lure of mischief called again. For once he was not the chief instigator. He had no problem going along, however, when a number of classmates, all frat brothers, decided to pile into two cars for a road trip to New Orleans for Mardi Gras. The young men, detained by the many charms of the Big Easy, extended their spring break longer than they should have. Classes had resumed by the time they returned, and school administrators considered expelling them for their impudence. Most likely they were saved by a faculty member whose son was among the revelers.

My father was also saved by his grades. He had finished his first semester with the highest grade point average in his class and had earned much respect and protection among Meharry faculty and administrators. At the Omega spring dance, his academic exploits were the subject of conversation among the Omega elders. Dr. J. B. Singleton, dean of the Dental School, speaking to Dr. Walter Davis, the president of Tennessee A&I, observed that John Cashin was leading his class. Dr. Davis asked him where his undergraduate loyalties lay. My father diplomatically but sincerely said he felt beholden to A&I, although he bemoaned that he did not have an undergraduate degree from either Fisk or A&I. Davis laid down a pointed challenge. He had been seeking university status from the state of Tennessee for his college and wanted "some real scholars" to help elevate the school's academic status. At the same time my father wanted an undergraduate degree from a fully accredited university. "Well, young man, if you continue to lead your class for the next four years, and if you claim us, I will give you a degree from Tennessee State University when you graduate from Meharry." It was a three-way wager. Davis would secure university status for Tennessee A&I in the next four years, Dad would lead his class, and Singleton would hold both men to their commitments.

Dad accepted the challenge. His reputation as both a genius and a partyer grew. Frat brothers at both the dental and medical schools would approach him for help with their coursework and he would oblige. He received an A in most of his classes, a few B's, and one black mark, a C in Dental Materials, a class he could have aced except that it met on Saturday mornings during his final semester. He would skip it most weeks in order to travel home to work with his father. The lone C did not knock him out of first place.

He had begun practicing dentistry without a license in his sophomore year. Initially, he would do fillings, relieving his father of the tedium that formed the bread and butter of their practice. Like his male forebearers, Dad used his earnings to pay his way through school. He also financed his friends' social life. He would return to Nashville after a weekend of work, flush with cash, his buddies waiting for his generous contribution to the liquor kitty and ready to begin their regular soiree of couples on Sunday evenings at the Seraglio. "We drank so much Canadian Club we nearly lost our citizenship," he would joke. By his senior year, he was undertaking any procedures that John Sr. hated to do, affording the old man something of a semi-retirement. Dad was making so much money that he was able to buy himself a 1950 Chevrolet convertible. It was robin's-egg blue, used but new to him. "That car was something else," Dad marveled. "But it didn't beat what Herschel got. After I worked my ass off and bought a car for myself, mother bought a brand new MG for him. *He* was the favorite. I was definitely number two." Speaking as a septuagenarian, with resignation more than resentment, my father is still the second son.

⌣: ∝ :⌣

The entire Cashin-Langston-Sykes clan was extremely proud of Dad, admiring his verve as much as his academic prowess. The Cashin cousins—Carroll

Langston before his death, Lil Sykes, Blinny and Betty-V—all felt the same way about my father. "He was the most electric, fascinating person we ever met," Cousin Blinny said of the brash young prince who would come to Chicago for visits in his Meharry years. He would take his young cousins with him on trips to Sixty-third Street, the liveliest thoroughfare in black Chicago, and within minutes someone would recognize him. The playboy attracted much attention—wanted and unwanted. As soon as he would hit town, the grapevine buzzed and the phone began to ring incessantly at Uncle Jimmy's house on Greenwood. Everybody wanted to see him, although he would claim that most of the calls were women hoping that he would be their emissary to Herschel, who had enrolled at Northwestern Law School.

Uncle Jimmy was also enormously proud of his nephew; in his estimation my father could do no wrong. There was a strong mutual admiration between them. In the one photograph I have of them together, taken by Betty-V as a child, my father sits at the dining room table eating their housekeeper Bertha's sumptuous food and Uncle Jimmy sits very close to him, smiling proudly at the camera as Betty-V "basked in the glow of my two heroes."

In the spring of his senior year at Meharry, Dad reminded Dr. Singleton of their wager with Dr. Davis at Tennessee State. They both confronted Davis, once again at the Omega spring dance. Would he honor his commitment to convert John's unusual undergraduate career into a degree of some kind, now that he had maintained his valedictory position? Both men were enormously proud of the younger Omega man. Dr. Davis, bemused and pleased that he had been taken at his word, sent my father to Dr. Carl Hill, the head of the Chemistry Department. They worked out the curriculum for a degree from TSU in natural science, counting some of his Fisk and Meharry credits, all classes in which he received A's.

When Grace learned the news, she said, "Oh, I'm so happy I finally get to see you graduate from college." The twenty-four-year-old sophisticate informed his mother that he was graduating from Meharry and would not be marching at Tennessee State. "Oh, yes you will," she told him. The son, like the husband, had learned that edicts from Grace were not negotiable. "So, just like she said," my father reminisced, "I marched at TSU one week, and I marched at Meharry the next." Grace and John Sr. happily made the two-hour drive to Nashville twice to watch their baby boy receive his diplomas.

They were even more pleased to see him receive the prestigious Alpha-Omega award for the rare feat of leading his Meharry class for four consecutive years.

In the early 1940s, John Sr. had built a two-story dental office adjacent to the house on Gallatin, creating a compound in which family and business were seamless. His son became instrumental as they practiced together, side by side, for nearly ten years. Dad filled the gap between his father's 1920s training and modern dentistry, taking on the difficult cases, and John Sr. taught him that it wasn't always necessary to "follow the rules" of dentistry or any other source of orthodoxy.

Three years into this arrangement, Dad was inducted into the military. The army was suffering from an acute shortage of dentists and gave him little choice in the matter. As an unmarried man with no prior service, he was a prime candidate. The letter from the Selective Service read, "Congratulations, you have been awarded a commission in the U.S. Army as First Lieutenant in the U.S. Dental Corps. If you accept this enlistment, you will report for active duty at Fort Sam Houston on May 8, 1955." A second letter sent days later informed him, "[I]f for any reason you decline to accept this appointment, you must report immediately as a Private, First Class to Fort McPherson." At an installation in San Antonio, Texas, that specialized in converting doctors quickly into commissioned officers, he underwent a boot camp of sorts and then was sent to serve at the Thirty-third Field Hospital in Fontainebleau, France, his first trip to Europe.

He was ecstatic at his good fortune. It was hard to imagine a more plum assignment than to be stationed in a suburb of Paris, although the patient load was heavy. By then the armed forces had been completely desegregated and he was the only military dentist for 6,000 people, including those in the military and their dependents. He ran a four-chair dental clinic night and day, with eight capable assistants. He endeared himself to his staff and patients because he was one of the hardest-working officers they had ever seen. He cut the three-month waiting list for dental care in half and, in typical fashion, did things his way. With a dental laboratory and two proven technicians at his disposal, he began doing gold bridgework for dependents and enlisted men, to the intense objection of his superiors. Typically, they would have had to make do with less expensive and less enduring amalgam fillings.

For the violation of standard practice he was given "an Article 15," a mild rebuke, which he appealed. His successful argument was emblematic of his unbending confidence: "First and foremost I am a dentist and if I assess a patient and conclude that a gold cast bridge is needed, I am going to do it."

Within six months, Dr. Cashin was promoted to captain and, as chief of dental services, a slot normally occupied by a lieutenant colonel, he enjoyed considerable privileges. He could write his own furloughs without seeking permission from a superior. By 1956, after three more dentists were assigned to work in his clinic, he wrote many furloughs for himself. A few of his patients who were flight officers in the air force made a habit of calling him whenever they were scheduled to fly a practice run and there was an extra seat on the plane. "Doc, we're headed to Stockholm, you want to go?" they would say. Invariably he said yes and went anywhere the military planes were going. The U.S. government took him to every capital in Europe and the British Isles, points on the Mediterranean from Algiers to Beirut, and even Saudi Arabia. As a scoutmaster for the base Boy Scout troop, he and his troop could also fly as passengers on the commander general's aircraft, a DC–3 that was equipped like a commercial airliner. He would take his troop on field trips, the most memorable of which was an aborted expedition to Egypt. They had just flown over the Great Pyramids and landed in Cairo when the word came that President Gamal Abdel Nasser had nationalized the Suez Canal, and a quick scramble to leave the country ensued.

The army wanted him to reenlist for two more years. Having had a taste of the world and wanting to see more of it, he said, "Only if you send me to Tokyo." His superior replied, "Cashin, I'm going to send you home by driftwood, you want it all." They promoted him to major in order to entice him to reenlist, a rank that lasted three weeks. Ultimately, he decided he would have felt very guilty being in Tokyo while a revolution was heating up in Alabama. The Montgomery Bus Boycott had begun in December 1955. For his entire life, he and Herschel had talked about what it would take to move the mountain of segregation in their state and this was the first time he had ever known blacks to take to the streets and demand change. He was impressed that Rosa Parks had refused to give up her bus seat and wished Martin Luther King Jr. well, but he viewed the race challenge in

Alabama as his and Herschel's fight. And now that the battle had begun, he was incensed that he couldn't lift a finger to help because he was under the control of the U.S. military. He decided that when his two-year enlistment was up in May 1957, he would return home.

Like many Negro expatriates, his social consciousness deepened with the humanitarian treatment he received in Europe. "I thought Huntsville was a pretty nice place until I went to France and was fully accepted as a human being," he told me. In Alabama, the Cashin family had accommodated to segregation. In his post-collegiate years he had not thought much about racism because he was largely exempted from it. As the scion of an upper-middle-class Negro family that operated largely in the black world and could afford the comforts it desired, he was not subject to all of the vagaries of segregation. He could do much of what he wanted to do. He drove his convertible to Nashville for parties with his frat brothers; he earned a handsome living; he had even crossed the ultimate segregationist fault line of the South, once fraternizing with a white woman. Mostly, he was a playboy who had enjoyed his life immensely, despite the strictures of Jim Crow.

Yet there had been the occasional reminder that "white supremacy" was still the dominant political and social order of the Deep South. On a Friday night in February 1953, he was returning to Huntsville from the national black high school basketball tournament at TSU. His first cousin, Juanita Brandon, Uncle Jack's daughter, was driving his brand new metallic-green Mercury convertible, while he slept in the back, recovering from the revelry and hoping to be able to face patients the next morning. Two other friends, Larry Carroll and Brent Dulan, Meharry dental graduates, accompanied them. A state trooper stopped them in Fayetteville, Tennessee. In open court the next day, the trooper told the judge, "I stopped them because no nigger had no business driving a car like that. And when he talked to me, he didn't talk to me like a nigger should so I hit him."

Knowing that Juanita did not have a driver's license, Dad had roused himself from his slumber and exited the car quickly to engage the officer in a conversation. The light-skinned Negro in the fancy car with his proper diction and confident manner had to be put in his place. As he was preparing to produce his license, the trooper clubbed him, knocking him unconscious. The trooper drew his gun, pointed it down at his victim, and contemplated whether to shoot him. Larry and Brent screamed, begging for their friend's life. With the "appropriate" order of white superiority returned, the trooper relented.

The wound required five stitches on the left front side of his head—the first time anyone in the family had experienced the violence of Jim Crow since Grandpa Herschel had been forcibly ejected from a train sixty years earlier. The family had caucused to decide who should accompany Dad to court. John Sr. could be hot-headed and was "notorious for starting things he would not finish," as Dad put it. Everyone was gravely concerned that the wound to his son's head might have shattered his ability to contain his anger at racism. Uncle Jack prevailed upon his brother-in-law to stay at home rather than risk an outburst that might make matters worse for his son. Instead, he proposed to bring his "eye for an eye" philosophy to bear on this situation. Jack Brandon had the means and the network to ensure that the state trooper received some of his own medicine. Grace prevailed on Uncle Jack to stay at home, too, and she accompanied her son to court. Her Christian belief in turning the other cheek was sorely tested, however. The court was not deterred by the trooper's brutality; perhaps the judge even approved of it. He sided with the officer, giving my father a $25 fine for disorderly conduct. Grace, who was never known to lose her composure, struggled to maintain it now. She mumbled through gritted teeth, nearly choking on curse words that Dad had never before heard her utter. They both took solace in the fact that they could have unleashed Uncle Jack on the trooper. Although they had no intention of exercising that option, it made the injustice of what had transpired more bearable because they knew they were not helpless.

There were no such moments in Europe. My father could go wherever he wanted, often in his new Chrysler 300, "a luxury car with real stamina" that he brought with him from the States. To be embraced or not, solely on the basis of who he was as a person, was a revelation. The freedoms of Europe clarified anew the artifice and injustice of American racism, especially its Southern-fried versions. It reinforced his resolve to return to Alabama to change it.

Paris was especially liberating. His entrée to the hip, expatriate crowd was Ollie Stewart, a writer who had a regular society column for the

Herschel Vivian Cashin, my great grandfather.

A charcoal rendering of a young Minnie Brewster Cashin, my great grandmother.

James Blaine Cashin, Jr. ("Uncle Jimmy"), with his father, "Grandpa Herschel."

Minnie Brewster Cashin, my great grandmother in her silver years.

Lillian Emmett Cashin, "Aunt Jack," in her youth.

Uncle Jimmy and Dr. Newlyn Edward Cashin, "Uncle Newlyn," in 1941.

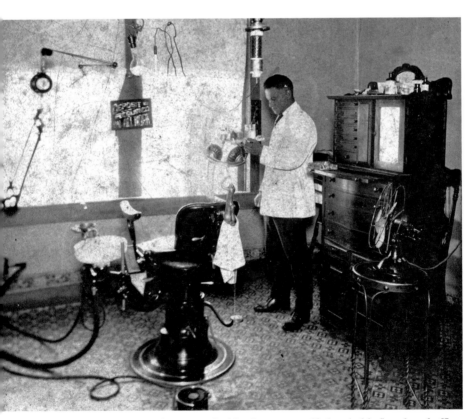

Dr. John Logan Cashin, Sr., my grandfather, in his first dental office.

Aunt Vivi and Uncle Tode stand
proudly with Carroll, who became a
Tuskeegee Airman.

Vivian Cashin Langston, "Aunt Vivi,"
watches Grandpa Herschel hold her
son, Carroll Langston, Jr., on the day
he was christened.

Carroll Langston, Jr., with his
beautiful wife, Marguerite.

My father and Uncle Herschel with a Brandon cousin in front of the new house Grandpa Claude Brandon built.

My father and uncle, standing in the same place a few years later.

Grace Brandon Cashin, "Grandma Grace," my fraternal grandmother.

Dr. John Logan Cashin, Sr., my fraternal grandfather.

Dr. Marie Ruffin Carpenter and Dr. Marcus Carpenter, my maternal grandparents, in 1955.

Dad and Uncle Jimmy in Chicago.

My father and mother, Joan Carpenter Cashin, at their wedding reception in 1957.

My grandmother, Dr. Marie Carpenter, with other civil rights protestors at the New York Stock Exchange, May 19, 1962.

My father's favorite family photo, taken in front of our home on Lydia Drive shortly before we moved out of it.

My parents
celebrate their
tenth wedding
anniversary with
the Drek Set.

Mama, me, and two
unidentified local
boys in Grenada,
Mississippi,
May 17, 1968.

Mama (center with
poster), Myrna and Don
Copeland (immediately
behind her) at the
Selma-to-Montgomery
March on March 21,
1965.

My brother John (holding sign), me, and Dad, at the front of a memorial march for Dr. King, April, 1969.

Dad, campaigning for governor in 1970.
(Credit: Wesley Swift)

Dad, a successful NDPA candidate, Rev. Ralph Abernathy, and Rev. Hosea Williams, celebrate victory in the Greene County Special Election, Aug. 11, 1969.

Chicago Defender. As usual, there was a Meharry connection. Ollie's brother was a Meharry classmate and an M.D. in Gadsen, Alabama. Virtually all of the black sophisticates making their way to Paris from the States, for a permanent stay or a short respite from America's burdens, would stop by to see Ollie, ensuring that they would be mentioned in the *Defender.* He and my father became good friends, sharing an appreciation for jazz and enjoying the company of the many black musicians who played gigs in Paris.

It was a sweet life for a free and single black American. Through Ollie, my father met most of the black expatriates in Paris, including James Baldwin, who was fast becoming a famous writer. "We would see somebody every weekend at Gavin Haynes's International Café," he recalled. "It was owned by 'Roughhouse' Haynes, a Morehouse football star who married a French girl. The joke was that the Haynes Café was like the Red Rooster in Harlem." The main attraction at the Red Rooster, a restaurant and bar on 134th Street, was a bartender who was "as funny as Richard Pryor," according to Dad. Harlemites went there to drink and find old friends because "anyone who came to town would stop at the Red Rooster." In Paris, the Haynes Café was the place where brothers and sisters would go to feed their souls. Roughhouse did the cooking. A frequent topic among black Americans was the difficulty of finding "chitlins" in Paris, and Roughhouse served them, along with po' boys, chili, pork chops, and beans.

The café was also the place to go if you were trying to find a certain black person in Paris. All you had to do was hang out at Haynes Café for a little while and they'd show up. It was located in Pigalle, a north Paris neighborhood where anything one wanted could be purchased with the right number of francs.

They called the neighborhood "Pig Alley." Some Negro expatriates spoke French fluently. Others spoke it contemptuously, including my father. "We deliberately corrupted everything we touched," he said. "Paris" was purposely distorted to "Pa-ass," sometimes just to infuriate a white affluent would-be hipster couple in their midst. Corrupting the name of their adopted city was of a piece with the dissonance in their hearts. American Negroes who lived in Paris delighted in its freedoms. But they were homesick. "There was an overwhelming sadness about these people," Dad said of his new friends, because it was obvious that they had come to Europe to be treated as equals and longed to be able to return to an America that offered similar dignity.

Through Ollie, Dad became a regular in a crowd that included the writer Richard Wright; Mezz Mezzrow, a colorful soprano sax-man whose record, *Bonjour Tristesse,* was a hit at the time; and Art Simmons, a jazz piano player from West Virginia. On the weekends, if they weren't at the restaurant, frequently they were at Wright's home, where Dad was often invited to Sunday dinner. As a southern Negro who was openly committed to returning to change his home state, Dad provoked debate about America's race problems. He and Wright would talk frequently, whether walking the streets of Pigalle, taking in the delights of Montparnasse, or at Wright's dinner table.

Wright had given up on the United States, and Paris was now his permanent home. He would remind Dad of what he was going to face when he returned and, as he had described in his autobiographical *Black Boy,* he knew firsthand the violence-backed regime of which he spoke. From Wright's perspective, nothing had changed. He was as pessimistic as his novels, doubtful that any racial progress would be forthcoming. But his bitterness did not define him. He was a charming man who was in love with his wife and devoted to his two daughters.

When Wright invited Dad for his last Sunday meal before returning to the States, he made a special request. "John, my daughters have never seen a black officer in the U.S. Army, would you please wear your uniform to dinner?" Wright knew that it was a request that ran counter to my father's instincts. The Algerian Revolution raged and rival factions of nationalists were waging a guerrilla war literally in the cafés of Paris; among the gangland-style killings, a few French soldiers in uniform had been attacked. Yet Dad was happy to oblige. Once again, he and Ollie ascended the birdcage elevator to the Wrights' modest apartment in Montparnasse. Wright's wife, a quiet, diminutive French woman who was very supportive of her husband, answered the door and the good-bye party began. Art Simmons was there, as were a few other friends. Wright spoke to his daughters. Alternating between French and English, he pointed at Dad and explained the significance of the uniform and the power to command hundreds that came with it. A black officer was very rare, he told them. "But he ain't too black," Ollie joked of his light-skinned friend. At the end of the evening, Wright wished Dad well, and that was their last communication.

While stationed at Fontainebleau, my father learned that his brother Herschel would be barred from taking the Alabama bar exam. The same forces that had orchestrated the Alabama Constitution of 1901 also saw to it that there would be few Negro lawyers in the state. In 1907, they enacted an ostensibly race-neutral statute that required anyone who would be attending an out-of-state law school but who intended to take the Alabama bar to notify the state bar association "upon entering" law school. It was an effective subterfuge, as there were virtually no law schools in the state that would admit blacks and few out-of-state law students, including Herschel, knew about the provision. He learned of it when he applied to take the bar in his senior year. Meanwhile, anyone who graduated from the University of Alabama School of Law was automatically admitted to the state bar. For decades, this plank in the state's Jim Crow regime was extremely effective. In the 1940s, Arthur Shores, a civil-rights stalwart from Birmingham, was the only black lawyer practicing in the entire state. The regime also ensured that most lawyers in Alabama would be homegrown residents who knew only white supremacy as a way of life.

The entire family was very upset by this turn of events. Here was a clear impediment of segregation that could not be mitigated by mere retreat into the black world or reliance on its supportive offices. The Cashin brothers were especially livid, foiled by the very regime they had vowed to tackle. It took eight years of maneuvering by Dad before Uncle Herschel would have the option of taking the Alabama bar exam. By then, he had made a life for himself in Texas. The (female) distractions of Chicago drove him to transfer to Texas Southern University during law school. He moved from the protective wing of Uncle Jimmy on the Cashin side in Chicago to that of Aunt Margaret on the Brandon side in Houston. While studying at the "separate but equal" law school that the state of Texas built for Negroes, a quiet clerk-typist who worked in the library caught Herschel's eye. He fell in love with Georgia Pumphrey because she had a singsong voice that mirrored her girlish sweetness, and she never deployed her considerable gifts to pursue him. They married and then began a family that would stretch to five children, whom I would know as "the Texas Cashins," my beloved first cousins. Aunt Georgia became a schoolteacher, and Uncle Herschel built a successful law practice. They bought an ample house on a one-acre lot in LaMarque, Texas, that offered its own grove of fruit trees. In this semirural hamlet near Galveston, they focused on raising their children well and remained largely in the black world.

When my father pressed his brother about taking the bar and moving back to Alabama, Herschel was moved to tears because he knew that he was not going to be able to hold up his end of the pact with his brother. His life had taken a different course; he no longer had the heart for the fight in Alabama. It pained him terribly to leave his younger brother alone in that struggle, but Dad understood. His brother had a wife and children to care for, and my father felt that he was more than capable of fulfilling their pact on his own. When Herschel and his wife started "having babies," Dad had decided that he would never marry or have children in order to devote himself to their fight. He was prepared for any violent forces he might face. But he did not want to place a wife and children at such risk. Without a family, he reasoned, no one would be able to intimidate him. I would hear about his professed intention never to marry or have children repeatedly, typically after he and Mama had had a fight and he felt the need to remind her that she had agreed to join him in a struggle. When Dad told me the story of Uncle Herschel's tear-filled decision to remain in Texas, I thought about the fact that my father ultimately did choose to have a family and we did endure some of the danger and consequences he had hoped not to visit upon us. I also thought of the tribulation we might have avoided had Dad had the benefit of his brother's sobering influence during the NDPA years, but it was not to be. Uncle Herschel died in December 1969 of a brain tumor, when the NDPA was in its infancy.

~: ৵ঌ :~

June 14, 1956, was momentous. On this Bastille Day in Paris, my father would finally have a first date with a young woman, Joan Carpenter, whom he had eyed from a distance in Nashville but never succeeded in taking out because she had a boyfriend who guarded his prize closely. She was eight years younger, a Fisk co-ed when he was an upperclassman at Meharry. Like Dad, she had been admitted to Fisk at a tender age. The Basic College program, founded by the Ford Foundation, brought exceptional Negro high school students to college a year early. She, too, had skipped a grade and was fifteen when she arrived on the Fisk campus, twenty when she completed the five-year program.

Mama had grown up in Jersey City, New Jersey, a child of privilege because she was the daughter of a flamboyant Howard-trained medical doctor, Marcus Carpenter. In addition to a medical practice that included a weight-loss clinic, "Papa" ran a business empire that included a Laundromat and a dry cleaner's. There were a lot of similarities between Marc Carpenter and John Cashin. Both men tended to live life on their own terms, drove fine cars, and were committed to their people. But Papa was the more dramatic character. He was a consummate charmer, if he had not had too much to drink. He once walked into a luxury furniture store in Manhattan and quickly proposed to purchase an extremely expensive dining room set. When the salesman demurred, suggesting that Papa could not afford such an extravagance, he climbed on the table and rained down invective on his newly appointed underling until his purchase was accepted, to the astonishment of the white folks.

Papa did not accompany his daughter to Paris. She had just graduated from Fisk and was on a two-month journey throughout Europe with her mother and two godmothers—her graduation present from Papa for a job well done. Marie Ruffin Carpenter was as genteel as her husband was flamboyant. "Nana" was also well educated. She was the valedictorian of her class at Virginia Union and earned a Ph.D. in education from Columbia University. Joan inherited brains and looks from both her parents. In the fall, she would pursue a master's degree in child psychology at Columbia. She was tall and slender, a quiet, somewhat reticent beauty who dressed elegantly and moved like the swan she portrayed in her ballet recitals. Friends from the Nashville smart set had made her promise to look up John Cashin when she arrived in Paris. "You'll never meet another one like her," they had warned my father. He was intrigued not just by her beauty but by her

familiar pedigree—well-educated black people who took social contribution seriously.

Dad showed her all the sights of Paris and his favorite haunts, including
a smoky nightclub that shared a wall with a police station. As an accommodation to the authorities, the patrons were required to snap their fingers
rather than clap to applaud the jazz musicians. They followed the lead of all
the other Bastille Day celebrants, walking the streets of Paris until dawn and
then going to breakfast, at which my father abruptly blurted out, "Let's get
married." She said, "Oh, you're crazy." "No, I mean it," he replied, "and I'm
going to prove it to you." He was unfazed by the uproar he encountered
from his future mother-in-law and the two attending mother hens when he
returned their young charge after keeping her out all night.

Like all couples, the story of their first date became part of their lore.
After she or he would tell the story, he would always claim that a year of
interracial exploits in Europe and being deprived of the charms of a beautiful black woman went to his head. He had planned never to marry or have
children, he would remind us. Paris and Joan's smile weakened him.

He showed up at several points on her itinerary, including Nice and London. The home movie he shot shows the two lovers lying side by side on
the beach in Nice, each propped up on an elbow, turning toward each other,
laughing and smiling, both at the height of their physical beauty, looking
unbelievably young and thin in the eyes of their daughter, observing them
decades later.

Dad was handsome, barrel-chested, and capped with a head of jet-black
curls. Joan seemed to tower over him when she wore heels. She was
attracted to his charisma and his craziness but wary because she knew of
John Cashin's playboy reputation. In Nashville, he had once tried to entice
her to attend one of his parties at the Seraglio, but she had refused when
he asked her to come without her boyfriend. She had not been looking forward to being tied to three middle-aged women throughout her trip, and
she viewed their date as an opportunity to breathe free. She did not take his
marriage proposal seriously, although she admitted to herself that he might
be the man of her dreams.

He wore her down; by the end of her trip, she had agreed to marry him.
Over the following year, she received precisely one letter and two postcards

from him. She kept them in her own box of treasures, which did not disappear thanks to her careful safekeeping.

He was not much of a letter writer but he loved her, more than he had ever loved any woman. Perhaps he intended to back out of his proposal, because upon his return to the United States in May 1957, he did not contact her. Within two weeks of returning to Huntsville, he started a voter registration drive. He was ready to get to work on his mission. Mrs. Fearn, a neighbor who was the principal of Councill High and a convenient emissary for the white establishment, had warned him, "John, you're doing something dangerous. Be careful, I don't want you to get hurt." Although he was not deterred, the warning may have contributed to his hesitation about calling Joan in New Jersey.

He encountered her, quite unexpectedly, on a weekend trip to Nashville. She had just completed her master's program at Columbia and was celebrating with friends. Nothing had changed. He felt the same compulsion. This was the woman he was supposed to marry, even if he didn't want marriage. Besides, she was tall. She would put an end to the curse of shortness in the Cashin line. Her long, straight legs would compensate for his short bowed ones. And she was dark enough that no one would mistake her, or his children, for white. Such were the practical calculations of a man committed to activism and a certain form of eugenics. He had once broken up with a blue-eyed, blonde, and Negro girlfriend, out of concern that if he had relented on his pledge to remain a bachelor and married her, her apparent whiteness would cause problems in Alabama. The breakup was also fueled by his rebellion against the light skin in his own family. If he were going to procreate, he wanted his children to exhibit more than a hint of the blackness he identified with.

Several very serious conversations ensued between my father and mother. Dad explained his lifelong commitment, how he was destined to finish his grandfather's work, to return blacks to power at the ballot box and free them of all the strictures of segregation, and why marriage was not part of this vision. One of these conversations occurred while they were driving from Nashville to Huntsville, Mama said. Dad held the steering wheel between the index and third fingers of his right hand, his usual driving posture, even at breakneck speeds. With his free hand he drew heavily on a cigarette, although he rarely smoked. Mama eyed her fiancé carefully. He seemed uncharacteristically nervous and unsure of himself, and she began to suspect that his feet were turning cold. He told her he would marry her only if she committed to moving to Alabama and joining him in the struggle to change it and only if she was sure she could handle the risks that might ensue. "I told him I was committed and I could handle it," Mama would always say. It was a pact I would hear about throughout my life, sometimes when they were being nostalgic, more often as a defense Dad would raise when the toll of his activism on his family grew heavy.

She hadn't needed convincing. Her parents had been in the vanguard of Negroes who organized themselves to exert influence in their state and local Democratic Party, and with Papa's support, Nana had begun to accumulate a string of "First Negro To's" after her name, including serving on the Jersey City School Board. They had always taught Joan, "When you are blessed, give back to the community and remember where you came from." Both of her grandfathers had worked as railroad porters and had done all they could to ensure that the next generation prospered. Nana and Papa, in turn, felt obliged to give back so that other people's children would also prosper, and they had passed that sense of obligation on to their daughter.

My parents eloped in Birmingham on October 12, 1957, ruining Nana's plans for a grand wedding with 300 guests in Jersey City. They had roused the Reverend J. C. Wilson at 11:00 PM to perform the ceremony in his parsonage around the corner from the A.G. Gaston Motel, named for its owner, Birmingham's black business baron. Harold Drake, my father's best friend, came along to serve as the best man. One night on Negro main street in Birmingham was honeymoon enough for Mama. She said of their decision, "I knew I was missing out on hundreds of wedding gifts, but your father was complaining about having to wear a 'monkey suit' and when he said, 'Let's just go get married,' I thought I better go with it."

Although Nana and Papa had also eloped and even kept their marriage secret for several months, my grandmother cried when Mama and Daddy arrived at her doorstep in Jersey City, ostensibly for an engagement party scheduled the next day, and flashed their wedding rings. She regrouped only by forcing them to go to her church and repeat their vows in an impromptu ceremony with her minister so that she could assure herself that in God's eyes her daughter was, indeed, married. Then she transformed the engagement party into a wedding reception. Few people other than my grandmother could procure a three-tier wedding cake with less than a day's notice. Nana and Papa's elegant three-story home was the backdrop for black-and-white photos that became iconic in my memories because my parents and their guests wore a sartorial grace and happiness that I would admire when I looked at the pictures as a child. All of Mama's people were there—generations of Carpenters, Reeds, and Ruffins who were meeting for the first time this young man who was stealing their Joanie to move her south. After taking in the full measure of his confident brio at the party, their general consensus was that Joan Carpenter had married a man just like her father. Not quite. My father was not an alcoholic. My grandfather was. Papa was also more inclined to spoil his wife, possibly out of guilt about his reportedly frequent dalliances and the tempestuousness he occasionally brought to his marriage. On an impromptu stroll into Tiffany's, he once announced, "I want to buy my wife an eighteen-inch, double strand of pearls with a diamond clasp and I don't care what it costs"—one of several exquisite luxuries he bought her that eventually would pass from Nana to Mama to me.

At the time, my father was twenty-nine, an ancient age for a bachelor in that era. Uncle Herschel had already named his second son after his brother, so confident was he that Daddy would never produce his own heir. At twenty-one, Mama was more typical of a newly minted, 1950s housewife, except for the unconventional men in her life. She moved from her flamboyant father's house to her flamboyant husband's.

Their prenuptial pact enabled a leap of faith that resulted in nearly forty years of marriage. Through countless highs and lows, their marriage endured until Mama's death in August 1997, the same day Princess Diana died. At her funeral, Dad recounted that when he brought Joan Carpenter to Alabama, he "hitched a show horse to a plow." Together they tilled, planting the seeds of black political emancipation in the state.

Civil Rights

M ama and Daddy began their married life together in one half
of a duplex on Scruggs Street, in the Grove, not far from Dad's
boyhood home in Huntsville. Aaron and Eltia Smith, also newlyweds,
rented the other half. "God never created better neighbors," Dad said of
them. Eventually, the Smiths would follow the Cashins to a new, one-street
subdivision carved out of farmland in Grandpa Claude Brandon's ances-
tral village of Brandontown.

Lydia Drive was an act of familial self-empowerment. Dad and his first
cousin, Charles Brandon, had a vision for what they could do with their
grandfather's considerable property *if* he would let them develop it while
he was alive. He could definitely see the good sense in his grandsons' vision.
He was especially fond of Dad. Once, he had intercepted my father on
Grace's front porch and handed him a paper bag, saying, "John you've
never asked me for anything and it occurred to me that if anything happened to me, you would be the one taking care of me and I just wanted you
to know how much I appreciate it." Dad sat down and opened the bag as
Claude hovered. It contained $5,000 in mixed bills, emergency cash that
my great-grandfather must have been accumulating for years. Dad choked
up at the thought of his grandfather correctly perceiving that he was prepared to take care of his elders, and hugged him tighter than usual.

Now Dad had asked Grandpa Claude for something. There were very
few places for Negroes to live outside of the Grove and central Huntsville.
His grandsons would transform land he was leasing to black cotton farmers

into the first modern subdivision in Huntsville for blacks, and he was happy at the thought of it.

"We acted like a family," Dad would say. With twenty acres of Grandpa Claude's land and a $5,000 initial investment from Marcus Carpenter, Dad's enthusiastic father-in-law, they founded "Brandon, Cashin, Carpenter, Inc." Because John Sr. was easing into retirement, his support for the project was moral rather than financial. Every aspect of the construction and financing came from Negro sources. Daddy and Cousin Charles oversaw the work. If they needed more financing they went to Marc Carpenter, their passive investor. Once the dead-end street was graded, the sewers dug and other infrastructure laid, they named the street after Charles's youngest daughter at the time, Lydia.

Major Bevels, an electrician and contractor, built the first house. Dad built the second—a modest but smart, three-bedroom, two-bath redbrick home on a large lot that welcomed all entrants to the subdivision. One by one, Dad and Charles personally recruited most of the families that would live on the street. Many were headed by Omega men. All were middle class. They had the means but had lacked the organization to build their own community, until then. Lydia Drive became an enduring middle-class black enclave. Fifty years later, it is a street of widows, widowers, and empty nesters who look forward to seeing their children and grandchildren.

Daddy and Mama moved to Lydia Drive shortly before their second son was born. Their first child was born prematurely. Gigi Marie lived three weeks, never making it out of her incubator. When Mama decided she was ready to try again, Dad decided to leave nothing to chance. With Uncle Herschel ensconced in Texas, Harold Drake became my father's closest co-conspirator. Dr. Drake was five years senior, the only son of Dr. Joseph Fanning Drake, the venerable president of Alabama A&M, and Anne Quick Drake, Aunt Pat's closest friend. Harold did not harbor activist ambitions, but he and Daddy thought alike on most subjects. Both were Meharry graduates, Harold an M.D. Both were pilots. And both men were supremely confident in their abilities. They thought they were smarter than most people, and in many ways they were.

Harold was a diabetic and sterile. He couldn't produce any of his own children, so he invested in Dad's project of procreation. They assumed that, as Meharry graduates, they knew as much as anyone about genetics and gender selection. They decided to prove that they could determine both the sex and date of birth of John's progeny. He wanted three children, and he wanted a sequence of two males and one female. His thinking, and Harold's, was that the older boys would protect their younger sister.

The zodiac was as convenient a framework as any other for picking the target birth dates. Of course, they wanted an Aries boy first. Harold's birthday was April 14, John's April 16, so April 15 was their target date. Since they were both fire signs, they decided that the two other children should also be fire signs. They planned a second son, a Leo, for the next year on August 15, and a girl Sagittarius on December 15 the year after that. In their arrogance, they did not inform Joan of their grand designs. They did, however, wish to document the success of their science project. They wrote up their plan and the proposed mechanisms for determining sex and birth date, sending a copy by registered mail to each other. Not surprisingly, the registered documents are now nowhere to be found. With no firm evidence of the experiment, I am left with Daddy's oft-repeated tale, the veracity of which is open to interpretation. But he was forever consistent in the telling of the story.

Their methods involved diet, controlling temperature, close observation of the ovulation cycles of the "patient," and a contraption they designed to control the polarity of the magnetic field in which John's sperm was produced. He would strap the battery-operated device to his loins for twenty-four hours prior to precisely timed relations with his wife. A certain polarity was set when a boy child was desired, the opposite when a girl was intended. Mama displayed her skepticism by rolling her eyes whenever her spouse would regale his children with the story of how they were precisely planned.

John Marcus was born on April 19, a few days past his intended due date. "Uncle Harold" delivered him. Dad was present—the same teamwork they would employ with future births. When the risk that the child would emerge a Taurus became clear, they did what they could to induce labor. They got their Aries boy.

Carroll Langston arrived a year later on August 16. They were a day off-target but quite proud of the extremely pretty baby "they" had created, naming him after John's fallen first cousin. I was born the following year, on

December 15. Daddy insisted on being the first person to lay hands on me. He finally had his daughter, on the precise date intended. Their methods vindicated, they revealed to my mother what they had done. She was going to be as famous as Madame Curie, they argued, once they published the results. Mama was not amused. Yet she knew her husband was crazier than most. In the end all she could do was laugh, and insist on choosing the name she desired for her daughter, Sheryll Denise.

To the extent there was any competition between my brothers and me for the affections of our father, it was not a fair contest. As the youngest, and the only girl, I won, hands down. My brothers never seemed to care. There was enough of his kid-like enthusiasm to go around. He showered them with trains, planes, kites, or whatever toy he might help them build. He showered me with pure love. Mama vindicated his stories of ardent attention to his infant daughter: "He would let his sons cry in the middle of the night. Any cry from you and he would wake me up, 'Don't you hear your daughter?'" His version was that *he* would be the one to get up in the night to see to my needs.

With the task of procreation complete, my parents' attention once more turned to the issue of civil rights. Grace and John Sr. had reluctantly accepted segregation as the Southern way. For them, the black world, with its Princess Theater, its many businesses, its elegant parties and teas in the homes of high Negro society, its schools and institutions of higher learning, its fraternities and sororities, its church life, was more than enough. In the security of blackness, they also avoided the indignities of "colored" water fountains and public restrooms that were markedly inferior to those designated as "white." Yet they were supportive, proud, even amused by the actions their son and daughter-in-law began to take to undermine Jim Crow.

When Huntsville built a new municipal golf course in the summer of 1958 and turned away the precious few Negroes who actually desired to play, my father bought a set of clubs. In 1972, he told an interviewer, Hardy Frye, who was writing his dissertation about the NDPA, "I went out there and said, 'Let them turn me away. Let them put me in jail. I hacked around the course two or three times, playing golf like I'm killing snakes.'" No one stopped Drs. Cashin and Drake from playing, and as other blacks returned to the course, the city decided to give Negroes their own "day." "But along came Labor Day and all the white folks wanted to play on our day. So we just started playing on their days. The next thing you know, the golf course had become completely integrated."

They also integrated the public library this way, simply by walking in and demanding to use it. Every other realm of public and private life in Huntsville remained segregated. Dad often found himself asking city fathers to do what was right for the Negro. He was tired of begging and ready for a revolution. He recalled, "I was an entirely different person when I came back from the service. I had shed my middle-class partying attitude, you know, who had the longest Cadillac, who could throw the biggest damn parties. When the sit-in movement came to Huntsville, I jumped in. I was glad to see 'em."

An outside force jump-started their intended life of activism. The Student Nonviolent Coordinating Committee (SNCC) and the Congress of Racial Equality (CORE) had orchestrated successful sit-in movements throughout the South in 1960 and 1961. More than twenty-five cities in Texas, Tennessee, and North Carolina had desegregated public accommodations, and the student-led movement was growing like wildfire. Alabama, like Mississippi, was a harder case.

In the "Heart of Dixie," no local movement had succeeded since the Montgomery Bus Boycott. Beyond local transit in Montgomery, the realm of public accommodations in Alabama was explicitly and often virulently segregated. When John Henry "Hank" Thomas, a twenty-year-old field secretary for CORE, came to Huntsville in early January 1962, intent on organizing a sit-in campaign, he and his co-workers were told to get in touch with Dr. Cashin, a local Negro leader who would be sympathetic to the cause. Dad suggested that they start at a bus station lunch counter because the Supreme Court had recently clarified that the Constitution's ban on segregation of interstate travel carriers extended to travel facilities *within* states.

Dad was sanguine about the likely outcome, despite the blood-soaked Freedom Rides of the previous year. Huntsville was not Anniston, where a busload of freedom riders had been firebombed, or Birmingham and Montgomery, where they endured beatings and assaults in 1961. He viewed Huntsville as substantially more progressive. About half of his dental patients were white, as had been the case for John Sr. since he began his practice in the early 1920s. For three decades, blacks and whites had been sitting together and literally rubbing elbows in John Sr.'s dental office. It was unusual and yet normal for their patients. Most people in the South, including ardent segregationists, had had intimate dealings with someone of the other race in their lifetime. A patient of the elder or junior Dr. Cashin had to bring that cultural dexterity to their waiting room, or seek care elsewhere. In the early 1950s, a Huntsville city councilman had tried to force my father and grandfather to set up separate waiting rooms for their white and black patients but they refused, saying they would go to jail first, and the councilman had backed down.

The timing of the Huntsville sit-in movement was fortuitous. The city had an image to protect. Werner Von Braun and the German scientists he brought with him in the early 1950s to advance the nation's rocket and missile program had helped to transform Huntsville from a sleepy mill town to the "Rocket City." By 1960, its population had mushroomed to 72,000, up from 16,000 a decade before. In May 1961, President John F. Kennedy had launched the race to put an American on the moon, and the Rocket City had been assigned a key role. Dad thought city fathers would want the Kennedy administration to think that this was a progressive, open boomtown. Many whites who were moving to Huntsville to work for space-related contractors like Boeing, Lockheed, and McDonnell Douglas were scientists who had never lived in the South and were not especially enamored of segregation. Several had become Dad's patients.

He was shocked when, in early January 1962, two Negro students who participated in the first sit-in were arrested and about seventy-five others were denied service at four different establishments. Walgreens, Woolworth's, G.C. Murphy, and W.T. Grant—places that were happy to take Negroes' money but unwilling to allow them to sit to eat a hamburger—were unrepentant.

Dad posted bond for the two arrestees, Frances Sims, a freshman at A&M, and Dwight Crawford, a sixteen-year-old high school student, who would become the "most-arrested" of the Huntsville sit-in movement. Not wanting to fill the jails, the police department released any demonstrator who posted an appeal bond. Over the next seven months, Daddy and other black men of means would serve as regular bondsmen for these and other impatient pioneers.

The *Huntsville Times* initially called for calm on all sides, applauding the lack of violence, hoping that if the merchants simply ignored those sitting-in, the demonstrators would somehow realize the folly of their agitation and just go away. They did not. By January 9, the *Times* had had enough. "It's Time to Call a Halt," it argued in a lead editorial. Echoing the incredulity of the white power structure of the city, it stated, "We cannot believe that anything like a majority of the responsible colored citizens here either endorse or support the [sit-ins]." They failed to perceive Huntsville's indigenous resolve.

After the first wave of arrests, homegrown Negro leadership in Huntsville organized the Community Service Committee (CSC). They made it clear to CORE that they would take over, organize their own effort, and raise their own money to pursue open public accommodations in their city. They were motivated by a confidence in their own abilities and wariness about the efficacy of national organizations that were being undermined by the state government. One week before sit-ins began in Huntsville, the state attorney general succeeded in procuring a court order permanently barring the National Association for the Advancement of Colored People (NAACP) from doing business anywhere in Alabama. In an unrelated case, Judge Frank Johnson had found CORE in violation of a similar state prohibition because it had sponsored the Freedom Rides. Even a liberal federal judge could sometimes be constrained by cagily crafted state legal edicts.

The CSC would fill the vacuum left by such court orders. It quickly became a disciplined organization with deep roots in Huntsville's black world. Scores and sometimes more than a hundred people would turn up for the weekly "mass meeting" on Monday night at First Baptist Church on Church Street, pastored by the Reverend H. P. Snodgrass. They would hear from an inspirational speaker, receive instructions on upcoming demonstrations, and take up a collection for the cause. Students were the most public of foot soldiers. Mature adults who had more to lose found clandestine ways to contribute.

The CSC's leadership consisted of seven of the least vulnerable or most committed blacks in town. They called themselves the Steering Committee, with Reverend Ezekiel Bell, pastor of Fellowship Presbyterian Church, as the chair. He was a hardworking, natural leader whose congregation was made up of a young and rising black middle class, many of whom were employed as teachers or in the space industry. The other members of the Steering Committee were Randolph Blackwell, a lawyer on the political science faculty at A&M; Dr. Sonnie W. Hereford III, a Meharry-trained physician; J. E. Harris, a manager for Atlanta Life, a black-owned insurance company; R. E. Nelms, owner of Nelms Funeral Home; and John and Joan Cashin. They met on Wednesday evenings at 8:00 PM to plan strategy, often at our home on Lydia Drive, the sessions sometimes extending into the early morning. They planned pickets, or "poster walks," arranging for demonstrators to walk all day, every day, with homemade signs echoing their cause. At places like Sears, Grants, and G&G Cafeteria, these walks would continue for months, mainly because young A&M students refused to be deterred. And they organized sit-in demonstrations, concentrating their energies on the main shopping corridor in downtown Huntsville, which surrounded the courthouse square. Their goal was to keep the pressure on city leaders and break through the news blackout that the *Huntsville Times* had imposed after the first few weeks of the movement.

Dad was enthusiastic about involving his wife in the movement. At twenty-six, she was the only female member of the Steering Committee. With three children under the age of three, she became a full-time civil rights worker, devoting more time to the cause than her husband, who had to attend to patients.

She blossomed with the fight. In March 1963, she told the *Southern Patriot*, a civil rights monthly, "When John proposed, he said there was one condition—that we live in Huntsville and try to make it a better community. I said I'm willing to go, but I'm not a crusader and I'm not optimistic about changing the South."

Reverend James Lawson inspired her to think in more visionary terms. He had trained student demonstrators throughout the South in the methods of nonviolent direct action. When he led a workshop for the CSC, Mama said, "His faith in humanity and the human spirit stirred my interest." Civil rights became her religion. In a 1962 speech she made to a group of co-eds at Oakwood, a local, predominately black Seventh-Day Adventist college, she explained the credo that motivated her to embrace the movement. The philosophy of nonviolence was grounded in Christian principles, "to achieve aims through redeemed suffering and love of mankind."

She added, "My personal belief is that *all* of life is a religious experience and therefore I have dedicated myself to this cause."

She would need such fortification. During the first week of protests, the *Huntsville Times* identified Dad as a leader of the effort. My parents received their first phone threat within days of the first arrests. My mother described her reaction to a reporter, decades later: "John said, 'I want to send you and the children to New Jersey to stay with your parents.' I said, 'No, I am not leaving.' I said I was committed." She had reason to be fearful. Birmingham had already earned the moniker "Bombingham" for the scores of bombs that had been directed at black residents in an attempt to keep its Negroes in check. Although Huntsville was not a hotbed of Klan activity, supremacists in the Rocket City surely would have been aware of such tactics. I suspect Mama's desire to be with the man she loved motivated her as much as her commitment to the cause.

Mama was put in charge of coordinating student demonstrators, and Dad became chair of the Planning Committee. He preferred to call it "the Committee on Psychological Warfare." He would call Mayor R. B. Searcy or Police Chief Chris Spurlock to tell them what the CSC wanted them to know, or to divert them from actions they wanted kept secret. The mayor mistakenly began to think he was an informer. Actually, the point of informing the mayor and police chief in advance of any planned demonstration was to ensure that there would always be a police presence. Huntsville police were far different from the forces of Bull Connor, the malevolent Birmingham public safety commissioner who would turn fire hoses and attack dogs on unarmed children a year later. Chief Spurlock was a marine reserve officer who vowed to do everything "by the book," and the U.S. Constitution was one of the guidebooks he had pledged to uphold. In Huntsville, the police watched from the sidelines and were never violent. They arrested demonstrators only after a merchant invoked the city's vagrancy law, which rendered any demonstrator who had received a warning to leave the premises a trespasser. The presence of uniformed policemen also limited possibilities for violent reprisals from committed segregationists.

My father's "psychological warfare" often reflected his sense of humor. When the city made the mistake of allowing Huntsville's White Citizens Council to convene a meeting at a publicly owned recreation center in Big

Spring Park, he viewed it as an excellent opportunity to "integrate" the council. The park was at the geographic and psychic center of Huntsville. It was an idyllic commons adjacent to downtown, and the Grove surrounded the literal spring that had drawn Huntsville's founder, John Hunt, to the area.

Dad called the mayor. "Hey man, are you going to be attending the White Citizens Council meeting tonight?"

"No, I hadn't intended to."

"Well, I'll be there! We'll have quite a few people there." As expected, the mayor called Chief Spurlock to ensure there would be no disturbance.

The CSC followed a carefully planned strategy. Its leaders had arranged for some of their white supporters to arrive before the meeting opened and stand near the entrance. When Mama sought to enter the meeting, followed by a dozen or more black CSC members, the appointed gatekeeper for the White Citizens asked, "Are you a member?"

"No."

"Well, you can't come in." Mama looked at one of her white allies who had entered the room and asked, "Are you a member?"

"No." She looked at another, "Are you a member?"

"No." The police stopped the farce and informed the White Citizens that they would have to entertain all comers because it was essentially a public meeting in a public building. The CSC entered just in time to hear the ruminations of the guest speaker. Jim Clark was the sheriff of Dallas County, home to Selma, and infamous among Negroes for leading a violent campaign of intimidation against blacks who attempted to register to vote. Every time he garnered applause from sympathetic White Citizens, black CSC invaders would stand and cheer, to great consternation and confusion. Whether the Negroes were cheering for their own oppression or making fun of the white man's way of life, either possibility was unsettling to the good White Citizens.

The CSC's tightly orchestrated, peaceful demonstrations continued daily. They walked the courthouse square with signs demanding freedom. At lunch counters downtown and at the Heart of Huntsville Shopping Mall, the city's newest retail venue, young protesters would sit and wait to be arrested or ignored. At a downtown movie theater, four A&M students learned that they could tie up the ticket line for an entire afternoon simply by going repeatedly to the box office and returning to the back of the line each time they were refused entrance. White patrons typically ignored the picketers, or stayed away from venues where the demonstrations were occurring. Occasionally a white person would walk by and whisper, "Keep it up. Good for you."

The whites that were most riled worked at the sit-in venues. At the White Castle on the courthouse square, a waitress grew enraged when she observed a white woman enter with Mama and other demonstrators. The waitress grabbed Myrna Copeland, an ally from the Unitarian Universalist Church, and shook her. "You're a traitor to the white race!" she yelled, as a policeman watched passively. Mama relied on her civil rights training and used her body rather than her umbrella to separate them.

She would take my brother Johnny with her on occasion; he was almost three. At a Kresge's lunch counter, he did not understand why he was made to wait for his treat. "When are we going to sit down? I want a Coke," he whined. The manager glared, enraged that Mama had put him in the position of having to respond to such innocence. She met his stare and spoke conspicuously to her son. "Oh, they're going to let us be seated in a few minutes," she said. With her eyes she dared the manager to defy her words. My brother did not get his Coke that day.

The few isolated attacks on CSC protesters were clandestine. Marshall Keith, a white employee at Redstone Arsenal who had participated in a sit-in at a drugstore, was dragged at gunpoint from his home at 1:00 AM that night. His abductors drove him to a remote area, forced him to disrobe, sprayed delicate areas of his body with a chemical that caused first-degree burns, then beat him with a blunt instrument he could not identify. He survived, although it was the *Birmingham News*, not the *Huntsville Times*, that reported the story. Hank Thomas was also hospitalized for burns he received from a chemical that was sprayed on his car seat after an all-day sit-in at a Woolworth's.

Most of the assaults were verbal. All of the CSC's leadership endured relentless threatening phone calls. They assuaged their fear by reminding each other that anyone who would call to make a threat was probably a coward who would talk but not act. My parents kept a listed number because they wanted to be in touch with their community and learned to live with frequent, menacing phone calls that would continue through the NDPA years. A caller would say, "Your husband is going to need a dentist because we are going to knock his teeth out." Or, "We are going to kidnap your children." Or, "We're going to burn your house down." Mama would say, "Come on, we're ready for you," and hang up. Dad had more fun with it. He would try to engage the caller in a conversation or, if the situation warranted it, say, "Come on, we'll use your ass for target practice," after which the caller would typically hang up. The Kennedy administration's FBI did exhibit considerable concern. Agents would call regularly to keep tabs on what was happening, and this gave my parents a modest sense of security. Subsequently, the FBI would keep tabs on my father for more insidious reasons.

In the event an opponent did attack, my parents were prepared. With three young children, they hired only babysitters who knew how to shoot a gun and would do so if necessary. Their favorite babysitter was an ex-marine. And they stashed guns throughout the house. My father carried a .357 Magnum with him wherever he went, along with his gun permit. He did not see any inconsistency in advocating nonviolence and carrying a gun. It was for protection, but mainly it gave him a psychological edge. If it was a well-known fact that Dr. Cashin carried a gun, there was little likelihood that he would ever have to use it. Eventually, he felt no need to carry it.

Once, a few opponents were inclined to act on their hatred. At the time, Lydia Drive was essentially in the country. There were no businesses in the vicinity. Except for the fact that Mama was armed and potentially dangerous, we were especially vulnerable in the evenings before Dad said good night to John Sr. at the dental office and returned home. One night she happened to look out of the bedroom window, anticipating her husband's arrival, just as a car turned into Lydia Drive with its headlights turned off. Again she followed her civil rights training, turning off the lights inside the house so she couldn't be seen through the window. She saw someone get out of the car and grabbed a gun from under the mattress before calling my father. "I'm coming right away," he said, slamming down the phone.

She shuddered at the thought of her husband confronting potentially multiple intruders with that Magnum. A bad scene playing in her head, she instinctively turned on the floodlights over the back patio. In that instant, she realized that it was the only outdoor lighting they had, and it might lead the trespasser directly to our front door. Luckily, the interloper was spooked when the lights came on, turned, and walked fast to the car, which a second person, the driver, had readied for exit from the dead-end street.

My father never needed an excuse for speeding, but this time he had a good one. When a police car stopped him, he opened the window and yelled, in his ever-colorful vernacular, "Follow me, somebody's fuckin' with my wife." The policeman happened to be one of his patients. As they floored it, another police car joined the caravan. They arrived, jumped out with guns drawn, and surrounded the house. Mama came out and announced that the interlopers were gone.

After that, Dad installed a makeshift alarm, using the same mechanism deployed by gas stations to alert an attendant to a new customer's arrival: a rubber hose that rang a high-pitched bell when the customer drove over it. He laid one across Lydia Drive so that he or Mama would hear the familiar "ding-ding" when any car entered what was at the time a two-house subdivision. Any entrant necessarily had to drive down the street to turn around, giving my parents a chance to react to any suspicious vehicle. Dad claims he also installed two cases of dynamite in a sewer pipe under the road, just in case he needed it, although I think he may have been puffing on this point. He was not exaggerating, though, when he suggested that he would have met deadly force with deadly force if he felt it was necessary to protect his family. Even Mama learned to be bold. I was an infant at the time, but I recall a night during the NDPA years when my brothers and I were watching television and she appeared in the family room wielding a handgun with an assurance that conveyed her determination to use it if she needed to. She pointed it toward the ceiling as she scanned the room and told us to stay put. Dad was not at home, and she was certain she had heard something unusual. As I watched her proceed purposefully to inspect the other rooms of the house, without any hint of fear, I felt safe and continued to watch TV. In that instance she found no interloper.

The movement continued, as did the harassing phone calls. Neither the CSC's leaders nor its followers were intimidated. Their primary challenges were monotony and a lack of concrete progress. As the weeks and months wore on, the numbers of demonstrators began to drop. They had begun with a core group of three dozen frontline troops. Under city codes, it was illegal to promote an economic boycott. The protesters' strategy had been to mount daily demonstrations and sit-ins in the main downtown business corridor in an effort to disrupt commerce and call attention to their cause. Rather than fill the city jails and attract press attention, the city would release any demonstrator who was arrested, if he or she posted bond. The city and the merchants figured they could wear students down with this tactic until the end of the spring semester, when many of them would disappear for the summer. The state of Alabama also cut into the CSC's troop strength by summarily replacing the president of A&M, Dr. Drake—Harold's aging, sick father—with a candidate committed to disciplining any students who participated in the sit-ins. The tactic had worked and the CSC frontline had dwindled to the hardcore faithful. At the same time, Dad's practice began to suffer, not because his patients were disloyal but because he was so consumed by the movement that he could no longer carry the heavy patient load for himself and John Sr. By then, my grandfather had reduced his practice to doing only dentures because they required no surgery and paid rather well. During the movement days, Dad would send many of their patients to another dentist and rely on the income he received from a three-employee dental lab he operated out of the ground floor of the dental office.

The CSC leadership invited Dr. Martin Luther King Jr. to speak, correctly intuiting that his oratory would revitalize their troops. He was not yet an icon. Mama and Daddy knew him as Martin, a man whose sense of humor was as powerful as his speeches. Dad had first met him through Joe Lowery, his childhood friend, who had become an intimate of King's in the Southern Christian Leadership Conference. Through Lowery and the SCLC, my father was becoming acquainted with a network of civil rights activists who were committed to nonviolent social change across the South. Little did he realize that in five years he would be attempting to convince these leaders of the necessity of moving beyond voter registration to forming their own political parties.

Oakwood College was the only venue with a sufficiently large auditorium to host King, and as a private school, it was insulated from manipulation by the state or the city. Over 2,000 people attended his speech on an evening in March. He called on Negroes who had been sitting on the sidelines to enter the fray, noting that freedom was "worth losing a job for" and "worth getting killed for," if only to spare one's children "from a life of psychological death." Then he spoke to all of God's children: "If there is a victory it would not be a victory merely for 20 million Negroes. It would be a victory for justice . . . And it will make a better nation for everybody because the festering sore of segregation debilitates the white man as well as the Negro."

The mayor heard him. After King spoke, he finally agreed to a demand the CSC had made in the first week of the boycott. He would appoint two whites to serve on a biracial negotiating committee, with the black representatives to be chosen by the CSC. The speech did not alleviate the collective fears of white Huntsvillians. The mayor informed the CSC that he couldn't find a single white citizen who was willing to serve.

Students, ministers, and ordinary citizens continued to picket with renewed vigor and no evident progress. A regular reader of the *Huntsville Times* would never have known that sit-in demonstrations were occurring daily downtown. Merchants were hurting, but neither the white power structure nor white Huntsvillians were feeling any meaningful compulsion to upset a decades-entrenched regime of racial separation.

The protests had occurred daily since early January, and the members of the Committee on Psychological Warfare decided they needed a dramatic event to break the logjam. They conceived a special sit-in that could not be ignored. On April 11, two doctors' wives entered Hutchins & Hutchins Walgreens on Washington Street in downtown Huntsville, where many arrests had occurred. Mama carried me, her four-month-old daughter, and Dr. Hereford's wife, Martha, carried an ample pregnancy. Frances Sims, who had been arrested eight times, accompanied Mama and Mrs. Hereford, with every intention of being arrested again. Four ministers including Reverend Bell rounded out their protest. As arranged, a photographer was ready to capture the scene.

As they sat down at the lunch counter, the Walgreens staff ignored them, answering their request for coffee and hamburgers with silence. The owner, William L. Hutchins, arrived. He had had much practice in dealing with demonstrators. The city attorney had carefully instructed all merchants on how to invoke the city's vagrancy law. "I am warning you to leave," he said, "if you don't leave, I will have you arrested." They sat in silence. Twenty minutes later, the police arrived; they promptly escorted the women out the back door, trying to avoid drawing attention to the extraordinary scene. At the back door, they told Mama she should get someone to take the baby. Once before she had taken me to a sit-in and had handed me off to Nurse Dent, a registered nurse who seemed to take care of the entire Negro community. This day would be different. Mama said, "No, the baby has to stay with me." She had brought diapers and bottles and was prepared to keep her daughter with her in jail. Nana had come down to take care of my brothers and offer Mama moral support. Grace and John Sr. supported the plan because their son had hatched it and they knew he would not endanger his little girl.

As the women were being herded into a police car, a plainclothes detective tried to use his raincoat to prevent the photographer from capturing the image of a woman with a baby being arrested. His obfuscation failed. A week later, *Jet* magazine, black America's national weekly, reported the story, unfortunately without the picture that I forever heard about but have never seen.

Often my father or Dr. Hereford signed appeal bonds for arrestees, enabling them to leave jail within hours of their arrest. Dad had signed so many bonds that he began a bail bond business that he also ran out of the first floor of his dental office. There was not much risk to their property because the cases rarely came to trial. The city was simply trying to use arrests to discourage the demonstrators.

The four ministers were each released under a $300 bond. The three women did not ask for an appeal bond, placing the police in a quandary about what to do with their unique inmates. After considerable deliberation, the police chief announced to the women that he was releasing them "on their own recognizance." At four months I had gone to jail for the cause, and slept through the entire episode. Mama, baby and diaper bag in hand, walked four long blocks from the city jail to Daddy's dental office on Gallatin Street. He was disappointed to see her. Looking up from a patient's mouth, he said, "What are you doing here? You're supposed to be in jail."

They got their wish the following week. Having refused to post bond, Mama, Martha Hereford, and Frances Sims were required to appear for an arraignment. At the hearing they again refused to post bond; the court had no choice but to order them to jail. This time Mama did not have me with her. Nevertheless, their incarceration was rather effective.

Attempting to avoid publicity, the city sent them to a filthy county jail. Their jailers tried several tactics designed to encourage them to post bond and leave. The mattresses in their cell had been removed, forcing them to sit on bare springs. The women piled their coats together to give Martha some comfort. Periodically, a jailer would come by to harass them: "What do you want for lunch? You want steak?"

Howard Barley and his Sweet Shop saw to it that the women were fed well. He and other supporters delivered three meals a day, in quantities so copious that the women shared the excess with prostitutes in the cell across the hall, all of whom happened to be white. There were no racial barriers in the sharing of a soul food feast.

A day passed and Mama's jailers grew increasingly exasperated with the unwanted attention. The CSC had organized a telephone committee and the jailer's phone rang incessantly: "Is it true you have mothers in jail, you have a pregnant woman in jail?" "What are you doing with professional wives in jail?" The mayor finally called my father, imploring, "John, why don't you get your wife out of jail?" "She'll get out when she's ready," he replied drily.

With the jailing of prominent doctors' wives, one visibly pregnant, the *Huntsville Times* finally broke its silence on the boycott, under the head-line, "Trio of Negroes Choose the Jail Instead of Bail." National press picked up the story. And Marc Carpenter made sure that the New Jersey papers covered his daughter's arrest. He was quintessentially exuberant in sharing how he felt about the matter. To the *New Jersey Herald News,* he said, "This time they made a big mistake. . . . They arrested a Carpenter and I'll back my daughter all the way. We are proud of her stand in this matter and stand ready to take this case to the highest court in the land." To the *Hudson Dispatch*, he announced, "I don't care what it costs—perhaps $20,000—but I'll fight it all the way." To another paper, its name lost from Mama's tattered scrapbook, he said of his daughter, "She's militant on the subject of segregation as I am." And from the nationally circulated *Afro American:* "Dr. Carpenter complained from his Jersey City home that while the federal government is spending millions of dollars in Huntsville, local officials are still allowed to flout the rights of colored Americans."

By day two, L. D. Wall, the county sheriff, was feeling considerable pressure to squelch his embarrassment. The sheriff's deputy arrived at their cell and announced to Mama and Mrs. Hereford, "Collect your things, you're being released." As they were escorted down the stairs to the jailer's office, Mama whispered to Martha, "We are not leaving here, if Frances is not also released." As they sat on the couch in the jailer's office, he repeated his refrain, "We're releasing you."

"What about Frances?"

"No, we're not releasing her."

"Well, then, we are not leaving." The two women staged a sit-in in the county jailer's office that lasted for several hours. During that time the phone was constantly ringing. "Well, yeah, they're here, but they're being released," the sheriff's exasperated deputy would say to every caller. City policemen and emissaries of Mayor Searcy arrived and also tried to prevail upon the women to leave.

Then the sheriff's lawyer and deputy began a "good cop–bad cop" routine. The deputy was respectful and polite while the lawyer was tough, bordering on belligerent, saying, "Why don't you leave!" They would not budge. At this point Mama counted a total of nine men in or near the office. She turned to Martha and said, "Martha, if they touch us they are really in trouble," and leaned back on the jailer's couch, relaxing on her pillow.

The phone continued to ring. Black Huntsvillians who had managed to register to vote, including my parents, had supported Sheriff Wall and considered him to be a rather decent guy. He was running for reelection and wanted to keep his job. He called and asked to speak to Mama. "Mrs. Cashin, you know I am not responsible for this, you were arrested by the city police and they moved you to the county jail. Won't you please leave?" he implored.

"I'm sorry, no, I cannot leave without Frances."

They had reached a stalemate. If the ladies would not leave, the sheriff concluded, they would have to return to their filthy cell. Mama and Mrs. Hereford smiled. Returning to a dingy jail cell was proof of their power over a white establishment that was desperate to release them. As the deputy escorted them, he observed, "I have never seen anybody happy to go back to a jail cell."

The sticking point continued to be that the three women refused to request an appeal bond. The sheriff had tried to release Mama and Mrs. Hereford without a bond but had not been willing to give Frances, a multiple arrestee, such favorable treatment. The next day, their third morning in jail, the three women finally posted bail. Drs. Cashin and Hereford underwrote the bonds for their wives and Frances Sims. Mrs. Hereford went home and got in bed, giving herself and the unborn baby who would become my best friend, Lee, some much-needed rest. Mama led a march to the courthouse to publicize what had happened to them.

By sheer happenstance, George Wallace was campaigning for governor and was scheduled to speak on the square on this late April day. Mama and fellow marchers reached the south side of the courthouse first. All sides of the modern structure featured steps that rose high, but the south side had the best light, giving Mama the platform she deserved. Wallace arrived minutes later, riding on a large flatbed truck surrounded by an entourage of Confederate flag wavers. He tried to disturb the CSC rally by parking his truck opposite them and blasting "Dixie" over a loudspeaker. Wallace's crowd of supporters began to swell, threatening to overtake Mama's rally. Two days before, Dad had appeared on a local TV program in which a Negro host had convinced the imperial wizard of the Ku Klux Klan to debate him. He recognized the wizard in the crowd of supporters who had come to see Wallace, sans his white robe, and walked straight into a clutch of plainclothes Klansmen. He disarmed the wizard by quickly grabbing his hand to shake it and saying, "Hi, good to see you again." Even a supreme supremacist could have manners. He returned my father's handshake, and, flummoxed, grinned sheepishly as his fellow Klansmen looked on with bewilderment. Before they had a chance to react, Dad turned on his heel and quickly headed back to Mama's rally.

She yelled over Wallace's "Dixie" chorus and proved an equal competitor to the Confederate anthem. He was forced to move to the opposite, less advantageous north side of the courthouse. Decades later she chuckled at the scene, marveling, "How did I have the guts to do it?" She and the many souls who poured their hearts into the Huntsville sit-in movement were on the brink of victory.

Within days, the mayor finally succeeded in appointing two whites to serve on the biracial negotiating committee. "Blue Jean Sunday" expanded the prospects for negotiation. Usually, Negroes bought the nicest clothes they could afford for Easter Sunday. This year they would deprive merchants of their dollars and wear denim. Dr. Hereford had heard of the success of the concept in Nashville's sit-in movement and brought the idea to the Steering Committee. What better way to show your sacrifice in the season of Lent than to give up material finery for a worker's fabric? The CSC evaded the ban on promoting economic boycotts by circulating leaflets with an elliptical message that made their point: "Are you *spending* for segregation or buying for freedom?"

Normally, a Negro would never commit the sacrilege of wearing blue jeans in the sanctuary of a black church. On this Easter Sunday, ministers preached the gospel wearing overalls. Their flocks reveled in their neatly pressed jean skirts and trousers.

Dr. Hereford captured the scene with his movie camera. Families posed amusedly in washes of never-worn denim blue, proud and emboldened by their solidarity.

The merchants felt the pinch. Most Negroes were buying out of town or not at all. White patrons were also staying away from downtown, probably to evade Negro demonstrators rather than support them. The business community finally agreed to cooperate with the biracial negotiating committee.

J. E. Harris and R. E. Nelms of the CSC steering committee went to work, demanding complete and total first-class citizenship for black Huntsvillians. The two white negotiators, both representatives of Huntsville's oldest money, requested anonymity as a condition of their appointment. Their names were James Johnston of Johnston Concrete Products and Harry Rhett, a real estate baron. They argued for incremental change, whereas Harris and Nelms demanded immediate, absolute desegregation. No more white and colored restrooms and water fountains. Full access to lunch counters, hotels, restaurants, bowling alleys, movie theaters, or any realm open to the white public. Now.

If the white leadership was having difficulty imagining an integrated order, most ordinary Huntsvillians seemed to greet change with a shrug. As the negotiations meandered, a few realms of the white world were desegregated by individual acts of defiance, with no reaction or resistance.

Mama and Kimela Hereford started it. The Herefords' three-year-old daughter was participating in a poster walk on the courthouse square and needed to relieve herself. Mama volunteered to take her to a restroom in the courthouse. Facing the "colored" and "white" signs, she decided impulsively to walk into the whites-only restroom, taking Kim with her. "I wanted to see if it was cleaner," she told Dr. Hereford. And it was. From that day forward, Negroes started using the best restrooms at the courthouse and began to take matters into their own hands in other environs. On Mother's Day, Reverend Bell and Dr. Hereford took their families to Big Spring Park. There were no parks anywhere in Huntsville designated for Negroes. Some whites stared when they observed colored children take to the slide and swings on the playground. But no one objected. And that was how Huntsville desegregated its city parks.

It would take more pressure before the city's leaders began to accept as inevitable the integration of privately owned venues. The CSC decided to extend its psychological warfare to Wall Street. Marie Carpenter, my nana, helped organize the effort. As a pioneer in Jersey City, she was delighted to pinch-hit for her daughter.

Marie and a hearty, integrated group of twelve picketers converged on the New York Stock Exchange on May 19. She was an exceedingly elegant civil rights protester, wearing her signature crown of expertly coiffed jet-black curls, a silk jacquard dress, matching embroidered handbag, pearls, and spiked black pumps with delicate bows. The sign she carried read, "Don't invest in Huntsville, Ala., it's bad business." And it did not interfere with her fashion statement.

The Associated Press wire service picked up the story, and city leaders were rather chagrined by the negative publicity. If daily poster walks and sit-ins were not a sufficient reminder to city leaders that the CSC was not going to relent, they received another pointed message when Dr. and Mrs. Hereford and other CSC members staged a similar protest at the Chicago mercantile exchange. They passed out 2,000 handbills that began with the caption, "I ordered a hamburger and was served a warrant in Huntsville, Alabama."

On July 10, 1962, without fanfare or publicity, Huntsville became the first city in Alabama to desegregate most of its public accommodations, nearly two years before President Lyndon Johnson signed the Civil Rights Act. To ensure that Huntsville's revolution was bloodless, negotiators arranged for testers to appear at designated establishments at a secretly appointed hour. Negro stalwarts arrived to eat and make history, and there was no violence and no "massive resistance."

Mama and Daddy and a few other couples were assigned to integrate the Eleganté, the swankiest restaurant in town. She called ahead to ask whether there would be any problem if they included a white couple in their party. "That's what we're doing, aren't we?" the proprietor responded evenly.

Indeed. An overwhelmingly peaceful change of order had taken place in north Alabama. Perhaps this region in the Tennessee River Valley, with its hills that had not been conducive to a plantation economy, was reasserting the kind of enlightenment it had displayed in the populist era of the 1890s. There was money to be made, and the race issue could not stand in the way of progress. Maybe this attitude was hastened with the space industry's infusion of non-Southern scientists. Whatever the reason, the Rocket City proved the weakest link in the chain of diehard segregation in Alabama and Mississippi. Police dogs and fire hoses would be unleashed in Birmingham the following spring. Those ugly images, transported internationally, created a tectonic shift in political and public attitudes, making way for the Civil Rights Act of 1964, a national edict of universal access on a nondiscriminatory basis.

The CSC did not rest on its laurels. Huntsville's unfinished "race" business included public education, public swimming pools, and politics—realms still imbued with the ideology of white supremacy. On the education front, its members began at the graduate level. Mama applied to be admitted to a continuing education course on foreign affairs at the University of Alabama at Huntsville, a satellite of the state's flagship university. Faced with evidence of her degrees from Fisk and Columbia universities, UAH could not deny her admission based upon a lack of qualifications. They found another excuse. A month after she applied, she received a letter in January 1963 informing her that the course had been canceled due to a lack of available speakers. The *Carolina Times*, *Chattanooga Observer*, *Louisville Defendant*, and *Jet* magazine saw fit to cover this episode as a transparent rebuff of a would-be integrator. The *Huntsville Times* was silent on the matter.

Two days before Mama received her rejection, George Wallace gave his inauguration speech in Montgomery. The scrappy little judge from Barbour County had won decisively in the Democratic primary—the only election that mattered in Alabama—by "out-seg'ing" the competition. On the campaign stump, he had repeatedly promised to defy any federal court desegregation order and personally stand in the schoolhouse door if necessary. He reaffirmed his purpose at his inauguration.

Some white people must have shuddered along with black Alabamians. Everyone remembered his most passionate statement: "In the name of the greatest people that have ever trod this earth, I draw the line in the dust and toss the gauntlet before the feet of tyranny . . . and I say . . . segregation today . . . segregation tomorrow . . . segregation forever." Between the lines, my father also thought he heard Wallace call for a volunteer militia that would aid the state in resisting school desegregation. He began to rethink the CSC's education strategy because he believed in his heart that Wallace's officially sanctioned volunteers would slaughter Negro schoolchildren if this was their first line of attack in desegregating public education in Alabama. He thought the safer strategy was to first desegregate higher education, and he wanted to deny Wallace and his legions the politically potent symbolism of massive resistance. If Wallace was determined to have his stand in a schoolhouse door, the most unfriendly stage for him would be the entrance to graduate education at UAH, because Dad and Police Chief Spurlock had shaken hands on Spurlock's commitment to arrest anyone, including the governor, who attempted to obstruct a court's desegregation order.

According to Dad, his suggested change of strategy did not go over well with Jack Greenberg of the NAACP Legal Defense Fund. Thurgood Marshall had led the "Inc. Fund" to win *Brown v. Board of Education* and legions of other civil rights cases. He had chosen Greenberg to succeed him when President Kennedy decided Marshall belonged on the bench. Nine years after the *Brown* decision, every public school in Alabama remained segregated. Greenberg and other Inc. Fund lawyers were prepared to mount desegregation test cases to force Alabama school districts to yield to the U.S. Constitution. As usual, my father went his own way.

He had recruited two black professionals to serve as plaintiffs in a suit to gain entry to UAH. Marvin Carroll and Dave McGlathery were federal employees involved in missile research. Both had applied to take postgraduate courses at the University Extension Center in order to better perform their jobs in advanced technology. He also recruited Chuck Morgan to represent them. Morgan was a well-respected white Birmingham lawyer who was not averse to taking on Negro clients with a cause. In a matter of months, he would be forced to flee Birmingham after he publicly blamed middle-class whites for their complicity in the underground violence that fueled the Sixteenth Street Church bombing that killed four little girls.

It would be the first of many times that my father would reach into his own pocket to help finance a cause he believed in. With Dad making up the difference between what they could raise from the ACLU and other sources for legal fees, Morgan filed suit in federal district court seeking to have Carroll and McGlathery admitted to UAH in June, well before public school desegregation was contemplated in September. Carroll dropped out for personal reasons, but Dave McGlathery persevered. The Inc. Fund filed its own suit for admission of Vivian Malone and James Hood to the main campus at Tuscaloosa, also for the summer session. The cases were consolidated, and the court ordered immediate admission.

Mama and Daddy always referred to Wallace's stand at Tuscaloosa as an unnecessary farce that gave him the national stage he had been looking for, one that laid a foundation both for Wallace's presidential candidacies and the Republican Party's ultimately successful "Southern strategy." Future Republican presidential candidates would accumulate electoral votes by exploiting the racial anxieties of Southern whites. In the interim, the Kennedy Justice Department must have had its own reasons for orchestrating a carefully choreographed showdown with Wallace at Tuscaloosa. At Wallace's behest, they even asked McGlathery to switch his entrance from UAH to the flagship campus, University of Alabama at Tuscaloosa, so that Wallace could stand in front of all of them. Dave said no. In accordance with an agreement negotiated with Wallace by Justice Department officials, McGlathery waited for two days after the show at Tuscaloosa to enter UAH, where he encountered no opposition. Another color line was broken in Huntsville without violence, hysterics, or racial showmanship.

In September, Sonnie Hereford IV became the first black child to enter public school in Alabama. His father accompanied the six-year-old to Fifth Avenue Elementary, at the corner of Gallatin Street and Governor's Drive, just east of the Grove. Wallace had ordered state troopers to block school doors in Huntsville, Birmingham, Mobile, and Tuskegee. The national guard and Chief Spurlock's local police were there to protect the Herefords, but their services were not needed. Although the Herefords received half a dozen death threats that day, most Huntsvillians went about their business. Unlike Little Rock in 1957, or Boston in 1965, or scores of other school districts where pioneering colored children were met with invective or worse, in Huntsville a local public school was desegregated without incident.

Desegregation of politics in Alabama was another, tougher matter. The CSC began its political assault in May 1962, during the height of the sit-in movement. Dad and other black compatriots made it clear that they would not be satisfied merely to sit at Huntsville's lunch counters or at the linen-draped tables of the Eleganté. Thirteen men and one woman—a veritable who's who of the black world—ran on a slate for all of the seats on the Madison County Democratic Executive Committee. Most of them were ministers, entrepreneurs, or doctors who did not depend on white institutions for their livelihood. Under the headline "Negroes Seek County Party Posts," the *Huntsville Times* took pains to identify Drs. Cashin, Hereford, and Drake; funeral home owners R. E. Nelms and Charles Ray Sr.; Robert Adams, a contractor; ministers Amos Robinson and E. D. White, and one "Lola P. Dill, Negro woman." They knew they had little chance of winning, but they had a point to make. Even if the party still operated under the official slogan "White Supremacy for the Right," it was the only vehicle of any import in what passed for democracy in Alabama and they intended to return blacks to their rightful place as key players in politics. They also campaigned in hopes of inspiring Negroes to register to vote. At a rally on the grounds of Charles Ray's Memorial Funeral Home, their mascot was a mule with a sign affixed to his midsection that my father always recalled fondly: "I can't vote because I'm a mule—what's your excuse?"

The Madison County Democratic Party operatives did not attempt to block these black upstarts from running—the ultimately unsuccessful tactic attempted by their counterparts in Birmingham. Instead, they simply advertised the roster of "white candidates" in the *Huntsville Times*, ensuring that most votes would be along racial lines. No black candidate won, but the election did increase black voter registration and it validated my father's hypothesis about the potential of political engagement.

Organization was key. It was clear to Dad that Negroes could be transformed en masse into voters *if* they had candidates that sincerely represented their interests. He and his buddy Harold Drake decided they had to keep up the pressure. In 1964, the next election cycle, Dad ran for mayor of Huntsville on a slate that included Dr. Harold Drake and Reverend L. C. Jamar for seats on the city council. Again, they had no illusions about winning. Their mission was to continue expanding the ranks of registered black voters *and* to agitate for more change. In the summer of 1964, they used the primary election season to focus attention on the last bastion of segregation of public accommodations in Huntsville: public swimming pools.

The pool at the Big Spring Park recreational center was the most obvious target. It was minutes from the Grove and had always been surrounded by black children who were never allowed to use it. On the first day of the summer season, the CSC arranged for several black families to attempt to enter. They did not succeed.

The Committee on Psychological Warfare assessed the city's opening move and countered with an aggressive play by several black knights. They sent a delegation of physically impressive gentlemen who could swim, most of whom happened to be A&M football players. As Dad handed the delegation a $100 bill to buy swimsuits, he instructed, "Make them let you swim or close it down." This time no Negro was denied entry.

Huntsville power brokers were not yet ready to accept the idea of black and white youth sharing the same recreational water. The next day the pool was closed for repairs, and it stayed closed for the entire summer of 1964. That closed swimming pool became an important symbolic issue in the mayoral race. Dad, Harold, and Reverend Jamar invoked it repeatedly in their collective campaign, altering the political realities in Huntsville even as the legal realities of constitutional law and the new Civil Rights Act were becoming more concrete for white Southerners.

Glenn Hearn, a former FBI agent who ultimately won the mayoral race, and Chris Spurlock, who came in second, both took the position during their campaigns that public property belonged to the public. They had both pledged that if they were elected, the swimming pools would be open to all comers. Hearn followed through with his commitment when he became mayor.

By the NDPA years, I had learned to swim and had grown used to being parked, along with my brothers, with Grandma Grace, our most frequent babysitter when Mama and Daddy had to be where the party called them. When we became old enough to leave her nest unaccompanied, Grandma would send us off to the Big Spring pool to get us out of her hair. We could walk to it from her house. I have no memory of any white kids swimming. Even the lifeguards were black by then. After a rest break, a multitude of black children would plunge into the water. Once, my brother Carroll backed into me when Johnny was splashing him. As he evaded the taunts of his older brother, he knocked me face down onto the side of the pool. The concrete busted my lip and left me with a chipped tooth I would live with until my mid-twenties, when vanity prevailed. The blood tasted salty; the lessons of my "integrated" childhood were just beginning.

CHAPTER ELEVEN

Integration

Dad says we "acted like a family" once again when he volunteered to move us from Lydia Drive in order to provide a retirement home for his elderly Aunt Vivi and Uncle Tode. It made sense for the Langstons to return south in their silver years. The debate in the family had been whether they should live in Nashville, Tode's hometown, Decatur, near Aunt Pat, or in booming Huntsville. John Sr. wrote Vivi to lobby for Huntsville as the place where all his remaining siblings should live out their days.

It must have been his first and last missive to her. Aunt Vivi kept everything. Her cache of family correspondence ran from the 1910s to the 1960s, but it included only one letter from her brother John Sr., written in December 1963. He was recovering from an operation and contemplating another. He was "a little apprehensive and nervous" and tried to mask his fears with a few pleasantries. Then he reminded her that "none of us is getting younger and we (all of us) must look to the future. . . . we can't take care of big homes and to build a sort of motel together might just be the answer. . . ."

He died six months later at age seventy-two, from complications of a hernia operation that Dad had tried to talk him out of. He always said that his father could have lived forever with the truss he had been wearing. "He could be called a lot of things but 'hypocrite' was not one of them," Dad would say of my grandfather's oft-repeated insistence that he did not want his funeral to occur in a church. Grandma Grace respected her husband's disdain for organized religion by holding his wake and funeral in the dining room of their home on Gallatin Street. The black world came to pay its respects. They filled the space where Grandma's ornate mahogany dining room table had been and overflowed into her ample living room. Reverend Ezekiel Bell and other close family friends eulogized him. As Dad listened to Bell speak of the man everybody, even the white folks in Huntsville, seemed to love, it occurred to him that he was losing his best friend. As they worked side by side for a decade, John Sr. had replaced his brother Herschel as his closet buddy. Lord, he was going to miss him. Grandma's church family and sorority sisters, Alpha Kappa Alphas, consoled our family the way all black Southerners do when a loved one dies. They brought food.

With John Sr. gone, Vivi and Pat were the only siblings left to tell the stories of their father, Grandpa Herschel, and how he persevered. The generation once removed from slavery was dying just as the civil rights movement was bearing fruit. Vivi and Pat would be heartened that they had lived long enough to witness the beginnings of radical change. As for the loss of John Sr., they would find comfort in each other's company, now that Vivi had returned to north Alabama.

For the privilege of living on Lydia, Tode and Vivi paid $65 a month. Dad told them to send the rent check to his newly widowed mother. Grace had done everything in her power to secure a future for him, and he would be her safety net if she needed one.

We moved in with Grandma Grace and her father, Grandpa Claude, not long after John Sr. died. My brothers and cousins had called him Grand-poppy. I was too young to remember him. Dad's stories about him were what made him real to me—a small man for whom humor was a life force. "He was one of the funniest cats you'd ever meet," Dad would say of him. "At the holiday gatherings at Aunt Pat's house, he would often joke about who could pass for white. He would stand up and whip his head around and say, 'I got that blow-in-the-wind hair,' and the laughter was riotous."

Grandma must have enjoyed having us constantly about to distract her from her grief. Dad had promised Mama that the move would be temporary. When I was old enough to understand that a woman can have tensions with her in-laws, or her husband, and still love them deeply, Mama would tell me about her frustrations with this living arrangement. It lasted two years and drove my mother crazy. Four generations and one very spoiled Chihuahua lived chaotically under one roof.

This is where my sense of being in the world and my memories begin. Mostly, I recall happiness. Waking up at dawn before anyone else in the house had stirred to discover our Easter baskets on the kitchen table. Although I still believed in Santa Claus, somehow I knew that this abundance of colored eggs, chocolate, and candy on fake green grass was Mama's doing.

Daddy's cabin cruiser. He kept it on a trailer in the backyard and would take us for joyrides on the Tennessee River, until he got bored with it and started buying faster-moving toys. I never saw his gyrocopter leave the ground, but, a few years later, he would take me to kindergarten on his motorcycle. I would hold on to him in complete terror, burying my face in his back as we raced impossibly fast to Fellowship Presbyterian, a black church school, where the other kids were awed by my father's vehicle of choice.

My playhouse. It was made of corrugated metal and seemed miles from Grandma's house, given the expansive size of her backyard, and even farther on the few occasions we were allowed to venture out to it at night. Grandma's backyard was its own fortress, surrounded on three sides by a cinder-block wall that obscured a bank and other commercial properties that had begun to encroach on the Grove. Her prized flower garden softened the gray cinder blocks. That yard had everything three rambunctious preschoolers needed to fill a day's play. In the summer we would jump off a wooden crate into a rubber baby pool, over and over again, until the water had to be refilled. Or we would collect pecans from Grandma's trees or try to climb her magnificent magnolia. If we grew tired with outdoor exploits, there was always a game of checkers to be had with Grandma in her sunroom.

Sometimes Grandpa Claude watched us from a rocking lawn chair that Grandma would place out back just so that her father would be occupied by our spectacle. There were nine decades between us, and neither generation comprehended the other. When his great-grandchildren ran amok in bathing suits, he would admonish us in a weak voice, "Why don't you go put on some clothes?" He lived upstairs. We didn't go up there much when he was alive. It was his space and exuded the mysteries of a very old man with very old stuff. I don't remember seeing him climb those stairs, but he must have been spry enough to tackle them. Like an apparition he appeared every morning, dressed in a fresh shirt and trousers held up by suspenders, and ascended magically at the end of each day.

Grandma Grace slept in the front bedroom on the ground floor. A bathroom separated her room from the guest room that became Mama and Daddy's bedroom. Instead of being the queen of her own castle, Mama had become tenant of a smallish room with three entrances, none of which locked. Through one door was a back room where Johnny and Carroll shared a sofa bed and I slept in my crib, despite my three years. I earned my first set of stitches by jumping with my brothers on that sofa bed. I fell and split my temple on its iron foldout frame, one of many injuries I would incur from trying to keep up with my brothers.

The second door opened onto the kitchen, the place where Grandma Grace ruled supreme and did not think much of her daughter-in-law's gourmet cooking. I never told Mama, but Grandma's food was simpler and better to me, especially her heavily buttered green beans and corn.

The third door led to the ground-floor bathroom that three children, two parents, and one grandparent shared. For Mama, the lack of privacy was maddening. When I was an adult, she related one of Grandpa Claude's more irritating idiosyncrasies. "He would burst into our bedroom, no matter what we were doing," she said, sometimes to pinch a cigarette off his granddaughter-in-law, although his Seventh-day Adventist religion forbade such practices. His hypocrisy was a source of amusement. When he could not live up to his own piety, he would go to Mama to cadge occasional smokes or nips of Canadian Club.

Daddy loved our living arrangement. "Those were the happiest years of my life," he said of the time when all the people he most treasured lived together. He could walk across the driveway to his dental office and return home as often as he wished. In retrospect, had we continued to live with Grandma, or had she lived longer, some of the darkness that fell in subsequent years might have been avoided. If Grandma sometimes irked her daughter-in-law with her dominance, she was a steadying presence on her son.

According to my father, the imperatives of finding an appropriate grade school for Carroll, who was hearing impaired, prompted our move to Owens Drive. There was only one elementary school in the city with the requisite resources, and Dad was determined to get his kid into that school. Blossomwood Elementary was untouched by desegregation, as was the neighborhood that surrounded it. For two years Daddy tried to buy a house in the Blossomwood district. No one would sell to a Negro, much less an uppity one. In 1966, there were no federal or state laws to which he could turn for recourse. America had relented when faced with the moral imperatives of the civil rights movement—but not on housing. Daddy prevailed by returning to the techniques of psychological warfare.

He frequently used the word "sincere" to describe committed people who were worthy of his trust. He had recruited the most "sincere" white people among his dental patients to support Huntsville's sit-in movement. Those who responded most ardently were Unitarians, and they became intimates. Daddy and Mama were attracted to this group of scientists, academics, and liberal thinkers who were intellectually curious and, in the vernacular of the day, groovy people. We became regulars at the Unitarian Universalist Church of Huntsville, the only black family in that community. I would find God later, in black churches. In the meantime, I learned humanism from the Unitarians.

Sas Rissé, a great friend from this circle, was more than happy to purchase a house for us with our money, once she was able to convince her recalcitrant husband to go along with the ruse of pretending to be the real buyers. My father beat the housing segregationists at their game by buying a house without seeing the inside of it. As an artist, Sas was able to provide Mama with a detailed rendering of the house we would live in for the next seven years. It was a modern yellow-brick, two-story rambler, perched high on a hill with a wraparound balcony off the second-floor living room that offered a bird's-eye view of the street—a salutary feature for a black activist who was about to enter the apex of his battle with Alabama.

It caused quite a stir when we broke the color line in southeast Huntsville. Apparently our invasion was worth a special trip for racial voyeurs who lived elsewhere. A steady stream of onlookers drove by the house for weeks. Daddy wanted to be sure they knew where the Negroes lived. Because we were a family of mostly light-skinned people, he invited the biggest, blackest friend he had to stand with him on the balcony. Albert Lee Kelley's size had proved useful in his work for my father as a bail bondsman. As cars slowly passed our driveway, Dad would look back at each voyeur through binoculars while Albert provided tangible proof that the neighborhood had changed.

Cowards called the house constantly with threats, although I was oblivious to these hostilities. Within ten days of moving in, someone shot a bullet through our front picture window while we were sleeping. In our somnolence, no one heard the shot. Dad surmised that the gunman had used a .25 pistol, a "woman's gun" in his estimation. It created a small, neat hole that I liked to place my finger on. We never replaced the pane. The hole was a reminder, something we would show visitors as a proud marker of our defiance. The specter of violence was never real for me because I was safe in the house of a father I thought was invincible.

Our neighbors contributed to my confidence about our new surroundings. Mrs. Parker, who lived across the street and two houses down, greeted us enthusiastically on the day we moved in. She stood in our kitchen smiling, the mother of four kids with whom we would bond. The family next door promptly sold their house rather than endure such close proximity to black people. The Goldens, a Jewish family, moved in, and we got along well with their four children, poodle, and cat. Other families on the block were equally welcoming. Practically every family, including ours, had a black housekeeper who came daily to clean, cook, and mind the kids. In this sense, our neighbors were quite familiar with black people. Allowing a black child to come over to play, or allowing their own child to spend time at the sole black household on the street, was no great leap.

In many ways it was an idyllic place to grow up. It was the last block on a street that stopped where a woods at the base of Monte Sano Mountain began, enabling a childhood lived out of doors. Summer days would stretch to dusk, when the "light'nin'" bugs would come out. We played kick ball and dodgeball in the street, collected frogs, turtles, and butterflies, picked blackberries from the wild bushes that grew thick in the woods. Every kid claimed his or her mother made the best blackberry pie. I forced Mama to make her first. Every family used a bell to call children in for dinner at the end of the day. Ours had a sonorous alto ring that could be heard no matter how deep into the woods or how many blocks we had strayed from home.

For the first five years, race never mattered, at least not to me. I was confident in my blackness and confident about my uniqueness, in large part because of Daddy. Over and over again he told me that I was special. I was his "Missy Poo," and there was nobody else like me. I could do anything I set my mind to. Even the year of my birth, 1961, was special, he told me. It was a palindrome-like year, in that it read the same when you turned it upside down. His words were backed up with copious daily affection and a near-daily affirmation, "Daddy loves you." Being his M. Poo enabled me to assert myself, especially in school. Mrs. Hovik did not seem surprised when the only black student in her second-grade class was also the one who read the most books that year, sixty-two. She extolled my achievement to the class and defended me when four-eyed Marty errantly claimed that most of the books I had read were "for babies." I didn't mind being teacher's pet that day or any day because I liked reading and learning, and Daddy had taught me that I was supposed to be first at everything.

The "race matters" started in the fifth grade. I found myself being frozen out of school social cliques that I had been at the center of previously. I became invisible or was reduced to a convenient note-deliverer in the inchoate game of romance that was emerging around me. There was also an occasional epithet, hurled by an older blond boy across the school playground. "Jungle bunny" was his preferred term for me. I had shed my pigtails and was proudly sporting an Afro. Sometimes I even came to school wearing a red and gold dashiki Mama bought me. The name hurt enough for me to complain to Mama about it.

"Just call him a blockhead," was her ineffectual reply. This was her way of making it clear to me that I was not to up the racial ante by calling him, say, "peckerwood," or worse. I decided that a dignified silence would be my best comeback, although the tomboy in me wanted to slap him.

Once we were old enough for sleepovers, I was no longer invited to birthday parties. A classmate with whom I was tight began to retreat when she received taunts from others about her acceptance of a sleepover invitation from me. Her father called for her, delicately explaining his daughter's distress. True to her peacemaking ways, Mama was empathetic. It wasn't fair to expect a young girl to have the courage to stand up to peers who were propagating an age-old racial order, even as that order was crumbling. Daddy was indignant. "Forget about her," he said angrily. "She's not worth it." "This girl is," Mama protested. Ultimately, I adopted his worldview. The people who were beginning to take exception to my color weren't worth any loss of self-esteem. Among the families we knew from Fellowship Presbyterian and Unitarian Universalist, I had friends, black and white, who valued me. Most of all, Daddy valued me and, in my girlhood years, his love was more than enough.

Being ambidextrous in our race relations, the Cashins negotiated the color line better than most people in Alabama, or so it seemed. Excepting my parents and a few of their friends, everyone seemed to stay on their side of the line when it came to socializing. As integration pioneers, our family often moved between all-black environments and ones that were completely white, until we arrived.

On forays to Atlanta, we always stayed at Paschal's—a black-owned hotel that seemed to be at the center of black life in that town. Usually we were there to see Daddy's good friends Cannonball and Nat Adderly play at a nightclub in the Atlanta Underground. Or on a weekend night in Huntsville, we might spend time with a black family with whom we had a history, typically the Gardners. Their daughter Vanessa and niece Felicia were my buddies from Fellowship Presbyterian, home to the children of so many up-and-coming black Huntsvillians. Deborah Gardner, Van's mother, had been our kindergarten teacher. Her husband, Stokely, would cook us "scrapple"—a delicious, thick white gravy with chunks of ambiguous red meat served on toast. We would wolf it down on Sunday mornings after a sleepover, and then hurry to church at Fellowship, where Stokely sang in the choir. The night before, the adults would have been hanging out in the Gardners' family room. Their music was the Stylistics, Les McCann, Quincy Jones. Sometimes they would play a Red Foxx album with blue references that I would overhear from upstairs but fail to comprehend.

Another night we would hang out with the "Drek Set"—Mama and Daddy's white hippie Unitarian friends. "Drek"—"a Yiddish word for shit," they told us—was an appropriate self-selected name for a group of intellectuals who were irreverent *and* committed. Most of them were scientists and engineers who had descended on Huntsville to aid in America's race to put man on the moon. Mama and Daddy, Harold Drake, and an anti-poverty worker named Spruce who would soon marry a Finnish scientist were the Negroes in this biracial crowd. All of the members of the Drek Set found trust and camaraderie in their deep-seated fervor to bring about radical change, and they embraced the Aquarian Age with a vengeance. Civil rights and the NDPA would be their vehicle for making America live up to her professed ideals, but there was also fun to be had.

The Drek Set was responsible for desegregating the Grand Ole Opry. It was another oft-told tale in our house, and it all began with a car. When Papa decided to replace his 1952 Rolls Royce with a new one in 1962, he sold the older model to his son-in-law for $4,000, then a princely sum and a bargain for a Silver Dawn. The car's elegant silver and black lines evoked ostentatious old money. It was also a source of amusement because an onlooker's stare would transform to a gape when he noticed its Negro occupants. Among the schemes the Drek Set would hatch in late night circles of alcohol- or marijuana-enhanced deliberation was how to make clever use of the Rolls.

The Nashville annex to the Drek Set included a well-placed city government operative who suggested the Opry as a target. He procured four front-row center seats for a Saturday night radio show that had been running since 1925, with few if any Negro attendees. Mama and Daddy would fill those seats along with Myrna and Don Copeland, should their plan work. Myrna was a New Yorker, the daughter of a Teamster organizer who began her activism by mounting a successful integrated ticket to the student government of her high school. She interrupted college to follow Don, an engineer, to Huntsville with the understanding that she wanted to be an activist in the movement. She had bonded with my parents during the sit-in campaign. Like the Rissés, the Copelands became a constant presence in our lives. Our families—the five Cashins, the five Rissés, and the four Copelands—marched, organized, and played together.

When the Rolls sauntered up to the old Ryman Auditorium, where every country music star began his or her career, all eyes followed the car with eager anticipation. Don jumped out of the driver's seat, dressed in an impressive chauffeur's uniform. Myrna emerged from the front passenger seat dressed as a maid. Don hustled to open the rear door with a flourish, and out stepped my parents, a stunning black couple dressed in evening finery, John in white tie and tails.

It was 1963. A black harmonica player named DeFord Bailey had been a star at the Opry in the 1920s, but he was long forgotten and Charlie Pride had not yet permeated country music. Generally, either as performers or attendees, black people were not expected or allowed. Don threw a $100 bill at an attendant, pressing him into service as their valet. "Just park that," he said, pointing to the Rolls. If the gatekeepers had any thought of objecting to Negroes entering, they were not prepared for this scene. My father moved swiftly, presenting his tickets and stating his case, "This is my trusted chauffeur and butler." "Oh, and I have to have my maid," Mama added.

They had reframed the issue. Would their white servants be excluded? Of course not. An usher respectfully escorted the foursome to their seats. A country hoedown was in full swing, a warm-up before the official program. As Mama and Daddy strode down the center aisle, followed by their servants, a hush fell over the audience. Another lily-white realm had been conquered through bloodless audacity.

When we moved to our house on Owens Drive in 1966, it became a frequent locale for the Drek Set's parties. Mama would serve her favorite hors d'oeuvres and, like other women of the era, she actually used her fondue set. I enjoyed submerging bread in the pungent concoction of wine-laced melted cheese. And I would help her carve melon balls that she would serve in a hollowed-out watermelon, which she would spike with vodka and Drambuie. It was the hit of their parties. The Drek Set would lie on their stomachs in a circle and drink from the watermelon with straws.

Music was part of their zeitgeist of freedom, love, and change. It filled our spacious living room. Crosby, Stills, and Nash. Miles Davis's *Bitches Brew*. The Woodstock album. Marvin Gaye. Bob Dylan. Iron Butterfly. They were ecumenical and open-minded in their tastes. I was never privy to it, but years later I would hear the legend of "Huntsville Green," a strain of marijuana one of the Drek Set's scientists cultivated in his own home. It had a "one-toke" potency that far exceeded "Acapulco Gold," contributing mightily to the Drek Set's liberalism and the expansiveness of their parties. Sometimes they were still there, strewn about the living room floor, when I woke up the next day.

The Rissés, the Copelands, and the Cashins were at the center of this milieu. Their kids were dear friends. My first crush was Greg Rissé, a beautiful, long-haired white boy, although I didn't see him as such. I would learn to see color soon enough. Until then, the baby Drekkers had their own set. While the adults played, danced, and imbibed in the living room, the kids were usually making trouble downstairs in our family room or sometimes sleeping outside in our camper van. We put on plays for the adults in the Copeland's living room, the same room where Mama and Daddy renewed their wedding vows on their tenth anniversary in 1967. Mama wore a green minidress with a print that was an ode to both Africa and Pucci and a garter belt on her exposed thigh. Jim Anthony, our Unitarian minister, conducted the ceremony, celebrating the children and change that their ten years together had brought forth. They reaffirmed their marriage with a kiss and a sip from a shared glass of wine as the baby Drekkers hurled flowers at them, and then they delighted us by throwing the glass into the fireplace. The authorized breakage made us cheer.

They left us behind a lot. Three sets of children preyed upon one babysitter for a week when our parents went to the Bahamas without us. The Drek Set was among the thousands at the second march for voting rights that succeeded over the Edmund Pettus Bridge in 1965, after the first one did not. They were there again to march in solidarity with Dr. King and sanitation workers who were striking in Memphis, the day before King's assassination. They drove back to Memphis after they heard the shocking news, evading a curfew to get into the city with the help of Ezekiel Bell, who had become a minister in the city of blues.

It was Myrna who told me this story, because by the time I began collecting the Drek Set's memories, Mama was no longer here to answer my questions. Dad and Don slept on Reverend Bell's living room floor, while Mama, Myrna, and Sas shared a foldout couch in the attic that must have been three decades old, Myrna thought. They could feel every loose spring in their backs and did not sleep much that night, the mattress sinking in the middle to fold them in like sardines. As they each jockeyed for space, they talked and giggled about stupid things to keep from crying.

That night, rioting broke out in the nation's capital, a wave of violence that would quickly engulf over 100 cities. At Fourteenth and U streets, the center of the black world in Washington, D.C., shouts of anger had turned into looting on the evening of King's death, and within four days, twelve people lay dead and 1,200 buildings had burned. A nonviolent movement threatened to disintegrate in the flames.

Memphis was different. James Earl Ray had lodged his bullet just after 6:00 PM, and the city had imposed an official curfew in an attempt to prevent violence. Crowds did not appear on the street until the next morning, when they gathered to mount a memorial march that the Southern Christian Leadership Conference had hastily scheduled.

Dad, Don, Reverend Bell, Mama, Myrna, and Sas agreed that they should stick together during the memorial. They approached the front of the assembling march, found Reverend Hosea Williams, an SCLC veteran, and asked him what they could do to help. The crowd was agitated. Williams asked them to talk to people to help soothe them. If the SCLC could not put on a calm, nonviolent memorial for its fallen leader, they would suspend the march.

The Drek Set walked through a throng of thousands who were snaking through downtown streets that had been blocked off for the march. At the front, things had been relatively calm and organized. But as they moved backward through the crowd, nerves seemed ever more frayed. They had participated in many marches, ones that had always been propelled by a hopeful feeling of Christian love. This gathering was suffused with menace. The people were on the verge of losing control. At the back of the crowd, they encountered a group of young black men who were yelling, "We should be out here with guns and baseball bats!" "This should be a war, not another march!" Their anger was intense, their disgust with an America that had killed a prophet of nonviolence deep-seated. Reverend Bell approached them and asked if he could pray with them. He began his prayer before they answered, reaching out to touch them. As the Drek Set joined hands with them, the angry youths parked their feelings of outrage, responding to cadences of the black church that must have been familiar. Bell asked God to put peace in their hearts and all of the people within earshot seemed to relax.

As Bell completed his prayer, Myrna instinctually began to sing, "Woke up this morning with my mind stayed on freedom," from a civil rights folk standard made famous by Odetta. Daddy added his silky operatic tenor, and the song began to echo from the back of the crowd toward its center. Mama was not much of a singer. Neither was Sas. But they had organized many poster walks during the sit-ins, and they began to herd people into lines of twelve to fourteen across, readying them to march. As with the movement, the NDPA, and later, her own family, Mama always tried to bring a sense of order to chaos. Many in the crowd had been marching for the garbage strike and they responded to her gesture. Everyone there found a reason not to indulge his or her anger. The march was peaceful. The Drek Set left the memorial with renewed dedication to make King's dream come true. They grieved together for several days, returning to Huntsville to change clothes and then driving to King's funeral in Atlanta.

The fallen King's Poor People's Campaign became their vehicle for honoring his memory. Dr. King and his compatriots at the SCLC had hatched the idea of a mule train in Marks, Mississippi—the poorest hamlet of the poorest county in the nation. Reportedly, King was moved to tears when he observed a day care worker divide one apple to provide lunch to four hungry children. Then and there, he determined that his anti-poverty campaign should begin in Marks, with a caravan of covered wagons headed to Washington. The mule and the covered wagon would be the most potent symbol of dirt-poor black farmers of the South who had yet to receive the forty acres that General William Tecumseh Sherman had ordered as reparations for their formerly enslaved forebearers.

After his assassination, Reverend Ralph Abernathy and King's other loyal lieutenants were determined to realize his vision of bringing caravans of poor blacks, whites, Native Americans, and Mexican Americans from their isolated corners to the public spotlight of the national mall to demand that Congress redress their mutual hunger and deprivation. The Mule Train was a noble idea and one of Dr. King's last wishes. Scores played a role, but my father found the mules. And pressed the Drek Set into action.

A week before the announced date of the Mule Train's departure, Reverend Hosea Williams was testifying before the U.S. Commission on Civil Rights at a field hearing in Montgomery. Dad was there as a member of the Alabama Advisory Committee to the Commission. At the end of his testimony, Williams asked if anyone could help the SCLC. They were having great difficulty locating mules. Dad called Reverend Randolph Blackwell, his fellow conspirator in the Huntsville sit-in movement who had become a full-time organizer for the SCLC. Blackwell confirmed their predicament. He was family, and my father did not want Blackwell or the SCLC to be embarrassed. He told Blackwell that if they would postpone their departure date for two weeks, he would get the job done.

The SCLC had been looking in the Black Belt of Alabama and Mississippi for mules, but that had been the wrong place. Mules were more readily available in middle Tennessee and north Alabama, where, in hilly terrain, a mule could plow as well or better than a tractor. Once again, Dad's activism cut into his dental practice. He spent a week working the phones from his office. As he began to call around, the word got out and the price for a mule rose from $75 to $125; the price of wagons also skyrocketed.

Then the story becomes comical. Someone called the FBI, accusing John Cashin of attempting to corner the market on mules. When the local FBI began to investigate, an agent concluded that it might be easier to call Dr. Cashin directly and ask him what was going on. Dad asked what crime he had committed in buying mules for a campaign against poverty. The FBI relented. In a week he had located and paid for sixty mules and fifteen wagons, most of which were bare frames that had to be outfitted with baseboards, seats, and hoops for the covers. Some of the mules had to be transported from as far away as Kentucky and Arkansas. He paid for all required hardware, the animals, and their transport to Marks in cattle cars and flatbed trucks. And he leased a truck with a hydraulic lift that would carry supplies for the Mule Train in its trek to Washington.

He put Myrna in charge of assembling and making wagon covers. For two days she oversaw a team of ten Drek Set volunteers, including Mama, who worked on four sewing machines at Myrna's house. When they went to Marks, they encountered people with heart and much disorganization. By default, Dad became the chief carpenter and quartermaster. The honors graduate from Meharry did not mind working in the Mississippi mud to assemble wagons and install hoops. "I decided that this thing had to be done," he told me, and after two weeks, as promised, the Mule Train was ready to leave its station.

Unwittingly, he had also become chief financier for this spiritual mission. After paying all of the SCLC's major creditors, he had spent $27,000, which in 1968 was more than half the cost of the house we lived in. At the time he was rather flush with cash. A few years earlier, friends in New York had let him in on a sweetheart stock deal that had multiplied his investment almost thirty times. In 1996, he explained his unreimbursed altruism to Roland L. Freeman, a cultural documentarian and freelance photographer who had covered the Mule Train. My father had had conversations with King and Blackwell about the concept of the Mule Train before King's death, he said: "I had promised Martin that I would do it if anything happened to him. Keeping your word to a dead compatriot is an extremely important duty in my culture."

It took the Mule Train almost a month to travel from Marks to Atlanta. A willing band of about 100 men, women, and children left behind their hardscrabble lives for a tough journey through Dixie. They were an open, easy target, moving at a pace of about twenty-five miles a day. Their painted wagon covers sported urgent messages that were easily read when viewed on network television. "Stop the War, Feed the Poor" and "Jesus Was a Marcher Too" were Dad's favorites. Lest they miss the main event in the nation's capital, in Atlanta the riders, wagons, and mules boarded a train to Alexandria, Virginia, for the final trek into Washington. The trip inspired a people who had been demoralized by King's murder. Through their own acts, they would diminish any doubts that the movement would continue.

Mama and Myrna rode the Mule Train only on its first day. Mama fell off a lead wagon when the mules broke away, exhibiting their distinct displeasure with walking on asphalt. It was a minor mishap compared to what happened to her in Resurrection City, the makeshift tent camp that was home to 7,000 on the Washington Mall as part of the campaign. She narrowly escaped being raped one evening at the camp. My parents and Myrna had gone there for June 19—Juneteenth—Solidarity Day for the campaign, deliberately scheduled on the day slaves in Texas learned of their emancipation and their descendants commemorate freedom. At dark, after the culminating rally of the campaign, two men grabbed her and they struggled in the mud. She broke loose, screaming. This was a part of the family lore that she chose not to talk about.

Decades later, when I discovered a fresh, unused mule bit and harness in my parents' attic, I would dust off the memory of my family's involvement with the Mule Train and of one particular day in Mississippi when I was allowed to tag along. My parents and Myrna had driven to the town of Grenada to help weatherize the covered wagons, which at that point had stopped in a muddy field. Constant rain had soaked the wagons and made the riders miserable. Dad came up with the idea of outfitting each wagon with a layer of plastic to make the long trip bearable. I sat on a wagon and played with a stray puppy, trying to ignore a pervasive odor of mule dung while the adults reworked the wagons and tended to rather unhappy looking mules. I was proud to be included. For once I got to go on one of my parents' trips while my brothers were left behind with Grandma. When they couldn't take all of us, sometimes they took only one child, and unlike my brief encounter as a four-month-old jailbird, this time I was six years old and could appreciate some of what was going on. Mama had tied my hair with a red bandana that matched the ones she and Myrna wore as insignias of their solidarity with the sharecroppers; our emancipation would not be complete until they, too, were free.

When I brought the unused mule bit and harness down from the attic, Dad let me have the contraption. For ten years, I hung it on a wall in my foyer in Washington, D.C., and enjoyed explaining it to any visitor, until my husband prevailed upon me to replace it with more attractive artwork and draw inspiration from it in the home office where I write. Virtually none of our guests had ever heard of the Mule Train, and only a few knew something about the Poor People's Campaign. Without a King to offer a rousing speech on the Mall, that campaign, with its message of economic justice, was largely erased from our nation's collective memory. Our guests' ignorance about it contrasted sharply with the urgent passion my parents and the Drek Set had brought to this cause and reminded me that in an activist's life, the victory, if there is one, is often in the mere act of trying.

Dad occasionally expressed bitterness about not being repaid. Such ruefulness was borne of his extended history of emptying his pockets for a passionately felt cause. His ethos, and the Drek Set's, was to live their ideals intensely, to give rather than to acquire. It was one of many times that he responded to the urgency of a need placed before him with no thought of the consequences. Moral imperatives had to be answered with action. To sit in comfort on the sidelines would have been inexcusable. He was of a breed of altruists who would give past the point of hurting. The Copelands were the same way. They spent the last of their savings for the Mule Train, despite their obligations as parents to two children. In an interview with Roland Freeman in 1968, Mama talked about their commitment. She said, "If you once make the decision that you are going to be in it up to your neck, you can't worry about what's going to happen, because if you do, then you are totally useless in any strategy you plan. So we just decided to move out . . . and we don't look back."

They took my brothers and me to another march in Montgomery the following year. On the one-year anniversary of King's assassination, his followers needed something to do with their pain. It was raining. Daddy, Johnny, and I were at the very front of the march. Mama and Carroll straggled a few yards back in the crowd. We walked with Heywood Henry, another black Unitarian. I held Daddy's hand and was excited to be at the center of things, even as my feet were soaked.

We sang "We Shall Overcome." The song and its sorrowful cadences were quite familiar to me. The adults sang it at the conclusion of all their important meetings. It was supposed to be a hopeful song, but I always thought it was tinged with self-doubt. Maybe they sang "We Shall Overcome" to exorcize the pain of current injustices, or maybe to convince themselves that even if their "some day" dreams of overcoming did not come to pass, they could handle it. We must have attained some victories that mattered because, within a few years, we stopped singing "We Shall Overcome" and defiantly declared our Somebody-ness.

My parents were unrepentant in the face of our whining when they could not take us along. When I would complain bitterly about Dad's frequent absences, Mama would say in exasperation: "We are not like other families where the father works 9 to 5." This explanation never satisfied a young girl who was desperately missing her daddy. I was not yet old enough to appreciate that activism required sacrifice and that they clearly believed the sacrifices were worth it. If they had tried to explain it to me that way, I doubt I would have been convinced. I had not yet had my own epiphany about their activism, or mine. In my tender years, when they left home to make life better for other people's children, I saw it as action taken at my expense and I did not like it. It would take a while for me to develop the empathy that my parents wanted me to feel for others.

The ways in which we were not like other families were often evident to me, though. If the grocery store sold only non-union grapes, that meant we would not buy grapes. Mama would explain our solidarity with César Chávez and the migrant workers in California and I understood. When I came home from school asking for $2.50 to order a POW/MIA bracelet,

Daddy answered me with a pointed lecture. By then I was ten years old. The bracelets were becoming ubiquitous on the wrists of school classmates and I wanted one. He used allegory to make his point: "How would you like it if a foreign government dropped bombs on our neighborhood when we had done nothing to deserve the attack?" Again, I understood. The war was wrong, and immoral. I would not be allowed to dissemble by supporting a POW with his name on my wrist when the United States was killing innocent civilians in Vietnam. It was hard to accept that a POW or MIA might be a war criminal, but that was Daddy's position. His stance contradicted what we were told at school by the nice lady whose nephew was being held and "roughed up" by the North Vietnamese. Daddy's moral clarity on the question brought me up short. I was still in the throes of hero worship, and not yet ready to debate the complexities of any question with him, fierce and outsized as he was in his opinions. I bore my confusion in silence, accepting that I would not be following the crowd at school, and probably not in life.

~: ⚬⚬ :~

On Owens Drive we also stood out, and not just because we were the only black family within any distance an adventurous child could walk or ride on a bike. The kids in the neighborhood thought we were the richest. That was Daddy's doing. He did everything to excess. At the kite store, he would buy two dozen and spend the afternoon assembling them. As he completed a kite, he would lower it from the balcony, until every child below had one and the sky was dotted with primary colors. He would buy hundreds of dollars' worth of (illegal) fireworks for the Fourth of July. Again, the children of the neighborhood would congregate at our house. In the backyard, he gave each of us a mega-sized roman candle and we screamed excitedly as each ball of fire rocketed into the night. For hours, he kept the neighborhood lit and loud. M–80s exploded to covered ears and laughs at the police-be-damned boldness of Dr. Cashin.

Our image as "wealthy" was burnished with the Rolls. We were already the first black children to attend Blossomwood. Emerging from that car each morning at the school's curb added to our mystique. Jonathan Parker, our neighbor and the most irreverent one of his clan, was moved to ask me,

"Is your father a millionaire?" I did not know the meaning of the word. "I think he has a million dollars but I don't think he is a millionaire," I replied forthrightly. Jonathan explained my stupidity. *Well, he must be a millionaire,* I thought. There seemed to be no limits in any dimension of his life, such was his intellect, his ego, his largesse, and his bravado. I ran to Daddy with the question.

"Are you a millionaire?"

"Who asked you that?"

"Jonathan Parker."

He never answered my question. "Just tell him we are on welfare," he replied evenly. I knew this was my father's way of saying that our finances were our business and I dutifully delivered his response to Jonathan, who seemed to appreciate the dryness in Dad's humor.

The perception that my father was independently wealthy was probably cemented when he bought "85 Victor." It started with a speeding ticket. His race against Wallace for governor was literal because he tried to be everywhere in the state where there was a contingent of black voters. On an early morning drive through Birmingham, en route to an NDPA state convention, his Chrysler 300 was clocked at ninety-seven miles per hour. Reporters gleefully noted that he had been stopped at least four other times for speeding.

"Damn, John, if you are going to drive like a bat out of hell, why don't you get an airplane?" his lawyer-friend Chuck Morgan suggested after his driving landed him on the front page of the newspapers. *Why not?* Dad thought. He *was* a pilot. He was constantly in motion, pouring most of his resources into NDPA. His own plane made sense in terms of efficiency, and it would fulfill his dreams.

His buddy Harold Drake had bought a Cessna 172, a serviceable plane they took on leisure rides. These two grown men had always shared their toys, which had included elaborate model train sets, radio-controlled model planes, boats, and the Cessna. They had been flying together because, as a diabetic, Harold could not obtain his own license. I first learned that my father could fly on a trip to Atlanta with "Uncle Harold." From the back I observed that my father was seated in the driver's seat. "Is Daddy flying the plane?" I asked Mama. She answered me with a nod and an extended smile. I was awed but not surprised. In my girlish mind, there was nothing he couldn't do. He seemed to have mastered the whole of human knowledge. He prided himself on completing crossword puzzles with alacrity, in ink, with no errors or second-guesses. On any given subject, from bird species to English poetry to world history to the constellations, he seemed to know it all. Mastering the skies seemed a natural progression.

When buying his own plane he had to have the best. "If I was a little boy on my knees praying to Santa Claus on Christmas Eve, a Bellanca was what I would pray for," he told me. Charles Lindbergh had wanted to make his maiden voyage across the Atlantic in a Bellanca. Unfortunately, the manufacturer insisted on choosing Lindbergh's crew, and therefore Lindbergh chose another company's plane. The Bellanca model Dad savored was not rated for acrobatics, but a pilot who knew what he was doing could sustain certain acrobatic maneuvers in it. My father longed to do the slow rolls, loops, and circles he had seen his idol Chappie James complete. As a man who prided himself on being able to do most things he set his mind to, he had every intention of mastering these maneuvers once he had a plane that could sustain them. Flipping through the pages of *Trade-A-Plane,* he spied a Bellanca Super Viking at a fire-sale price. A doctor in Midland, Texas, was being forced by his irate wife to unload his second Bellanca. She had threatened to divorce him if he didn't spend more time with her.

The plane had only seventeen hours on it. Santa had answered his prayers. He bought his new bird sight unseen for $31,000—about half of what it was worth. She was turquoise blue and sleek. Dad always referred to his plane as "85 Victor," the last three digits in the plane's license call number.

Mama had grown used to her husband and Harold Drake doing whatever the devil told them to do, so she was not surprised when Dad informed her, after the fact, that he had purchased an airplane. He did not inform her how much he had paid for his indulgence, and in this instance she chose not to question him. She was not enthusiastic about flying in a small plane and her stomach never completely accommodated to it. She suppressed her nervousness in order to serve as his co-pilot, although she would scream at him if he ever tried any trick maneuvers while we were on board. Otherwise, I suppose she made her peace with the fact that flying in a small plane with John Cashin was about as dangerous as having married him in the first place. If she feared for her safety, or ours, she never showed it. And he wisely learned to reserve his daredevil stunts for well-planned trips with Uncle Harold, the most audacious of which was a 360-degree loop of the St. Louis Arch. I always thought this was a "big fish" story until I questioned him repeatedly about how he executed this maneuver. He and Harold planned and practiced for months until he was confident that he could fly under the arch, then rise, fast and furious, complete a circle, and fly back under the arch once again. In the annals of recorded Arch history a pilot was spotted flying beneath the arch on April 16, 1971, Dad's forty-third birthday. The account gives no further details. I was forty-four years old the first and only time I visited the Arch. I purposefully stood under it. Its vertigo-inducing lines rose up magnificently against a cerulean sky. Yes, I thought, the father I knew was crazy and skilled enough to thread this expansive opening; he had come through much tighter jams than this.

On rare occasions, I was his sole passenger. He would let me steer the plane, showing me how to keep us on course using panel instruments. Once we even landed on grass. In the summer of 1971, the Southwest Alabama Cooperative was holding its annual meeting in Livingston, the Sumter County seat, and my father was their keynote speaker. They carved a humble landing strip out of a cow pasture just for us. Dad suggested that they call it "Sheryll Drive." I don't remember his speech, but I do remember that he spent the next day giving airplane rides to anybody who could mark an X. Sumter County, like most places in the Black Belt, was dirt poor. Giving rides and buzzing the Black Belt to drop campaign literature became common in the NDPA years. As a septuagenarian, he would tell me that giving plane rides was his way of "showing affection" for the people of the Black Belt and "debunking stereotypes." He would encourage his passengers to take the controls and comprehend freedom. Reverend Thomas Gilmore, an NDPA stalwart in Greene County, said of Dad's flying: "I had never heard of black folks flying small planes. It hit me like the fire hydrant peeing on the dog. It was more to be admired than I can ever describe." Flying with Daddy was the best thing I ever did as a child. His flying would come crashing, literally, to a halt in a few years. Until then, when I got to soar with him I was ecstatic.

CHAPTER TWELVE

The National Democratic Party of Alabama

At some point the worries of adults began to weigh on me. I remember having a rather serious conversation with my father about death, the kind of conversation all children eventually have with a parent when they begin to perceive that life brings pain. I don't know what precipitated it. Grandma Grace had not yet left us. Mama and Daddy had not yet started their war. I was lying in the living room, in the corner of our superlong couch; its high arms and sunken cushions created a comfortable hollow into which every Drek Setter liked to curl. My father noticed his normally ebullient daughter sporting a furrowed brow.

"Missy Poo, what's the matter?"

"I'm afraid."

"Of what."

"Of people I love dying," my lip began to tremble. He inserted himself between me and the couch, encircling me with his brawn, and spoke with urgent concern.

"Pooskie, death is nothing to be afraid of. When you die, the people you love are waiting for you. When I die, my father will be there to greet me. And I promise you I will be there when it is your turn to die. We will all be together."

He didn't say anything about heaven or the afterlife. He was not religious, having inherited his father's cynicism about a certain breed of minister who used religion to accumulate wealth and anesthetize the radical impulses of the masses. He was enamored of the teachings of Jesus Christ, though, and always carefully distinguished "true Christianity" with its message of love for humanity from the business of organized religion.

It was clear to me that he meant it when he said he was not afraid of dying and that I would see him again if he did. I was comforted by the thought that I would never really lose the person I needed most in the world. As an adult, I still depend on this seminal conversation as I contemplate the abstract thing that I have most feared throughout life: the inevitable death of my father.

Dad once told me that he did come to Jesus in his own way, primarily because he wanted to learn to live without fear. He had been using techniques of hypnodontia on some of his dental patients. In lieu of anesthesia, a patient who was open to suggestion could be put into a trance. In researching the technique, he had come across references to early Christians who would enter into a trance in order to face slaughter by lions at the hands of the Romans without crying out in pain or exhibiting any fear. They would not flinch when confronted with violent death. This was just the measure of fearlessness he would need to take with him into battle in Alabama. Although he did not profess Christianity as such, he "made a pact with Jesus Christ," he said.

"Lord," he implored, "if you will just take away all fear I will do what has to be done." Of course he was thinking of completing the work of his grandfather. It must have worked. Daddy exhibited plenty of emotions, but fear was not one of them. He would say, with utter, guttural credibility, "I ain't afraid of nuthin'." He found an anchor in something that was larger than himself and seemed to believe he had a special dispensation from God. His unwavering commitment to the disenfranchised meant that he would give his all, and he seemed to believe that this would excuse any transgressions in his means.

He hadn't really been afraid during the sit-ins in Huntsville. The death threats he and Mama received on the phone had been mostly comical. The church bombing in Birmingham that killed four little girls was something entirely different, a watershed event for my parents and America. From that point on, my parents felt they needed to be prepared to face anything. That Sunday my father was the lead speaker at the Unitarian church in Huntsville. When he heard a report on the radio that the church had been bombed, he jumped into his Chrysler and sped to Birmingham to see the destruction for himself, greatly compressing what would normally have been a two-hour trip. Upon surveying a gaping hole in the back wall of the church, he thought about the manner of man who would do this. Direct hits on the homes of civil rights leaders in "Bombingham" were common, but an attack on a church during Sunday services suggested depravity. He bent down and picked up a hatful of broken stained glass that littered the ground. Mama would make a collage from his grave souvenirs, a memorial to the girls' involuntary sacrifice. She hung the collage on the wall in our study. I was a toddler when the bombing occurred. By the time I was old enough to pay attention to Mama's collage, the heavy bond paper she had used as her canvas had yellowed. "September 15, 1963, Sixteenth Street Baptist Church, Birmingham Alabama," Mama had typed below her hand-iwork. Jagged shards of beautiful disjointed color evoked the tragic violence of that day. The bombing had been an immoral, desperate protest against Negroes' insistence on full equality. It did not deter the children of Birmingham or the better angels of our nation. But it was a pointed reminder of the dangers of stepping on white folks' prerogatives. As my parents began to turn their activism toward politics, they knew they could face similar hostilities because obstructing blacks from gaining political power, by any means necessary, had been the signature imperative of segregationist Democrats in the state since Reconstruction. My father would need the anchor of his private agreement with God to steady him.

George Wallace made the National Democratic Party of Alabama—the NDPA—possible. His brand of "segregation today . . . tomorrow . . . and forever" politics meant that a black voter, or a liberal white voter, was relegated to discerning the least evil among candidates in the state Democratic primary—the definitive election in what was essentially a one-party system. By 1964, little had changed in Alabama politics since Grandpa Herschel had died. The Republican Party was a minor player, and most Democratic candidates ran as committed segregationists. Black voter registration had grown in small increments, largely because of the work of black voter leagues in urban areas. In rural hamlets, time seemed to have stood still. Sharecroppers in the Black Belt, who tilled the same "bell clay," the dark soil that had been worked by their slave ancestors, continued to toil under the weight of a rural feudalism that locked them out of politics or the means to get ahead. Those Negroes fortunate enough to enter a voting booth would find candidates for the Alabama Democratic Party listed under the party's emblem, a white rooster. The rooster crowed under a banner that read "White Supremacy," with "for the Right" ruffled below its feet—the party's slogan for nearly a century.

Even assuming a liberal Democrat could stomach this paean to the Southern Way, it was impossible to cast a vote supporting the incumbent president of the United States, Lyndon Baines Johnson. The Alabama Democratic Party offered a slate of uncommitted presidential electors who were all loyal to Wallace, who had mounted a vigorous run for president in the national Democratic primary.

Lyndon Johnson seemed to recognize the degree to which he was shut out in Alabama by "Dixiecrats" who disdained him. In planning his inauguration festivities, the only woman from Alabama who was invited to serve as a hostess was my mother. She and my father attended all three inauguration balls in January 1965 as a reward for their loyalty to the national Democratic ticket. Dad had paid his $1,000 to be a contributing member of the President's Club, and he and Mama had been working within the Alabama Democratic Conference (ADC), a caucus of black Democrats, to force liberalization of the state party. Mama enjoyed telling me the story behind the yellow silk beaded gown I would discover in her closet as a teenager, her favorite among the three gowns she wore because it evoked Jacqueline Kennedy's classic elegance. At the White House, Mama had been escorted down the stairs by a U.S. marine and formally introduced to the ball as an official hostess. "It was magical," she said of that night, her eyes lit with the memory. As she recalled the inauguration, two days filled with elegance and possibility, I saw a glimpse of the person she had been at the height of their activism. She was happy, vibrant, and excited by life, unlike darker times when getting through her day seemed an exhausting challenge.

After the inauguration, my parents returned to Alabama and continued to toil within the ADC. Everything changed in the spring of 1965 when 600 marchers had the temerity to attempt to cross the Edmund Pettus Bridge in Selma, their Via Dolorosa to voting rights. Bloody Sunday made the nation recoil, and thousands returned to Selma to complete the march, making political elites like LBJ take notice. The president took swift advantage of the new political context that the marchers created. Once the Voting Rights Act passed in August 1965, indigenous black leadership in the state sprang into action. All of the subterfuges of the past—including poll taxes and ridiculously difficult, unevenly applied literacy tests—were no longer a barrier to enfranchisement, so local civic organizations accelerated their voter registration activities. Helped by the Southern Regional Council, the Southern Christian Leadership Conference, the Student Non-violent Coordinating Committee, and a host of federal registrars, the ranks of black voters swelled to hundreds of thousands by 1966.

The impact was most dramatic in the Black Belt. My father first encountered Greene County, Alabama, by car in 1946, en route to Houston with Grandma Grace after his expulsion from Fisk. He drove, she relaxed. They played cow poker and enjoyed the sequential Burma-Shave signs, innocent poems for the road that made Grandma chuckle: "A peach / looks good / with lots of fuzz / but man's no peach / and never was / Burma-Shave." As they crossed the Black Warrior River, entering Greene County, headed toward Mississippi and seemingly backward in time, Dad thought of his cousin Juanita's joke, "Look at all those honest people." When playing the dozens, a common response to an epithet concerning the darkness of a man's skin was that he was "honest," meaning he was free of the dilutions of nighttime integration.

There were a lot of honest people in Greene County. There were also antebellum homes, monuments to the plantation economy that still reigned but was changing. Half of the people who were fortunate enough to have a job in the county worked on the land, and many of them earned less than $500 a year. As was the case in most of the counties of the Black Belt, in Greene County a few families dominated, their elite status maintained by timber and soybeans once cotton was no longer king. Before the Voting Rights Act was passed, it was not too difficult for these landed aristocrats, and the Democratic operatives who served them, to keep most Negroes out of politics. By 1965, the Reverend William McKinley Branch had founded the Greene County Civic Organization and a chapter of the NAACP, and was president of both. When not teaching history, math, and English to junior high students or preaching from a Baptist pulpit, Branch worked doggedly to register blacks to vote. But he and his organizations were having little success because a Negro had to be "a Philadelphia lawyer," Branch said, to manage the feat of completing the questionnaire the registrar would give any would-be voter. In a county where most blacks had much less than a high school education, intimidation or insistence on an impossible literacy had been rather effective.

With the new law, Branch invited the Southern Christian Leadership Conference to help his people mount a massive voter registration drive. He was a man prone to see democracy in biblical terms. They were coming out of Egypt as far as he was concerned, and the Lord blessed them. Like Jesus feeding the multitude, Branch and his disciples filled the people with the bread of a voter registration card.

In less than two years, the number of black voters in the county rose from a few hundred to over 4,000, nearly twice the number of registered whites, even accounting for the scores of dead white bodies that managed to stay on the rolls and vote. Similar miracles were being performed in Hale, Marengo, Lowndes, and most rural counties that boasted indigenous local organizations hungry for change. The second Reconstruction had come and, with Dr. King and the SCLC urging Negroes to participate, fifty-four black upstarts through-out the state decided that they should run for office as well as vote.

Thomas Gilmore, Rev. Branch's young cousin, was one of them. He ran for sheriff of Greene County in the Democratic primary in 1966. He was twenty-five and one proud black man who had studied theology and would eventually become a minister. For now, his religion was politics. Working for the Student Nonviolent Coordinating Committee in the civil rights movement had lit a fire in him. He knew about what Stokely Carmichael and the SNCC were doing with their "Black Panther Party" in Lowndes County, but he was determined to make the Rooster Party include him.[1] In Lowndes, none of the Black Panther candidates succeeded in the 1966 election. Some blacks were frightened by the all-black party and simply stayed away from the polls. Others thought the party suffered because Mr. Carmichael's attentions were diverted by the need to explain and reexplain the "black power" mantra he had coined a few months before and by his elevation to national chair of SNCC, which he would soon lead in a direction of militant black separatism.

Gilmore was also stymied in his bid to become sheriff of Greene County. He lost in the primary and tried again in the fall of 1966 as a candidate on the Greene County Freedom Party ticket, a local independent party Branch and others founded. But the probate judge left his name off the ballot. He was angrier than he had ever been. "They stole it as if they had a right to do it," he said. He was not alone. As white supremacy Democrats returned to tactics of voter intimidation and economic reprisal that had been honed for a century, including threatening to fire or evict black people who voted, only four of the fifty-four Negroes who ran for office throughout the state were victorious.

A disempowered people will always have disagreements about how to proceed against forces that dominate them. Whether to ask for *or extract* the change they desire becomes a point of debate. Whether to proceed incrementally or insist on radical change? In the same way that black Republicans in Grandpa Herschel's era fissured over strategy, black Democrats in the 1960s feuded over tactics. Like his grandfather, Dad allied with the impatient, even militant black leaders of the state who were ready to put direct pressure on the political system to let the black man in.

Orzell Billingsley was one of those agitators. He was an Omega brother who thought a lot like my father. I remember him for his hound-dog looks. His eyes were always bloodshot, his countenance saggy. He drank a lot. But he was a brilliant lawyer who could accomplish more while under the influence than most sober lawyers. He had provided counsel to Dr. King during the Montgomery Bus Boycott and successfully challenged all-white juries in the case of *Billingsley v. Clayton*. A Negro could call "Lawyer Orzell" when no one else would come, and he was as tough as iron. He took a lot of cases on principle, regardless of whether a client could pay, and kept at least one young black man out of the electric chair.

According to Dad, Billingsley was also a political genius. He had filed a case that forced blacks onto the Jefferson County Democratic Executive

Committee and he ascended to the chair of the Alabama Democratic Caucus, a black caucus to an Alabama Democratic Party that was also beginning to fracture on the question of how and whether to include the Negro. Dad was ADC's finance chairman, meaning he was opening his own wallet for yet another organization to which he was committed. Under Billingsley, the ADC began to press the Alabama Democratic Party for real change.

A committee of ADC standard bearers, including Billingsley and Dad, decided to invite themselves to a meeting of the Alabama Democratic Party's Executive Committee. They presented their unsolicited demands. They wanted blacks to serve on the state and local executive committees commensurate with their numbers in the population. They wanted that damned offensive white supremacy slogan off the ballot and recommended that the party replace the rooster with the national party's symbol, the donkey. Most of all, they wanted the party to support rather than obstruct blacks who wanted to run for office. They threatened to incite a boycott by black voters if their demands were not met.

Dad remembered the meeting as a vitriolic standoff, although he surely contributed to the tension. The party agreed to change its slogan to "Democrats for the Right." But that was reform enough. "This is as far as we can go. This is our party" was the message. My father took this as a challenge. He could be hotheaded, opinionated, and most unlikable when he wanted to be, and he knew it.

"I've got a lot of Jack Brandon in me," he once told me, referring to his mother's brother, who was famous in the family for standing his ground. In his choice vernacular, Dad also offered his analysis of the dynamics of progressive change: "Every successful movement has to have a son of a bitch. Without one there will be no progress. You need someone who is *your* son of a bitch to deal with the other SOBs."

My father proudly admits he played that role rather effectively for the NDPA. Ridding the Rooster Party of its white supremacy slogan was a potent symbolic victory, but it was not enough. He and Billingsley soon realized that they had the means to effect more dramatic change.

In the 1966 gubernatorial election, Richmond Flowers, then the attorney general, became the first statewide candidate in memory to openly court black voters. Not since Reconstruction had blacks had any meaningful impact in a statewide election. With a cast of characters running in the Democratic primary, including cancer-ridden Lurleen Wallace, who ran as her husband's surrogate, grassroots black folks, mostly working-class people from the Black Belt who had been foot soldiers in the civil rights movement, were inclined to support Flowers, while members of the black establishment rooted in urban areas mounted a backdoor campaign to support Carl Elliott, a labor-oriented congressman and ostensible liberal.

True to his boyhood empathies, my father sided with the grassroots and helped engineer the ADC's endorsement of Flowers. Even though Lurleen Wallace dominated with 54 percent of the vote, Flowers received 19 percent, an unprecedentedly large showing for a second-place candidate. It became clear that blacks wielded a potentially powerful block. Although they might not swing a statewide election in which white voters were still leaning heavily toward old-line segregationists, their numbers did underscore that rural black voters could dominate in their home counties.

Carl Elliott, who won the white liberal vote, had come in third with 8 percent of the vote. From Dad's perspective, it made no sense for blacks with their greater voting strength to take instructions from white liberal leaders about how they should proceed.

He had first heard of the idea of forming a statewide independent political party to tap new black voting strength in Suite 30 at the A.G. Gaston Motel in Birmingham, the place where Mama and Daddy honeymooned after they precipitously eloped. Like Paschal's in Atlanta, this establishment was a safe haven for civil rights leaders during the civil rights movement. It was owned by a legendary black business baron and located across the street from the eponymous A.G. Gaston Building, headquarters to an insurance company and bank that Gaston owned and half a block down from Gaston's radio station. Suite 30 was the only three-room suite at the hotel, and it soon became a favorite spot for an interracial group of change agents, including Dad, Orzell Billingsley, Chuck Morgan, Attorney General Richmond Flowers, and Jimmy Evans, Flowers's able assistant and a future Alabama attorney general. Whenever they were in town, they would call over to reserve the suite where they most liked to talk, think, and drink Old Forester bourbon, Billingsley's favorite poison. It was the only logical place in Birmingham for white and black progressives to commiserate, and party, without calling attention to themselves. Often they talked into the night and schemed about how they might drag the state of Alabama into the twentieth century. "We were all Alabamians who resented the rabid racist image that had been projected for our state," Dad told me. In their mutual agitation, they had bonded, and saw themselves as being in the vanguard for what Alabama could be.

Unlike the Drek Set, Suite 30 was an all-male club. As men who attacked life and injustice with a riotous sense of humor, they became good friends and allies. When Chuck Morgan was litigating *Reynolds v. Sims*—the case in which the Supreme Court rendered "one-man, one vote" the rule for legislative apportionment in Alabama and the nation—they had acted in concert. Dad and Billingsley were informal consultants. As attorney general, Richmond Flowers had supported the outcome of the case by not fighting it. When it was decided in 1964, the case struck the first blow against the Black Belt's landed aristocracy. After Morgan's coup, the planter class no longer wielded grossly disproportionate influence in the state legislature.

In assessing Flowers's strong second showing in the 1966 gubernatorial race, they ruminated on an idea that Morgan and others had been thinking about for several years. Why not end-run the Wallacites by skipping the Democratic primary and running black and progressive white candidates on a third-party ticket in the general election? Flowers's county-level results showed what such a party could do, especially in the Black Belt. The beauty of the idea was that an independent party could avoid the costs of the primary and protect its candidates and supporters from reprisals by delaying announcement of its slate until late fall. An independent party would also solve the perennial problem that liberal Democrats faced every presidential election—the unwillingness of the Rooster Party to field presidential electors who formally committed to the national Democratic ticket. A liberal in Alabama would thus be able to guarantee that his or her vote supported the national ticket; in addition, a new party would offer liberals state and local candidates who were truly responsive to their concerns. Most of all, an independent party could empower rural blacks, the majority of whom were functionally illiterate and easily intimidated or confused at the polls on Election Day. A separate party with its own recognizable symbol would enable semi-literate people to cast a straight ticket by simply marking an X under the party symbol. They would not need to ask for assistance from poll workers intent on leading them astray.

Chuck Morgan and Richmond Flowers talked incessantly about these strategic advantages. My father was the urgent idealist who kept saying, "Let's do it, let's do it!" "Y'all are talking. I'm serious. Why not?" He felt the ADC had had to do too much begging within the Rooster Party and had too little to show for its efforts. Like H. V. Cashin in 1901, he was not inclined to implore Democrats to treat black voters fairly. He had learned the efficacy of psychological warfare and self-empowerment in the sit-in movement in Huntsville and was ready to take matters into his own hands. Jimmy Evans researched Alabama election law for him, and they soon learned that it was rather easy to create a new party. Evans drafted the charter for the National Democratic Party of Alabama (NDPA).

Perhaps the political novice in my father propelled him. He didn't really know what he was doing, but he was done talking and determined to try. He and Billingsley made the mistake of publicizing that they were going to file the NDPA charter on December 15, 1967, my sixth birthday. They would actually file a few weeks later, although in Dad's lore, they filed on this date and that also became his oft-repeated truth. The NDPA was my "birthday gift," he always said. Just as he had planned meticulously for my birth on December 15, he hoped that the date that had brought him so much joy would also prove momentous for his newest creation. As an adolescent and young adult, I always felt ambivalent about this "gift" that I never asked for. Of course I was proud of what he had done. I simply felt that the price had been awfully dear. From my perspective, as I scrambled to find money for college because he was broke, I resented the suggestion that he had spent his fortune for me. I wrestled in silence with the fact that people other than his family seemed to have been his primary beneficiaries. I did not yet understand that the NDPA was, indeed, a family legacy—that in creating it, Dad was completing the work of radical Republicans like his grandfather and, he hoped, enabling his children, and generations to come, to live in complete freedom.

A charitable interpretation of what happened next would be to say that reformers in the Rooster Party sincerely wanted to give liberal voters and blacks more options, so they formed the Alabama Independent Democratic

Party (AIDP), solely for the purpose of offering a slate of presidential electors who would be formally pledged to the national Democratic ticket in the 1968 election.

Dad cast this move in more sinister terms; it was an effort by so-called good liberals to stop the Negro from freeing himself. He would follow the philosophy of his hero, Frederick Douglass: "Slave bondsmen, don't you know? If you will be free you must strike the blow." And, being flush with more than half a million in assets garnered from his sweetheart stock deal and desiring nothing from the white establishment, he was in a position to proceed. This party was going to create real black power without any nationalist trappings.

They filed the party charter in early January 1968, ultimately choosing an American bald eagle as their symbol because the AIDP preempted their choice of the national Democrats' donkey. The eagle was the next-best emblem to signal their national loyalties. The bird flew with wings arched high and wide, talons and head down as if ready to land on its prey, most probably a white rooster. "To end racism and poverty and bring democracy to Alabama," was their carefully crafted party slogan. The mission statement Dad filed with the charter had declared that "the hostile racial atmosphere" in Alabama was an "artificial situation . . . deliberately cultivated by our traditional political leaders [who set] the races against each other" in order to exploit and deprive the majority of Alabamians, both black and white. The Drek Set came up with the idea of issuing a party platform, a move then unheard of in Alabama politics. In a late-night session at our home on Owens Drive, hard-core Drekkers fleshed out a draft that stated an ideal of the perfect society they hoped to create.

In some ways they emulated radical nineteenth-century populists: To abolish tax advantages for industry, to impose a progressive structure on the tax system, to guarantee collective bargaining for the farmworker. In other planks, they sought guarantees of racial equality that eluded their Reconstruction forebearers: racially balanced juries and equal educational opportunities in completely integrated public school systems. Mainly, they were futurists, weighing in on issues of environmental protection, abolishing the draft and capital punishment, encouraging UN-led efforts to stop nuclear and weapons proliferation, and halting the Vietnam War. To ensure that this transparent statement of purpose was widely disseminated, they conceived a monthly newspaper, the *Eagle Eye*—a free rag that became "our paper" in the Black Belt. The platform was reprinted on the back page of every issue, along with instructions about how to join the party. Inside were Dad's tough, insistent editorials along with news of NDPA candidates throughout the state and general stories of interest to black readers. Dad financed the paper while a predominately white and very young contingent of loyal volunteers produced and edited it.

With the exception of my father, the NDPA's state executive officers were also white. Dad was the chairman. Mary Pandow, a world-renowned physicist whom I knew solely as the smart lady with three poodles, was the secretary. Joe Gannon, a Tennessee Valley Authority executive from Florence, became the treasurer, and F. Jackson "Jack" Zylman, a Unitarian minister in Huntsville, became the party's first executive director. Later, Thomas Gilmore and Myrna Copeland would become vice chairs. If it mattered to the grassroots in the Black Belt that whites were engaged in the party, they did not make much of it. The NDPA was 90 percent black, and it grew by tapping movement people in the counties who were empowered to lead their local chapters. Giving black people the means of democratic self-determination was seen as a godsend. And inclusion seemed the right thing if they were going to be credible opponents to a party that had been created by and for white people.

After his defeat by fraud in 1966, Thomas Gilmore doubted he could prevail within the established political system. He had learned from the civil rights movement that you had to be a little radical to accomplish any victory worth having. The NDPA was radical enough. It would tap a breed of revolutionary that descended from the disagreeable slaves who were sent to the Deep South, far away from their more compliant upper southern cousins. At least that is the colorful theory Gilmore learned from Doc Cashin. My father had reasoned that the Deep South slaves were cheaper because they were warriors and much more difficult to discipline. Those in this rowdy gene pool, Dad's *Homo sapiens Africanus Alabamus*, were capable of leading themselves to victory at the ballot box and deserved a party that would place them in control of their own destiny. Gilmore liked Doc's theory and felt that he personally must have inherited some of that radical impulse in the bloodlines of the Black Belt.

Gilmore liked the idea of the NDPA even better. To have a vehicle that enabled him and others to run as part of a statewide slate of candidates raised the aspirations of the people. He thought it was a little crazy, but he knew it would work for him. And he knew it could work for others. A lot of foot soldiers were tested in the civil rights movement and were ready for the next battle. They could use a technocrat who could relate and help them defeat a political system that had been set against them since time out of mind.

The idea became real on May 7, 1968, primary-election day. Lawyer Orzell had determined that under Alabama election law, NDPA chapters could hold nominating caucuses instead of using the ballot to select their candidates for the general election. In the seventeen rural counties of the Black Belt and in urban areas, including Huntsville, Birmingham, and Mobile, local NDPA chapters sprang to life. The caucuses were reminiscent of mass meetings that propelled the civil rights movement. Movement people had found their way to the NDPA.

People like E. D. Nixon—the Pullman car porter with a sixth-grade education, who was head of the NAACP in Montgomery when Rosa Parks, his secretary, refused to relinquish her bus seat. Whatever reading he had learned in school, the process of comprehension became real to him in reading the works of A. Phillip Randolph. Mr. Nixon knew that Randolph had moved President Franklin D. Roosevelt to issue equal employment standards for the defense industry with just the threat of a mass march. Nixon had launched the Montgomery Bus Boycott but deferred to Dr. King as the better spokesperson to articulate the concerns of Negroes and inspire them. My father loved Mr. Nixon. In observing the respect Dad accorded him, it was clear that I was supposed to revere him as well. At a Sunday afternoon dinner in a church basement, we sat on metal folding chairs and blessed the food laid out on a spare Formica-top table—white cottony Wonder Bread, chicken fried to a taut crisp, and green beans soaked with salt and butter. Mr. Nixon didn't talk much, but when he spoke his voice was deeply resonant. His words came out slowly, exuding the wisdom and scars of age. Dad sat at his side, earnestly absorbing his advice, leaning in to hear him, asking him if he'd gotten enough to eat.

He earned the old man's trust the same way he earned that of other grassroots people: He acknowledged and respected their innate abilities.

Each county NDPA chapter was an autonomous organization. The members led themselves, learning the difference between the art of civil rights protest and the block-by-block mechanics of corralling votes as they went. Dad advised and gave them money when he could.

On primary day, in more than twenty counties dozens of blacks and a few liberal whites met at courthouses and churches throughout the state to choose their candidates for local office and delegates to the first state NDPA convention. In July 1968, 200 delegates met in Birmingham to nominate a slate of presidential electors and delegates to the Democratic National Convention in Chicago. They also debated and approved the party platform and a biracial slate of candidates for state and local races. Among them was Reverend Branch, who was nominated to run for Congress.

When Daddy and Mama left for Chicago, I was aware of the tragedies convulsing the country, although I never internalized the pain that the adults around me were feeling. Dr. King had been assassinated in April, Robert Kennedy in June. The Vietnam War continued, seared in my memory by war correspondents who offered matter-of-fact reports for television viewers as tanks and echoes of gunfire rolled in the background. Even at six years old, I knew that "Burn, baby, burn" had something to do with riots going on in black urban neighborhoods across the country. Like most Americans, I experienced these scenes through television. Watching from my safe, pastoral universe on Owens Drive, the violence was no more real to me than that of the cartoons I absorbed on Saturday mornings. As I watched the violent upheavals in the streets outside the Chicago convention, I now worried about whether my parents would choke on tear gas. Grandma Grace assured me that my parents were safe inside the Chicago Hilton, with their windows tightly sealed. I was oblivious to what was going on before the Credentials Committee at the convention. Alabama had been allotted fifty delegates and three contingents—the Rooster Democrats, the AIDP, and the NDPA—were vying for official recognition.

The NDPA's delegation looked like America before America had even begun to contemplate serious inclusion. The Drek Set had come up with the utopian idea of creating a delegation that was equal parts black and white as well as female and male. The party faithful had endorsed the concept at the state NDPA meeting as a means of providing a pointed contrast to the tokenism of AIDP and lingering segregation of the White Rooster Democrats. Like the Mississippi Freedom Democrats in 1964, in 1968 the NDPA would not be recognized as the authentic arm of the national party. The AIDP's lawyers went head to head with Chuck Morgan and Orzell Billingsley and won with the argument that the NDPA was too liberal to represent the interests of Alabama and an erroneous claim that the NDPA delegates had not held their nominating conventions on Election Day, as required under state law.

The Credentials Committee tried to placate the NDPA by offering to seat four of its delegates. My father thought the offer was contemptible, but he presented it to the NDPA delegation, which voted unanimously to reject the offer. "No compromise with evil!" E. D. Nixon had shouted, and other delegates joined him in chorus. They wanted full recognition or nothing at all. "I was so damn proud of them," Dad told me. His eyes welled with hot tears as he looked out at this loyal band of true believers, many of whom had been heroes and heroines of the movement. They authorized him to take their fight to the floor of the convention and he was heartened by their vote of confidence in him.

The NDPA delegates broke into teams and canvassed other state delegations to explain why Alabama's Wallacite delegates were traitors to the national party and why the AIDP was not a real party. Mama and Myrna organized pickets in front of the convention hotels, reprising their work for the Huntsville sit-ins. The NDPA delegates carried handmade posters calling on other delegations to reject George Wallace and his racist followers and did their best to distinguish themselves from the anti-war protesters vying with Mayor Daley's Chicago militia. Dad pressed Willie Brown, who would later become the venerable Speaker of the California legislature, and Fannie Lou Hamer, the seasoned Mississippi Freedom veteran, into service. They roused the convention hall with passionate eloquence, speaking on national television about how and whether the Democratic Party was going to deal fairly with the children of Hagar.

FDR had wooed most Negroes away from the party of Lincoln. He had succeeded where the Populists failed in creating a winning, stable political coalition of white and black workers. Now the national Democrats were in a quandary about how to hold onto Southern white workers after supporting the civil rights of Southern black ones. With George Wallace running for president as an independent nationwide and a Democrat in Alabama, and Nixon poised to begin his "Southern strategy," a party led by Hubert Humphrey was fearful of being associated with grassroots people and anything that smacked of black power.

On the proposition of whether to replace the Alabama delegation with NDPA delegates, the NDPA lost the roll call vote: 1,605 against, 833 for. The AIDP delegates were seated as representatives of Alabama when the Wallacites of the Rooster Party refused to sign a loyalty oath. The long-haired members of the NDPA delegation decided to join anti-war protesters in the streets of Chicago and take their chances against the city's police force. Mama and Daddy joined them briefly, but their hearts were not with that fight. They were exhausted and dispirited after three grueling days of battling for NDPA recognition. In Grant Park, as the protests raged, Dad spied an equestrian statue of General John Logan, his father's namesake. The statue reminded him of the lengthiness of America's race struggles and their need to get on with whatever role they were destined to play in them. He and Mama decided to leave the craziness swirling around them and retreat to the balm of the black world. They ate dinner at a pleasantly turned out black-owned restaurant on the South Side before returning to the battle in Alabama.

The NDPA was mounting its first election campaign in the fall, and most of its candidates had never run for office. Mabel Amos, Alabama's secretary of state, made their first efforts even more difficult. She announced that the NDPA candidates would not appear on any November ballot because they had not complied with the Garrett Act, a law enacted in 1967 requiring that any potential candidate for office file a declaration of intent to run by March 1—eight months before Election Day. She also followed the lead of AIDP's lawyers, claiming that the NDPA had not held required mass meetings and caucuses on primary-election day. As usual Dad turned to his most trusted lawyers, Chuck Morgan and Orzell Billingsley. The purveyors of the status quo in Alabama had not anticipated an opponent who dreamed quixotic dreams and sometimes made them real, or that the judicial system would stand with him.

Morgan was ensconced as head of the American Civil Liberties Union's legal offices in Atlanta, which is where he landed after he had been forced to leave Birmingham following the church bombing. He and Billingsley filed suit against Mabel Amos in federal court in Montgomery on September 13, 1968. True to the irreverent conceits of Suite 30, they chose a sweet soul, Mrs. Sally Mae Hadnott, as their lead plaintiff. She was Alabama's answer to Fannie Lou Hamer, although perhaps more fragile. But she did not mind putting the truth out to her people. She lived, literally, on Easy Street in Prattville, Alabama, but the only thing easy about her activism was her tendency to advocate with a smile. A candidate for Autauga County commissioner on the NDPA ticket, she was an ample, brown-skinned mother of eight who covered her thickness with sensible shift dresses and spoke just as plainly. She had founded the Autauga chapter of the NAACP and added a room to her home so that there would be a place for blacks to meet and organize. Legend had it that she was personally responsible for registering hundreds of blacks to vote. Morgan and Billingsley thought her deserving of top billing in the case, but they also thought her surname, "Hadnott," appropriately resonated the "have not" condition of the NDPA's constituents.

After the suit was filed against her, Secretary Amos added the charge that the NDPA had not complied with Alabama's Corrupt Practices Act. Her claim that the NDPA candidates had failed to provide her with the names of persons designated to manage their campaign finances was laughable to Dad, because most of his candidates had no such finances. The district court ruled against the NDPA in a decision issued on Friday, October 11. With the general election looming, Morgan and Billingsley worked heroically through the weekend and managed to deliver an emergency appeal to Supreme Court Justice Hugo Black by the following Monday morning. Justice Black, a former U.S. senator from Alabama as well as an active Democrat (and briefly a Klansman), would have been familiar with the ways of Alabama politics. He recused himself from the case because his sister-in-law, Virginia Durr, was one of the NDPA nominees for presidential elector. She and her husband, Clifford, had posted bail for Rosa Parks. They had supported the sit-in movement and opened their home to Freedom Riders in need of a haven. In a 1972 interview with Hardy Frye, Durr explained that the NDPA appealed to her because she was tired of Alabama's "race politics." She had gone to the 1968 convention in Chicago as a member of the NDPA delegation and had done her best to advocate for the party. It had not been easy to explain the Byzantine nature of Alabama politics to her national contacts. For her, the idea that George Wallace could run for president in Alabama as a Democrat when he was really running against the national Democratic ticket "was just as crazy as plowing up the cotton and the corn and killing the pigs when people were starving."

The Supreme Court heard Chuck Morgan's oral argument on the following Friday, October 18. Billingsley sat by as co-counsel. Morgan emphasized the complicated nature of Alabama ballots. Even exceptionally literate justices had difficulty understanding the eight columns of candidates and parties that comprised Alabama's proposed general election ballot. Without the straight NDPA ticket, less literate souls who were inclined to support the national Democratic presidential ticket would have to first choose the slate of presidential electors offered by the AIDP, then go in search of state and local candidates offered by other political parties, few of whom were likely to be responsive to the concerns of black folks. Six justices were sufficiently persuaded of the efficacy of the NDPA's claims to issue an order the very next day requiring all of the NDPA's candidates to appear on the November ballot. A slate of presidential electors pledged to the Humphrey-Muskie presidential ticket and eighty-nine candidates for state and local offices now had sixteen days to campaign.

The NDPA launched into action. With its shoestring budget, the party relied heavily on the altruism of well-known civil rights figures and indigenous leaders in the counties. Sample ballots with the slogan "Mark your X under the Eagle" were passed out at mass meetings in black churches throughout the Black Belt. On the airways of black radio stations, Julian Bond, Coretta Scott King, and Ralph Abernathy offered urgent appeals to "Vote the Eagle Party."

On Election Day, Richard Nixon won the presidency with a "law and order" message that must have provided a salve to those Americans who didn't like what the 1960s had wrought. In Alabama, George Wallace swept Nixon at the polls, which meant he had continued to attract most white voters to the Rooster Party. In the face of this dominance, seventeen local NDPA candidates won, and all of those victories were in the Black Belt. The Marengo County NDPA chapter led the field with five justices of the peace, three constables, and the chairman of the board of education. Overnight, whether ready for it or not, Alabama boasted the most black elected officials of any Southern state. And, because NDPA candidates came in second in most of the other races, the party was entitled to appoint its own poll workers to participate during the next election. A funny thing happened in Greene County, however.

At 8:15 AM on Election Day, November 5, Dad's phone rang. It was Thomas Gilmore, then the Greene County NDPA chairman. "Doc, our candidates are not on the ballot!" Gilmore said. At Dad's direction, Gilmore and his precinct captains checked the ballots at every polling place and the NDPA candidates for local office were not on any of them. In each county, the probate judge was charged with certifying local candidates. The NDPA candidates for state and national office did appear. The four NDPA candidates for the all-powerful, five-member County Commission were left off, as were the two NDPA candidates for the five-member school board, on which one black incumbent already served. If the NDPA candidates had been listed on the ballot, and won, black officials would have gained control of county government. Incensed, my father placed a person-to-person call to Greene County Probate Judge Dennis Herndon:

"This is the NDPA state chairman and my Greene County chairman tells me that our candidates are not on the ballot," Dad said.

"That's right, they sure aren't," Herndon responded.

"But the U.S. Supreme Court ordered them on the ballot," Dad exclaimed.

"Well, I've got a copy of that court order, too, and in my opinion they are not legally qualified," Herndon replied.

"Man, what did you say your name was?" Dad challenged.

"My name is Judge James Dennis Herndon, that's who, the probate judge of Greene County, Alabama, and you can do any damn thing you think you are big enough to do!" the judge shouted in outrage.

And with an assurance he had inherited and carried all of his life, my father replied firmly, "My name is Dr. John Cashin Jr., chairman of the National Democratic Party of Alabama, and I intend to do exactly that." He hung up, and after a few moments of shocked disbelief, called his lawyers. The NDPA was headed back to the Supreme Court.

On November 15, ten days after the general election, NDPA's lawyers filed a motion to hold Herndon in contempt, to declare elected the seventeen NDPA candidates who won in other counties, and to order an unprecedented special election in Greene County. The second oral argument before the nation's highest court for an upstart party devoted to the least enfranchised occurred on an icy winter morning, the day after President Nixon's inauguration. As they waited for the Court's opinion, which would take a few months, the denizens of Suite 30 felt confident. They had not expected to end up before the Supreme Court of the United States, much less twice, but now that they had, they knew they were going to win. The architects of change had been on a roll in Alabama. Montgomery in 1955. Birmingham in 1964. Selma in 1965. And soon, Greene County in 1969.

Because NDPA candidates for statewide office and presidential electors did appear on the ballot, and votes cast for the "straight" NDPA ticket in Greene County outnumbered those cast for the Rooster Party, it was clear to the Court that the local NDPA candidates would have won had they appeared on the ballot. Justice William O. Douglas, the Court's most colorful white liberal, writing for a majority of six, found that the disparate application of Alabama's corrupt practices laws to impecunious black candidates ran afoul of the U.S. Constitution. Under the Fifteenth Amendment, the "right of people regardless of their race, color, or previous condition of servitude to cast their votes effectively," and the First Amendment right "to band together for the advancement of political beliefs," the people of Greene County were entitled to a new election and the NDPA candidates who prevailed in other counties were now "duly elected."

As for Herndon, the Court ordered the district court to initiate contempt proceedings against him. Throughout the civil rights movement, no public official, much less a judge, had been held in contempt of a federal court's desegregation order. By early 1971, Herndon's brand of Southern defiance of the imperatives of civil rights would be met with a conviction for civil and criminal contempt.

With the Greene County special election scheduled for Tuesday, July 29, 1969, the six NDPA candidates returned to campaigning and Dad called in as many favors as he could. As usual, he dug deep into his own pockets to help finance the campaign and called on others for donations.

In his telling and retelling of the most important fight of his life, the amounts always varied. In a 1972 interview with Hardy Frye, he put it this way: "I have spent, hell, $150,000 keeping [the NDPA] going. That's the reason NDPA is alive; because an honest son of a bitch like John Cashin said, 'People are more important than money; let's keep the damn thing alive.'" Before my digital recorder, as a fuzzy-brained septuagenarian, he remembered his contribution to NDPA as "a half million."

Whatever the actual amount, grassroots people marveled at how Doc spread his treasure across the Black Belt to help secure their political independence. "Don't take any money from anybody else," he would tell them, often retrieving a bankroll from his kneesock and peeling off a couple of $100 bills to solve a problem or help get more folks to the polls. The landed aristocracy had begun buying people off, recruiting a few "acceptable" Negroes to serve as tokens in newly created positions like deputy sheriff and co-director of the food stamp program, for a county government that otherwise employed very few blacks. He was determined not to let the Rooster Democrats stop a political revolution with a few modest gestures to select individuals.

With a special election occurring in a solitary county, the NDPA and civil rights veterans had the luxury of focusing their energies. Any personality differences were set aside as the specter of a historic victory unified leaders and followers. Once again, veterans like Ralph Abernathy and Hosea Williams of the Southern Christian Leadership Conference descended on Greene County. In mass meetings at black churches, oratory and song were brought to bear to urge ordinary folk to get to the polls on Election Day and take up their place in history. On the eve of the election, the First Baptist Church was filled to overflowing. The faithful and curious endured 100° heat for over four hours as speaker after speaker sought to inspire the masses. "We can change the course of history!" shouted Hosea Williams. Referring to the rough percentages of the black and white populations of the county, he continued, "It is not God's will that eighty-five black people be dominated by fifteen white people. The Eagle Party will prove that Martin Luther King's dream can come true!"

The day of the election, whites in the county seemed either apprehensive or resigned. Some fought the inevitable, bringing their maids and cooks to the polls early in the morning and telling them how to vote. Most blacks donned their Sunday best as a mantle of independence. They flocked to the polls, many giddy with the freedom of voting for the first time. "There was nothing that could turn them around. The people had an absolute fever for change," Reverend Gilmore told me as he reflected on that day. "Yet there was some fear. Younger people had shed all trepidation in the movement. But there were elders who had lived long enough to know how mean-spirited some whites could be." The people of Greene County had heard about the machinations in other counties the previous fall. In Lowndes County, black sharecroppers who had worked for generations on large plantations lost their jobs and homes if they attempted to register to vote or participate in politics. A local NDPA leader in Sumter County was beaten when he attempted to observe ballot counting. In Greene County, NDPA candidates were told they would never live to take office if they won the election.

For his efforts, Reverend Branch was fired from his job as a schoolteacher and his life was threatened. When he and Gilmore called Doc about the threats, my father summoned them to Huntsville, a three-hour drive. He had learned a few things about self-protection during the sit-in movement. He turned to Harold Drake to help him accumulate a cache of weaponry that would bolster the Greene County NDPA chapter's confidence. Gilmore and Branch's eyes popped when Dad opened his trunk to reveal a load of shotguns, pistols, and even one crossbow. Dad and Harold had borrowed every twelve-gauge shotgun they could find, including two from Glenn Hearn, who had become a special agent with the FBI after stepping down as Huntsville's mayor. Both Gilmore and Branch were men of the cloth committed in theory to nonviolence. Still, they distributed the weapons judiciously. The effect was psychological. Being prepared to act in self-defense gave them and their compatriots more backbone.

Most of the black citizens of Greene County moved past their fears on Election Day. But some people did need to be dragged to the polls. NDPA volunteers and SCLC workers from across the state cajoled whomever they could find in their quest to turn out every registered black voter.

Dad had a favorite story that became a fixture in his lore about the special election. About 3:00 PM he received a call from a block captain, "Doc, this lady probably has about eight or ten votes and you told us, for the tough ones, send for you." She was a community leader in Boligee, a hamlet in the county one might miss but for the railroad line that ran through it, and she could influence the registered but hesitant or fearful voters in her small domain. She lived in the first of a row of five shacks at the edge of a cotton field. As my father approached her shack, he cautiously observed a white man mounted on a tractor, plowing in the distance. His target voter lay limp on a swing on her front porch. She was thin and in her sixties, he estimated. She wore a gray plaid housedress that matched the dappled gray pattern of her hair, which was plaited into knotty braids that circled her head. She gave him every excuse in the world about why she couldn't go to the polls. She had had her wisdom teeth extracted the day before and her mouth was hurting. She was feeling all kinds of bad.

"I'm a dentist, I can do something for you on that," Dad told her. He made her sit up and inspected her mouth as he massaged her cheek. She needed a lot of dental work on the teeth she retained, and he instinctually assessed what he would have to do to overcome the years of neglect in her mouth, were she his patient. Then he reminded himself of his purpose and continued to make his pitch.

"Look, all you got to do is mark an X under the eagle," he said, showing her NDPA's sample ballot, which included pictures of Mrs. Coretta Scott King, Ralph Abernathy, King's successor at SCLC, and Julian Bond. He took her hand and moved her finger across the ballot, showing her precisely where to mark her X.

She looked at my father dubiously. "Are they colored?" she said, pointing to the pictures of civil rights heroes she did not recognize.

"They are colored," he said assuredly.

"Are you white or colored?"

"I'm colored," he laughed. She began to relax, the furrow evaporating from her brow.

"Well, they say you have to pay five dollars to vote. I ain't got no five dollars."

"They lied to you. You don't have to pay a damn thing."

"Well, how am I gonna git there?"

"I'll take you." The engine of his air-conditioned Chrysler was still running.

"Let's go, I'll try it." Dad lifted her into his arms, laid her down in the back seat of his Chrysler, and drove her to the polls. She was weak or putting on a good act, enjoying the attentions of the doctor. He carried her to the door of the polling station and placed her down onto her feet. He did not want to be accused of manipulating her, so he encouraged her to walk, unassisted, into the polling place while he remained outside. She teetered through the door, her legs threatening to collapse. As my father waited anxiously for her, thinking that he should have accompanied her, she reappeared in the door, beaming. Before she entered, she had been a cripple. Now that she had voted, she was rejuvenated—the kind of transformation he had seen faith healers bring about, or fake, for television.

She walked unassisted to Dad's car and let herself into his passenger seat.

"Okay, let's take you home," he said.

"I don't need to go home. Let me show you where to go." She directed him back to the row of shacks. Walking purposefully down the path, she entered each home, my father following along, trying to keep pace with her newfound urgency.

"They lied to you. You don't have to pay nothing at all! You need to go on and do it," she cajoled. She corralled about ten votes. The lady from Boligee was my father's hardest case that day but ultimately his most productive.

At sundown, Dad, Gilmore, and Branch huddled on the courthouse square. A white water tower announcing the name of the county seat, "City of Eutaw," in faded green letters, looked down on them. They were nervous, as were their White Rooster opponents. As the vote tally arrived from each polling place, a clerk posted it on a wall outside probate judge Herndon's office in the courthouse. "We were pretty sure we had won the election, but we figured we needed at least a 410-vote margin to prevent the absentee ballots from affecting the outcome," my father told me. There were 206 absentee ballots that had not yet been counted and Dad, Branch, and Gilmore greatly feared the chicanery the Rooster Democrats might resort to with those ballots. Dad assigned himself to watch the absentee box. Branch and Gilmore agreed to signal to him as each new vote tally was posted outside the probate judge's office, and he promised to do everything in his power to hold up the counting of the absentee ballots until all regular ballots were counted.

He entered a small room in an office on the courthouse square where a five-member committee was supposed to count the absentee votes. A few poll watchers were already there. As the committee prepared to open the box, Dad launched into his act. "I went crazy, I picked up a chair and shook it and told them they would be violating a federal law if they counted those votes before the regular ballots were tallied." Nobody wanted to test what the fanatical Negro might do with that chair, so Dad managed with thinly veiled threats to delay the counting of absentee votes for twenty minutes. He watched for Branch and Gilmore through a window; they were giving him hand signals every two minutes. Once they signaled that they had a spread of 410 votes, he sat down in the chair he had been wielding like a sword.

"Gentlemen, you can count those ballots now," he said.

"What do you mean?"

"It's over, we have won. You can count them and do anything you want." The stresses of the previous year began to drain from his body. Shouts erupted in the square as the final tallies were announced. With a clean sweep in the election and blacks gaining a controlling majority, it was the only unequivocal victory that most movement people had ever experienced.

The vote had been close. Despite a two-to-one registration advantage and a heavy turnout, the NDPA won the special election by a surprisingly narrow margin of only about 200. With federal observers and national news reporters swarming the county and the black electorate energized and organized, honest voters prevailed over all efforts to suppress or steal votes.

For black political aspirants throughout the South, Greene County was like the first domino falling. They were electrified by the possibilities. At the inauguration celebration, Ralph Abernathy declared his aspirations for this new political direction of the movement: "This is the first time since Reconstruction that blacks have taken over a county in the Deep South or in America. We are going to replicate this throughout the Black Belt!" Dennis Herndon saw things differently. "It was a black day for Eutaw," he told a *New York Times* reporter, apparently without intending any pun.

For my father, the Greene County special election would always be his most treasured victory. Mama did not reminisce much, and she didn't talk about herself without prompting. My father was more sentimental. He would return to the special election again and again, always seeming to feel that no one really appreciated the significance of the victory. By the time I was old enough to fully comprehend his tutorials about the Alabama Constitution of 1901 that had destroyed Grandpa Herschel's work, and what the NDPA had done to recapture it, I had stopped listening, consumed as I was with my own survival.

The Greene County special election, coupled with the NDPA victories from the November 1968 elections, had brought twenty-three blacks into public office, a quantum leap then without parallel in the twentieth century. When Dad called his brother Herschel the day after the election to share the good news, it quickly became clear that Herschel had his own preoccupations. He had been having problems with his eyes and had checked into a hospital at the University of Texas in Galveston for tests. They had not been able to diagnose his condition, he said. If my uncle ever knew he was dying, he didn't tell my father. Dad had stoically accepted that his brother's life path had taken him away from Alabama. Accepting Herschel's death five months later had been much more difficult. He was angry, convinced that if the doctors had been more aggressive, his brother might have lived longer. He would not have much time to grieve.

The seventeen counties of the Black Belt became a fresh battleground in 1970. The NDPA again ran a statewide slate of candidates and Dad ran for governor against George Wallace, not with any illusion of winning but as the spokesperson for voting the "straight NDPA ticket." For some, he was like an evangelical figure. He spoke fast and dressed sharply in white suits with white patent-leather shoes. He would fly in, literally. The people liked his flamboyance and they related to him, even though he was from a different socioeconomic class. They knew he had tied his fate to theirs, and they appreciated the hell he was giving the white establishment.

The black bourgeoisie hated him. He came on too strong. He was very self-righteous, they thought—talking fast and loud, telling people how it would be. His insistence on being respected by the white power structure and going head to head with them grated because, like the disciples of Booker T. Washington a generation before, they focused on advancing the race through economic uplift, especially their own, instead of political agitation. Old-line political elites in the black world had also grown used to being power brokers who would deal directly with the white establishment and instruct the masses through their constituent organizations on whom to support. The NDPA represented an end-run of both the white and black political establishment.

If my father was an irritant, my mother was a quiet, methodical, soothing presence and the backbone of the state headquarters in Huntsville, which at the time was in our dining room. The core of the Drek Set would work into the night. They were aided greatly when Bill Edwards, a white, twenty-three-year-old Vista worker, became NDPA's executive director in 1970. He lived with us for more than a year, occupying our guest room on those rare occasions when he slept. He worked for nothing, although Dad would give him cash when he needed it. We called him "Uncle Bill," and like the Drek Set, he became family.

By 1970, the NDPA had become a magnet for a congeries of Alabama liberals who had been in the wilderness: activist hippies intent on the legalization of marijuana, although Dad managed to convince them that for strategic reasons that goal needed to stay out of the platform; Vietnam Veterans Against the War; women's libbers; and even a few gay libbers out of Birmingham, joined with black voters to form a new "soul-type movement," as my father called it on the campaign stump. They were merging black power with coalition politics. He saw no irony in being a black supremacist who led a rather integrationist life and was inclusive in his politics. His inclusiveness upset some of the young black college students who came to Alabama to work for the NDPA the summer of 1970. They had come south thinking radical thoughts and anticipating an all-black party. Encountering more than a few earnest white volunteers conflicted with their notions of self-empowerment.

I remember the day their bus arrived in front of Grandma's house. Forty sleep-deprived, blue-jeaned and Afroed students spilled out onto the sidewalk clutching their belongings. They looked around expectantly, probably disappointed at the tameness of their first encounter with Alabama. A tall guy named Bruce carried a shotgun in a shoulder harness, just in case. The bus left, and after some generalized confusion, it was decided that they would spend the night at our house on Owens before being dispatched in the morning to all parts of the Black Belt. Bill Edwards pressed me into service, saying, "Sheryll, your country needs you." My brothers and I each directed a carload to our house. Mama and Daddy must have been away on a campaign trip because we had been staying with Grandma. It was fun to leave her watchful eye and hang with the big kids for several hours. They parked their belongings and their behinds in every nook and cranny of our home. At the time, I was a precocious eight-year-old and relished talking to them about their dreams and mine. They came from Harvard, New York University, Columbia, and any number of other elite institutions that had decided in the wake of the movement to widen their entryways. In them, I saw my future. I was going to be like them, to go off to some far-flung exciting place to gain an education, to see and do whatever I wanted, and then bring my energies back to Alabama. It made me giddy to think about it. Grandma stopped my reveries with a phone call. "Yeah," I said to her when someone handed me the phone, instead of the "Yes, ma'am" she had taught me. "You don't talk to me like that, young lady. You get someone to bring you back here right now!" My glimpse at independence was over, and I grudgingly complied.

∾ ⚶ ∾

Reverend Gilmore was one of many NDPA candidates in the 1970 election. When I interviewed him about it, he was a reluctant senior citizen. He said of his candidacy, "I knew in my heart after the Greene County special election that all I had to do was just live, just be alive and I could win in 1970, because of NDPA." He was right. Despite death threats, at age twenty-nine, Thomas Gilmore became the sheriff of Greene County, defeating "Big Bill" Lee. It was a tectonic shift. Lee or someone in his family had had a dynastic hold on the sheriff's office for fifty-four years. And he had ruled with a plantation mentality, having once literally whipped Gilmore for demanding the arrest of a deputy who had struck a black schoolgirl.

Gilmore became known as a "movement sheriff" who never carried a gun. His legend grew when he relied only on his persuasive powers to overcome a drunk, agitated husband wielding a loaded sawed-off, double-barreled shotgun. The crazed man's wife was attending a mass meeting at the county courthouse. Dad interrupted his speech to watch the scene from a balcony off the second floor. Inside the second-floor courtroom, most of his audience ran to the windows, clambering to see. Gilmore walked easily across the courthouse yard, approached the man, and said, "Why don't you get out the car and hand me the gun. You could be in prison for at least ten or fifteen years, you need to give that thing to me right now." His easy manner soothed the man and he complied. They walked together to the jail. Movement people put him in office, and movement people kept him in that office for three terms.

Reverend Branch became the probate judge, replacing Dennis Herndon in the most powerful office in the county. A black man was now chair of the County Commission. Among other indications of his power, *he* would oversee the preparation of ballots for elections. Decades later, for his long and faithful public service, Judge Branch was honored with the naming of the new William McKinley Branch Courthouse in Eutaw.

If the NDPA hoped to replicate the Greene County example elsewhere, many whites were determined to preserve the status quo. On Election Day 1970, college students who had been recruited by the NDPA to serve as poll watchers observed repeated acts of voter intimidation and fraud. A black Harvard student complained that in Hale County, "black people were constantly insulted and made to feel stupid [while] white people who made mistakes were informed of the correct way to vote." A student assigned to Wilcox County reported that the probate judge "required anyone who needed assistance in voting to vote orally, only after hearing all 135 names read off" and forbade poll workers from indicating which names were on the NDPA ticket. The U.S. Commission on Civil Rights found that white voter registration in many rural counties far exceeded 100 percent of the eligible white voting population. Against these kinds of odds, the NDPA outpolled the Rooster Party in four counties in the 1970 election: Bullock, Greene, Lowndes, and Macon. In Sumter, Perry, and Hale counties, NDPA local leaders were moved to file suit in federal court, alleging vote fraud and challenging the results. They were unsuccessful.

Although Wallace won by an overwhelming majority and the NDPA did not fare well outside the Black Belt, from the perspective of movement people, the impact was unbelievable. Suddenly one could drive across the state from Columbus, Georgia, to the Mississippi border and enter mostly counties in which the chief law enforcement officer was black. In Lowndes County, John Hulett, the former chairman of the Lowndes County Freedom Organization, was elected sheriff on the NDPA ticket. This was the same county where Mrs. Viola Liuzzo had been shot and killed by the Klan five years earlier for the effrontery of driving Negroes from the Selma-to-Montgomery voting rights march; Hulett exulted that Mrs. Liuzzo's death had not been in vain. A black sheriff meant that black boys were no longer beat up on Friday and Saturday nights on their way to a county jail on questionable charges.

People began to walk, talk, and act differently. "Everybody wanted to run for office," Gilmore said. Federal money for which the landed aristocracy had refused to apply began to flow. In Greene County, two Head Start early childhood education centers were opened. King Village, a fifty-unit public housing project, was built in 1971. The county broke ground on a multi-million-dollar 200-unit housing project that enabled residents to become owners through their own sweat equity. It began a youth job-training program with federal funds. The impoverished black electorate now had black representatives in official positions—probate judge, sheriff, school board, county commissioner, justice of the peace—that had a greater impact on their daily lives than the American presidency. And, for the first time since Reconstruction, two blacks returned to the Alabama legislature, one, Thomas Reed, elected on the NDPA ticket and the other, Fred Gray, elected under the Rooster Party. A feudalist miasma had been lifted.

"NDPA opened the door," Branch told me. "We realized that we had the voting power to win any election. With the door open, we walked in." Other Deep South states had had such black voting power, but not the apparatus to harness it that the NDPA afforded. Alabama is (in)famous for some things, but being among the states with the highest numbers of black elected officials is not one of them. By 1976, the number of blacks serving in the state legislature had risen to sixteen. Today, thirty-four African Americans serve in that body, eight in the Senate and twenty-six in the House, matching the numbers of their ancestors during Reconstruction.

The NDPA continued until Daddy's money ran out. After 1970, the Rooster Party became much more inclusive. In the Black Belt, poor whites were just as badly off as most black folks. As with populism a century before, the risk with the NDPA was that working people would get together and demand a whole pie. In some minds, such independence had to be squelched. In others, the power of the black vote was such that it simply made sense for the Rooster Party to reform in ways that included and attracted these voters. NDPA candidates won again in west Alabama strongholds in the 1972, 1974, and 1976 elections. The national Democrats turned the NDPA away again at the 1972 Democratic National Convention in Miami. Still, the fight was not in vain. Both the Rooster Party and the national Democrats ultimately adopted delegate selection rules designed to create precisely the kind of multi-hued and bi-gendered delegations that the NDPA had presented as the way things ought to be.

Yet it was inevitable that the NDPA would become obsolete. Once the Rooster Party and George Wallace were no longer committed to rigid exclusion, the NDPA began to lose its raison d'être. The party folded in 1976. As I was transitioning from child to preteen, Alabama was finally coming out of its racial infancy.

Ultimately, Reverend Gilmore taught me the true significance of my parents' lifework. Their idealism and that of many unsung heroes had been vindicated. They had led a life directed at something that mattered and brought about a radical transformation. "That's the most religion I ever had in my life, in the early days of NDPA," Gilmore told me. "I knew I could pick up the phone and call Doc when he was emptying somebody's mouth of their teeth and he would hand her off to someone else and come on down and see us and be available to me. After a while I could do that with Chuck Morgan. And Hosea Williams. And Ralph Abernathy. And Stokely Carmichael. With that kind of help I could get out and face the lions."

CHAPTER THIRTEEN

Altruism

My father's signature virtue was also his signature flaw. He was utterly selfless when his passions moved him, and that left all of us vulnerable. Another of his stories conveys his tendency to give without thought to his own interests.

It involves a diamond men's ring that John Logan Sr. won in a poker game—a reasonably impressive stone bracketed by four smaller ones, set in antique gold. But for its provenance, the ring conveyed a dignified gentility, the very quality Grandpa Herschel had sought to cultivate in his progeny. John Sr. wore it occasionally on his left pinkie and then gave it to my father when he was in college. He figured his second son would appreciate it more than his first because Dad had mastered poker and the cultural milieu in which his father played. Eventually, the old man brought home another ring with his poker winnings and gave it to Herschel.

My father loved his ring. Every young man in Nashville's "in crowd" had such a bauble, and if they didn't, they wanted one. He also wore it on his left pinkie because his hands equaled his father's in size and appearance. My brothers have the same hands—thick workmanlike palms and fingers marbled with large veins.

Dad was working for McKissack & McKissack, a black-owned construction company in Nashville that was building college apartments for Tennessee State. He and his friend "Dixie" operated the band saw, cutting pieces for the carpenters. They were paid $1.50 an hour, the best summer job a Negro collegiate could find in that era. Dixie had a propensity for getting into trouble. The cops were looking for him for stealing and selling fur coats. This time they were close on his heels. He needed to leave town immediately, and this being a Tuesday, he was broke until payday. He explained his situation to my father, whose pockets would also be empty until Friday. Sensing Dixie's desperation, Dad removed the ring he cherished and handed it to his friend. "Here, take this and pawn it and get it back to me when things settle down," he told him. Dixie bolted. This was my father, extending himself for a friend in need, regardless of the unsavory origins of his friend's problems. "Dixie was an honest thief," my father explained. "I knew he would get it back to me. I didn't know when and didn't care when. I trusted him."

"You see, your father is crazy! He will give the shirt off his back to anyone," Mama laughed, shaking her head with weary acceptance of her husband's idiosyncrasies as Dad told me the story. On this rare occasion, the beneficiary of my father's largesse actually repaid him. To his great credit, Dixie returned the ring fifteen years later, using his mother as an intermediary to deliver it.

My father continued to wear the ring for many years until he passed it on to my older brother. I remember it vividly. Dad always referred to it as "my father's ring." It elevated the appearance of his hands, which were always dry and slightly chapped, from years of using a gritty soap in his dental office that achieved excessive cleanliness.

Mama shared Dad's conviction about social contribution. By their actions, they both instilled in me that helping others, particularly the most deprived among us, is the rent you must pay for being on this earth. These were their family values. People who focused on contribution were worthy of our respect. People who focused on making money were not. We lived an upper-middle-class existence, but it seemed to matter to Mama and Daddy that their children should be able to relate to poor people.

Dad sponsored a softball team for girls who lived in one of the worst housing projects in Huntsville. People who lived elsewhere called those projects "Little 'Nam" (as in Vietnam). He paid for their uniforms and equipment and spent more time at their games than at mine. He even missed me play right field for the Blossomwood Eagles in our league playoffs in order to be in the dugout when his adopted girls played.

I was eleven then. My team was eliminated in the first round. Daddy jokingly derided our team as "sorry" in front of his girls, bolstering their confidence at my expense. Although I did not appreciate this put-down, I understood it because I understood him. His daughter had everything. They didn't. They deserved special treatment and he was going to give it to them. When we took his girls with us to Point Mallard—a water park with a wave pool—it was clear to me that most of them had never enjoyed such fun-soaked amusement. They stuck together, looking wary at first, as if they could not trust an adventure populated by so many white people.

"Would you rather be black or white?" one girl asked me, her tone connoting a test that I needed to pass, even if I was Doc Cashin's daughter.

"Black," I said without hesitation.

"Why?" she challenged.

"Because, black is better," I said simply. I knew she needed to hear this answer even though I didn't really harbor any racial superiority and had doubts about whether there was any empirical truth to what I was saying. I no longer inhabited that magical kingdom of childhood in which race doesn't matter, the one I began to exit not long after I stopped believing in Santa Claus. I knew that for the girls from "Little 'Nam," being white seemed to accord with getting to do and be more. So I contradicted their thoughts of inferiority with an unwavering racial boosterism I had learned from my father.

I also knew from hearing it so much that Dad did believe that black was better. He believed these girls were superior to their white peers, even if the world didn't. He was incensed when his own son had little to say to them and picked a fight with Mama about it. "He wouldn't speak to the girls!" he raged, as if Mama's own privileged upbringing somehow explained it. In truth, the privileged life we led placed all of the Cashin children at risk of elitism or, worse in the minds of our parents, a bourgeois mindset. My father was born into the upper echelon of the black world, but he had always empathized with the plight of his poorest brethren. Although he had been a partyer and a playboy, once he got serious about activism, he had little patience for people motivated by materialism, especially any Negroes of means who sat on the sidelines and did little to help their people.

I had my princess tendencies. On a ride in our camper van, returning from my brother's Cub Scout meeting, Mama looked at me with alarm and upbraided me when I volunteered that the scout leader's house was not as nice as ours. She began to "deprogram" me in subtle ways. In the appliance section of Montgomery Ward, I asked when we were going to buy a microwave oven, then a novelty that miraculously cooked hot dogs in one minute.

"When we can afford it," she said pointedly. The phrase shocked me. It had never occurred to me that there was anything we couldn't afford. "What do you mean?" I asked. I had watched her weekly exercise with Daddy. She would tell him about the clothes she needed to buy for her growing, chubby daughter, or sprouting sons, or the groceries, the art and ballet lessons, the boys' multiple sports uniforms. My father would take his bankroll out of his kneesock and peel off an appropriate number of bills. He always seemed to have plenty of cash. I had no conception of limits, economic or otherwise, when it came to Daddy. The microwave oven did appear in our kitchen, the first one on our block and a revelation to the other kids in the neighborhood. If we consciously sought not to be materialistic, we certainly enjoyed its trappings, as Mama would buy the latest innovation—a trash compactor, a waterbed—as soon as it became available.

As with Dixie, my father acted without hesitation once he decided he believed in something, or someone. Believing created its own imperative, justification enough for any action he might take. The money he spent on the mule train for Dr. King's Poor People's Campaign was minor compared to what he spent on behalf of Elijah Muhammad's Nation of Islam—the organization that cultivated Malcolm X until he turned to mainstream Islam.

Mr. Muhammad must have taken notice when blacks swept the special election in Greene County, even though his program was one of cooperative economics among black people and avowed separation from white society and politics. He wanted to buy farmland in his native South to begin a program of sustainable black agriculture and a county where blacks commanded government seemed a logical place to invest. He had been duped somehow into buying land in St. Clair County in north-central Alabama and realized that he had landed in unfriendly, Klan-infested territory when his water wells and cows were poisoned. He wrote this Dr. Cashin he had heard so much about, asking him to come to Chicago for a meeting to discuss better alternatives in the

Black Belt. Dad obliged, flying himself and Harold Drake to the Windy City in late December 1969.

They met at Mr. Muhammad's mansion on Greenwood Avenue, the same neighborhood Uncle Jimmy had infiltrated decades before. The house was grand, dark and imposing. I would sit for hours outside it at a subsequent meeting, banished to the car with my cousin Gwillin Grace because we wore miniskirts that would have invited opprobrium from the old man.

Even after hearing this story more times than I cared to, I continue to be astonished by what transpired. In his first encounter with the head of America's most prominent black separatist organization, my father came away committed to help the Nation of Islam purchase a farm in Greene County. Initially, he hadn't planned on using his own money. He had agreed merely to locate an appropriate property for Mr. Muhammad to buy. He identified a 3,600-acre farm, rich with dark bell-clay soil that impressed the Nation of Islam as a place to grow crops that would, in their vision, feed black America. In his enthusiasm to bring an independent black economic engine to the county, one that would employ blacks and bring revenues to the new black-led government, Dad purchased an option to buy the farm and returned to Chicago to present his findings to Mr. Muhammad.

The option had cost Dad $25,000, and it was due to expire in a matter of months. Mr. Muhammad's lawyer expressed a healthy skepticism that I wish my father had possessed about the prudence of attempting to raise the additional $350,000 required to exercise the option. The Nation of Islam was short on cash, owing to its misadventure in St. Clair County. "I want that land, Doctor," the diminutive Muhammad said in his slight voice, his eyes moist in Dad's retelling—an embellishment I think Dad needed to help justify his actions to his daughter, or to himself.

At their second meeting, my father and Mr. Muhammad reached an oral agreement. If Dad would help him finance the purchase of the farm, Muhammad promised to repay him with 20 percent interest within a year. In about a month, my father raised $243,000, an improbably large sum for anyone, much less a black man, to accumulate quickly in 1970. He tapped a close circle of relatives and intimates, including his mother and Harold Drake, who did not need much convincing because they had supreme confidence in him. My father poured his money, and theirs, into what he believed to be a guaranteed investment and bought the farm.

His thought processes were unconventional. He knew he was going to run for governor and could use the profit from the deal to infuse the NDPA with more cash. Ultimately, that did not happen. Mr. Muhammad died in 1975 without ever repaying my father. The risks of this alliance had been political as well as financial. As a true maverick, Dad was not concerned about the potential negatives of being associated with black separatists. In his view, the Black Muslims were not anti-white and his association with them would not undermine the NDPA because both organizations were "pro-black progress." Although he did not personally espouse a separatist ideology, he trusted Mr. Muhammad and believed in what he was doing. "I think that any man or any system that can go into the prisons and reclaim black people from a living death of narcotics addiction, and make contributing citizens out of them is worthwhile to be allied with," he told Hardy Frye in 1972. When I questioned him about why he entered this transaction with Mr. Muhammad, he simply said, "Because I believed in him." The first time I heard the story, as a teenager, his explanation angered me. My father seemed incapable of securing his flanks. His economic wounds appeared to be self-inflicted.

Although my father was never repaid, he had to repay the people he borrowed money from to invest in the deal. It was the beginning of our financial downward spiral. Before our reversal of fortune was complete, he became more ensconced with the Black Muslims. He turned the farm he held title to over to them to operate. He helped them procure a commercial airliner and a black pilot to transport their products, an involvement that was reported in *Jet* magazine. He passed up a chance to sell the farm and recoup his money because he had made a promise to Mr. Muhammad that it would not be sold. He was rather stubborn about his promises and his principles. This particular promise made no sense to me, but in Dad's moral code, it was essential to keep a promise to a revered elder.

His commitment to finish Grandpa Herschel's work was bound up in his promise to another sacred elder, E. D. Nixon. Dad would drive to Montgomery often to visit his civil rights hero. He could see that his friend was declining, and he savored his time with a dying breed of activist. Mr. Nixon was in the hospital when his wife called, "Doc, you better get here soon, he might not make it this time."

"Tell him I will be there on the first thing smoking," my father told her. He arrived at the hospital at about three in the afternoon. He embraced Mr. Nixon and then sat beside him, holding his hand. They would talk between the old man's intermittent naps. He must have known that he was dying. In a lucid moment, he left his hopes for the future with Daddy.

"Doc, will you please find some way to tell our people to stop celebrating before the job is finished? Finish the job and then celebrate." In my father's telling, these were Mr. Nixon's last words. He went to sleep and died peacefully that evening.

Of course, Dad agreed to do everything he could to fulfill Mr. Nixon's wish. The elder's sentiments perfectly mirrored his own. "I made a promise to E. D. Nixon" became a mantra of sorts. From Dad's perspective, this was sufficient to explain almost everything he did thereafter to advance the cause of his people.

I can now comprehend the impact of Mr. Nixon's deathbed plea much better than the first twenty, thirty, or 100 times I heard the story. "Finish the job and then celebrate," the elder had said. Given the conditions faced by poor black people in America, there would always be unfinished work to do. The moral imperative of Mr. Nixon's words proved devastating when uttered to a man seemingly without any instinct of financial self-preservation.

CHAPTER FOURTEEN

Reversal

I still remember the first time I ever saw a mother and father fight. We were at our house on Owens and it was the morning after another one of the Drek Set's parties. Gaby Rissé's father came charging up the stairs, screaming at Sas, her mother. Apparently, Sas had their kids over a weekend when he was supposed to be with them. They were in the process of getting divorced, and it did not seem to be proceeding amicably. Allowing the Rissé children to sleep over at the Cashins, outside in a camper van, fueled Mr. Rissé's ire.

They stood over Gaby and me, yelling back and forth. Proximity amplified their tension. I stared in stunned silence, my head vacillating with each parent's volley. Mercifully, their vitriol ended abruptly. "Well, I've got them now," Sas concluded. She was a slight woman with a well-earned name, more able than most females at checking a man.

Gaby collapsed in tears. I wanted to console her but I didn't know what to do or say. I ran to Mama, seeking my own comfort after witnessing such a scene. I was disturbed by their ferocity and by the thought that Gaby's father didn't like the fact that his children spent so much time with us. I was not yet sensitized to the possibility that our race may have had something to do with it. I simply abhorred conflict and the idea that I might be seeing less of Gaby.

"Sometimes parents fight," Mama said evenly, offering a statement of fact intended to ease my anxiety. As she spoke, she stood behind me, lightly touching my shoulders. Her caresses were always light—earnest, but not the full-throttled smothering I was used to receiving from Daddy. I preferred his bear hugs to her reserve because they were direct, uncomplicated displays of affection. Expressing romantic love toward her husband seemed to come naturally to Mama. With her children, she loved from an emotional distance—a gap I would come to appreciate as an adolescent when I began to declare my independence and Daddy's love could be suffocating. After the Rissés' fight, Mama's words and her caress had reassured me. Although I felt empathy for Gaby, I was thankful that my family was free of such volcanic eruptions. I would soon pay for my smugness.

> January 3, 1971—Dear Diary, Today I over herd [*sic*] my parents argueing [*sic*] my mother was crying my father was yelling the loudest well goodbye

I was nine, old enough to know how to use periods and commas. Grandma Grace would not have approved of my lack of punctuation, or my poor spelling. I wrote with the deliberate curlicues of early cursive, using a felt-tip pen that bled deep purple ink, appropriately enough. Deep purple was the color Mama's skin would turn when she bruised. We both bruised easily. My bruises were that of a tomboy determined to keep up with her brothers. Hers were evidence of something else.

"Mama, what happened?" I shrieked the first time I saw a large one. Like a cow's spot, it covered her entire right side. She was wearing a bra and slip, looking in a hallway closet for something, the urgent necessity of which had led her to forget to cover herself.

"Got hit," she said with evident embarrassment. She had intended to shield her children from the combat that was beginning in her marriage. Now that I had seen her bruise, I was dumbstruck and unsure how to respond because my loyalties were being tested. I loved both my parents dearly, but I was Daddy's girl and could not fully comprehend, or accept, that the same man who showered me with affection had done this to my mother. Before this moment, I had never known of any ugliness between my parents. This was new behavior and I did not know the origin of my father's demons.

I took my cue from Mama. Watching her carefully as she exited quickly to her bedroom without further comment, I decided not to follow her or ask questions. Subconsciously, I must have hoped that by not talking about it, whatever ugliness there was between my parents would fade with her purple spot. Eventually, she gave up on trying to shield my brothers and me. In the heat of their battles, she concentrated her energies on parrying my father's verbal assaults and lobbing some of her own.

I learned about "the violence," as Mama termed it, when I overheard a conversation she was having with Grandma Grace. I stood in the hallway outside of the kitchen, where they were talking.

"Did he tell you he hit me?" Mama asked. Grandma did not acknowledge the question. "I was going out the door and he grabbed me and said, 'Don't walk away when I'm talking to you,' and he hit me."

They talked past each other.

"I told him he needed to look after his health," Grandma said, her voice rising with concern. "Your health can change overnight." The only complaint she could muster about her son was that he was so hell-bent on his causes that he did not take good care of himself. In retrospect, it makes sense that Grandma Grace did not intervene to help her daughter-in-law. My grandmother would never have put up with such behavior from my grandfather, who had adored her and allowed her to rule their nest. Yet she seemed incapable of admitting any imperfection in the son she had raised to be an exception. Just as she had when my father was expelled from Fisk, Grandma Grace received this news in silence.

Mama and Daddy would fight like a storm that gathered fury and then rolled out to sea. The storm would be replaced by calm, but it always came roaring back with renewed intensity, only to grow quiet again once it hit land and exhausted itself. A fight might last an hour, a day, or weeks. It was always followed by reconciliation and tenderness. My parents would exhibit intense love and anger, often within the same day.

When I thought they were arguing, I would lie on the floor of my bedroom with my ear to the vent to our central air conditioner. Somehow it piped in their voices from the kitchen, which was down the hall, and I could discern what they were saying to each other and assess whether I needed to worry. Eventually, I didn't have to eavesdrop to hear. Shouting became standard. My mother was in her mid-thirties, my father in his early forties. In such relative youth, they naively believed that if they yelled loud enough and stood their respective grounds, the other would change.

There were consistent themes to their battles. She was angry with him for not spending enough time with his family, for flying off to whatever political meeting—or perhaps something else—he claimed he needed to attend to. Sometimes he said unbelievably cruel things. He used the B-word. Mama accused him of being with other women, often naming names. He denied it. Sometimes I believed her suspicions, sometimes I didn't. Although I didn't know it then, my father *was* quite similar to his father-in-law, Marc Carpenter, in that monogamy did not come naturally to either of them.

Usually I didn't take sides. I just cried and coped, sometimes by writing in my diary. I did come to believe that my father did not fight fair. He was a manipulator. The first time he discovered me crying because of their fighting, he tried to use it to his advantage. He found me in the bathroom, tears streaming down my face, and took me into the living room where Mama was lying on the couch. Her eyes were closed, her arm raised to her forehead, suggesting she was trying to get some rest before their next skirmish. He presented me as evidence and spoke of history repeating itself.

"Didn't you grow up crying in your room when Marc and Marie would fight?" This was supposed to be justification for her surrender.

"John, I am not going to let you bring her into this," Mama said calmly, never opening her eyes or changing her position. In these early years of their war, she stood her ground.

As much as I hated their fighting, I was proud of her for asserting herself. My father was a force of nature and her elder by eight years. Because she married at the tender age of twenty-one, I think Dad always saw her as the junior partner in their marriage. He might support her taking a leadership role in civil rights and political movements. But when it came to who was boss in their marriage, he would pronounce, "A woman cannot win an argument with her husband!" He would say it definitively, pacing as he uttered each word. To my budding feminist ears, this claim was insufferable.

One night I saw the violence with my own eyes. They were in the kitchen talking, and their voices became animated. I took my position at the air vent, assessing the temperature between them. It was getting hot. Mama began to bang dishes and scream for emphasis. She only reached such crescendos when she had exhausted herself of all patience with her hus-band. Otherwise she was an even-tempered woman, the person the Drek Set had always referred to as a peacemaker because she defused any dis-agreements that arose over NDPA strategy. Now as she crashed a dish against the counter and screeched at my father, I shuddered and prayed in vain that their fight would not get worse. They parried verbally, round after round, and eventually stormed down the hall past my bedroom and that of my brothers, into their bedroom, and behind the door they were careful to lock when they did not want to be disturbed. The air vent did not carry any sounds from their most private space. I climbed into my bed and listened to the muffled shouts that rattled my innards, waiting for a conclusion that would not come. Suddenly, without warning, Mama burst out of their bed-room and ran down the long hallway toward the kitchen, Daddy close behind her. She screamed and I leaped out of bed and ran into the hall. I saw my mother lying on the floor like a wounded deer. My father had pinned her under his knee. She lifted her head to look at me in jerking motions, clearly concerned that I was seeing this.

"Stop it, stop it, stop it," I sobbed hysterically.

"Are you sure? I'm doing this for you," Daddy said.

"No!" I bawled, my command echoing until I had no breath left. I called him on the ridiculousness of his logic and he relented, letting her up. Before my parents started their war, my relationship with my father had been rather simple. He adored me and I adored him. He still adored me and I still loved him, even in this ugly moment. But now I hated his ego.

Their battle continued, sans violence, into the wee hours that morning. At sunrise, the family awoke bleary-eyed and fatigued. Under the circumstances, Mama and Daddy were willing to let us skip school. I insisted on going.

"Aren't you tired, Pooskie?" my father asked. He seemed impressed by my resolve and remorseful about his role in wearing me out.

"No," I lied. School made sense to me at that moment because I excelled there and it gave me a respite from my anxiety about when my parents would erupt again. I didn't know at the time that turning to my schoolwork would become my chief means of self-preservation.

The violence worsened after Grandma died. She had been in and out of the hospital, battling a breast cancer that had overtaken her lungs. I would be middle-aged before I heard the story of my grandmother's attitude toward her impending death, a gem that emerged for the first time when I was plying my father with insistent questions about when and how his mother died. She had been told she was dying, and my father was in a quandary. The NDPA had another credentials fight to mount at the 1972 Democratic National Convention in Miami and he needed to be there. "What should I do, Mom?" he asked her. Grace was eerily calm, cheerful even. "It doesn't matter whether I live or die, either way I will be with one of my boys," she said, referring to her eldest, Herschel, who was in the spirit world, and her second son seated before her in the corporal one. She approached death the way William Cullen Bryant had counseled in his poem "Thanatopsis," Dad told me. He recited the last stanza of the poem to me, with a familiar verve that belied the mild dementia that had begun to overtake his brain. At seventy-nine, his short-term memory was disintegrating. Thankfully, he still retained his long-term memories, and the countless verses he loved. Grandma had great faith in God, he told me, and, like Bryant, she viewed death as "[lying] down to pleasant dreams." On her deathbed she squelched Dad's moral dilemma. "I am so proud of what you are doing, son," she told him. "I want you to go to Miami and win the fight."

In his lore, the Democratic National Committee breached its promise to hold a roll-call vote on whether to seat the NDPA, robbing him of the chance to prevail and of his last hours with his mother. My memories are different. We were all together at our house on Owens Drive the morning after Grandma died. Our first cousins, the "Texas Cashins," were there. Mama and Aunt Georgia gently broke the news to us. Perhaps Dad had been away to appear before the Credentials Committee, or perhaps over the years his bitterness about the NDPA's defeat in Miami became conflated with his grief over Grandma.

Her funeral was on July 5, 1972, the week before the convention. I remember the time of year because Daddy had already completed his annual ritual of buying too many fireworks and must have concluded that lighting them was an appropriate way to memorialize his mother. My cousin Lydia, the one we named our street after, chastised me for lighting bottle rockets on the day we buried Grandma.

Human death was new to me. I had succumbed immediately to grief upon learning that one of my three kittens had died. With Grandma, I was strangely numb, even after I stared at her corpse for an hour at the wake. She "looked good," everyone said. I thought so. Odell, Mama's hairdresser, had swept Grandma's thin hair into an elegant style that was nicer than the way she wore it when she was alive. She appeared to be sleeping, a resolute expression on her face that said, "Well, this is it and it's not so bad." The undertaker had placed her glasses on her face. *Why would Grandma need glasses in heaven?* I thought.

I sat next to my father and leaned into his arm. As much as I loved Grandma, I was spooked because I had never seen a dead person before. I think I was also unnerved by the finality of death. It was hard to accept that a life force could be gone in an instant. If Grandma could die, then Daddy could die. And Mama. Despite my father's prior attempt to reassure me about death, the world seemed less trustworthy and the people I loved less dependable.

That night we all slept at Grandma's house on Gallatin, to prepare for the visitors who would come by after her funeral the next day. I was relegated to the couch in the living room and lay in terror in the darkness as my mind returned again and again to the image of my grandmother's corpse. I had never been afraid of the dark. Now I was.

Daddy, Uncle Harold, Mama, and several Brandon cousins sat around Grandma's kitchen table, laughing and reminiscing. I could hear their revelry and was somewhat comforted by the normalcy of it. On a bathroom break, Dad noticed that I was awake and came to my side. I told him that seeing a dead body, even Grandma's, had chilled me. I was afraid to move, convinced that spirits of the dead would get me.

He tried to comfort me by taking me into Grandma's bedroom and placing me in the same spot where she had slept each night: "Grandma loved you and she is here with you now. She would never hurt you, you know that." Intellectually, I did. Her smell of Jean Naté was everywhere and my memories of her were joyful. But the idea of her ghost hovering about was too much to bear. As soon as my father left the room, I leaped from her bed and returned to the living room couch and my frozen watch for any spirits. As he returned to the kitchen, I overheard him betray my confidence.

"Sheryll says she's scared because she's never seen anybody dead before," he said dismissively. Listening to my father expose and invalidate my fear reinforced the confusion I had felt after seeing the violence. I had forgiven him because Mama had forgiven him. Because he had always been a loving father, I had compartmentalized the harm he had done to my mother and hoped that he would not do it again. Now as I listened to his small betrayal, I again realized that within the same man there might be "Daddy," my devoted hero, as well as another character capable of saying or doing things that were hurtful not only to Mama but also to me.

At Grandma's funeral, I saw something else in my father I had never seen before. I was seated next to him on the church pew at Lakeside United Methodist, Grandma's church. The cavernous, surprisingly modern sanctuary was filled with waves of black strivers who were as upstanding as Grandma. Dad spoke to me occasionally in muted tones, explaining the social protocols inherent in burying the dead. I was absorbing the pageantry when, midway through the service, he burst into tears, threw his face into a handkerchief, and sobbed.

I was stunned. Until that moment he had seemed invincible. I did not understand the extent to which forces were aligning against him or the ways in which he would contribute to his own undoing. Losing his mother seemed to accelerate the unraveling of much of what he had worked for.

After Grandma Grace died, her home became the de facto state NDPA headquarters and a commune of sorts for its most ardent volunteers. Another slate of 130 NDPA candidates was running in the fall. A party with candidates and local chapters in nearly every county in the state could no longer be run out of our dining room. Julian Bond, then the Georgia state representative with good looks and an emerging national reputation, and John Lewis, the civil rights hero who was clubbed on the skull on the Edmund Pettus Bridge, had urged my father to invest his treasure in building the party infrastructure. Early in 1973, a woman came to work for NDPA as an office manager, and she would eventually replace Mama as the party mother in a manner that did not seem right to me. She was a female version of Daddy—light-skinned with silky hair that suggested a mixed-race heritage, stout, and possessed of a larger than life personality. She was handsome, not pretty. Her eyes were set wider apart than they should have been, and she smoked filterless cigarettes because, she said, a real smoker wouldn't dilute the experience.

She came south from New York City and was charged with creating a formal, organized state office. Dad's explanation for why she was assigned this role and not my mother was that he had asked my mother to type a few letters for him and she had responded, "Why don't you get a secretary?" This story, another that I heard more times than I cared to, never rang true to me because I had seen my mother type, organize, and sweat for the party she believed in just as much as my father. For me, the story was a rationalization that allowed him to shirk responsibility for trusting someone who would contribute mightily to our reversal of fortune.

Dad bought a small house across the street from Grandma's home, and the new office manager oversaw its remodeling, the purchase of furniture, the setting up of files and systems, and the hiring of a temporary paid workforce. She was a taskmistress, and the office came into being in a matter of months. She brought with her a cast of hip characters from New York who worked out of Grandma's house while the new office was being renovated. My brothers and I all worked for the NDPA that summer of 1973, and she was our boss. I opened and sorted mail and read *The Adventures of Tom Sawyer* when the office manager wasn't nearby, the "engagement" between Becky Thatcher and Tom hastening my interest in romance. "You'll be screwing soon," the office manager observed, as I looked up from the book, embarrassed that she had caught me with my nose in it. "Uh-uh!" I protested about the repulsive act my first cousin John had described to me earlier that summer. Excepting this exchange, I always liked the fact that she talked to me like an adult. Although she was an obese woman, I was attracted to her style and her worldliness. Every day she wore colorful maxidresses and skirts created for her by a New York fashion designer, and she arrived at the office with her two large dogs, an Afghan named Logan, I assumed after my father, and a sheepdog named Moon. Frequently she brought me no-occasion gifts, surprises that evoked a tinge of the excitement a child normally feels only on birthdays. Whatever her motives, she succeeded in thoroughly charming me, as did her dogs.

I was eleven then, and I didn't have any concrete evidence that Daddy philandered. But I knew my father was emotionally disloyal with this woman and that my own loyalties were being divided. Mama was not banned from the NDPA office, though she may as well have been. A memo appeared on our refrigerator explaining in rather officious language why interference from volunteers with the office reorganization was counterproductive. It might have been intended for Mama specifically, or it might have been a general swipe at the Drek Set and other long-haired supporters, including Bill Edwards, who had also given their souls to the NDPA and did not appreciate being displaced by someone who was imposing a hierarchical order on their organic political party.

Daddy encouraged our closeness. Perhaps he wanted his daughter to be as fierce and independent as she was. Perhaps he merely wanted his daughter to like his paramour, although I was unaware at the time of the true nature of their relationship. She would become part of my parents' emotional baggage—the subject Mama would bring up years later when she felt like reminding Dad of his betrayals.

Our reversal had begun with Dad's purchase of that farm in Greene County for the Nation of Islam. Then the FBI began to investigate him. I learned about it from my brothers, who took pleasure in informing me that our phone was tapped, offering as unmistakable evidence the clicking sound we often heard on the line. They liked to think of themselves and their father as smarter than the people who were spying on us, and I adopted that attitude. We were amused at the thought of constant surveillance and would sometimes pick up the phone and say silly things to the agents we felt certain were listening. We never had any worry about Daddy overcoming any forces set against him. In our minds, he continued to be a dragon slayer.

My efforts to reveal the full extent of the federal government's surveillance of my father, using the Freedom of Information Act, resulted in a few pages of highly redacted reports. "John L. Cashin, Jr.—Congress of African Peoples, 12/1/71" was the name of one file created by the Birmingham office. The FBI must have looked into Dad's involvement with an organization that espoused black nationalism, although nothing came of it. Surely they were more concerned about the NDPA, and maybe they needed a nationalist angle to justify an investigation. In 1976, they would open another file, labeled "John L. Cashin Jr., Espionage, Miscellaneous." When he learned of it he called the FBI directly, demanding to know what the investigation was about. He volunteered to appear for an interview, and the agent described his attitude as "very confident" and his dress "excellent." In the end, the agent concluded that he had no basis for suspecting that Dad was an agent of a foreign government attempting to purchase missiles, "however, the whole conversation and meeting was [*sic*] very unusual," he noted. "Cashin advised that being from Huntsville, which he considered to be the missile capital of the world, his interest in missiles is more than the average citizen." I laughed when I read this, recognizing both my father's propensity for psychological gamesmanship and his belief that his scientific training enabled him to master almost any subject. He did have more than an average interest in anything that could be propelled into the sky and he had had a conversation with a redacted third party about the possibility of him becoming a consultant for hire on missile technology. That person apparently did not comprehend or appreciate my father's idiosyncrasies and had contacted the FBI about his suspicions that my father was a foreign agent.

The FBI was a nuisance compared to the Internal Revenue Service. Shortly after his run for governor in 1970, two IRS agents stopped by Dad's dental office informing him that he owed $780,000 in back taxes. Dad thought the claim was laughable. The IRS did not. They based it on the evidence of income Dad had offered in conjunction with purchasing that farm for the Black Muslims. He had overstated his income in order to finance the purchase. And his involvement with recruiting black militants to Alabama, or cultivating indigenous ones by offering them their own political party, apparently had attracted attention from what he and Mama called "the white power structure."

The agents arrived at our house on the following Saturday morning to interrogate him. "They walked in like they owned the place," Dad recounted. Immediately, he reverted to psychological warfare. Leaving the agents in our two-story foyer, he proceeded upstairs and called the man he always turned to when he smelled trouble: his lawyer-friend, Chuck Morgan. He stood in our living room, not far from a balcony overlooking the foyer, and spoke with unmistakable purpose.

"Chuck, the IRS has just barged in, can I shoot 'em?"

"Just be sure they are in your house," Chuck responded with a chuckle.

By the time he returned to the foyer, the agents were on the street. "We're going to get you, you son of a bitch," my father recalled them saying.

"Okay, just be sure you've got a way back home 'cause that's going to be your problem," he rejoined. The IRS was not amused. For five years they pursued him. Dad's accountant advised him that the charge was specious, but the federal government seemed determined to treat him as a "jeopardy assessment," meaning they would aggressively attempt to seize all of his assets. They were convinced that he was financing his political party with drug money. That claim was also false, although my father would endure years of harassment before the IRS ceased to believe their own assumptions.

I was aware that the IRS was after my father because I heard the adults speak of it often. "They came to see me," Mrs. Blackburn, our housekeeper, told Dad wearily. Virtually all of Dad's friends and allies reported such visits from the IRS. Mrs. Blackburn was like most of his friends in this regard. She remained loyal to the boss who treated her like a member of the family and called her "Groovy Granny" because she was a grandmother who wore miniskirts.

According to Dad, the IRS interviewed virtually anyone who wrote him a check between 1970 and 1975, and always asked whether a purchase of narcotics had been involved. He gave the two IRS agents who were spending so much time at his dental office a key and some office space on the ground floor where his bail bond business was located. "Investigate all you want, you aren't going to find anything," he told them.

In one sense he did prevail. After five years, the IRS concluded he owed only $40,000 in taxes, instead of nearly $800,000. He continued to challenge them and refused to pay. Through lawyers and accountants they battled to a draw, but by the time the IRS finally dropped the investigation, the NDPA had folded and Dad was broke. In this sense, the investigation took a grave toll. He evaded the jeopardy assessment by placing most of his assets in a trust. His chosen trustees, one being his paramour–office manager, turned out to be untrustworthy. Ultimately, he was defrauded of his assets, and my mother would file a lawsuit to have them returned. I was sixteen when her lawyer put me and my brother John on the stand to help make her case. Mr. Huckaby was his name. He seemed nice—a lanky white man with an easy manner. He asked me questions about "the violence."

"Have you ever seen your father hit your mother?"

"Well, not hit her," I said, thinking literally.

Mr. Huckaby's questions did not lead me to tell the story of the one time I saw Dad attack Mama with my own eyes. I did testify that I had *heard* the violence and seen its effects, remembering the bruises and once some blood spattered on Mama's bright yellow bathrobe. During the trial, my father sat at one table with the office manager who defrauded him. My mother sat at another table because she was suing both of them, although my parents were still together and their intent was that she would prevail in order to get our assets returned. On a few occasions when she could no longer endure the violence or the absurdity in her marriage, Mama had left us. Each time, my parents had reconciled after a few days. And they remained a tempestuous team in the courtroom. Although they had agreed on strategy, my father clearly was discomfited by his daughter's testimony against him. He made sighing noises as I spoke, as if to say, "I'm not as bad as this sounds," although he knew that I was speaking the truth. I felt no qualms about testifying. By then I was rather angry with him about our reversal of fortune, and the role his paramour had played in it.

I vented in my diary about the injustice of our situation. My father's paramour had gained title to our homes on Owens and Lydia. We moved back to Lydia Drive and she moved into the house on Owens and subsequently tried to have us evicted from Lydia. No one explained these absurdities to me. She took possession of many of Grandma's antiques, silver, and other heirlooms, ostensibly to clean and repair them while the NDPA office was being organized. The heirlooms disappeared, and she claimed that they had been stolen. Among the many family treasures we lost, Dad always said that she had absconded with Grandpa Herschel's ebony box. "How could Daddy do it?" I wrote with anguish and anger. By the age of sixteen, I was old enough to recognize that my father had had an affair, and I knew vaguely that he had had to deed property to others to evade tax problems. "But to risk so much," I wrote, made no sense to me. I could not excuse the loss of "family heirlooms that never would have been stolen if my father hadn't given them to her." I struggled mightily to reconcile my anger with my love. "I respect my father, I love my father—more than any daughter alive," I wrote. Even in my private diary I found it difficult to articulate how I felt about what had transpired. Had he been disloyal to his family, and to the ancestors whose heirlooms he had failed to protect? Or had he been duped and his judgment clouded under the weight of a conspiracy to destroy him?

I don't know whether my court testimony made any difference. I was a junior in high school by the time the case was finally resolved. In the end, the only asset Mama ever regained title to was our house on Lydia Drive. She secured not just the roof over our heads but she also kept us together as a family until the day she died. All families need such saviors, people who make the right decisions in a crisis. Mama was ours.

My race became more apparent as all the boys and girls around me began to notice each other. At school and in the neighborhood on Owens Drive I was a convenient, implicitly neutral keeper of romantic secrets for my friends, but never the object of anyone's affections. As my interest in this boy-girl business grew, I discarded the color-blind consciousness of the Drek Set and became thoroughly, happily, black. Fatigued with schoolyard exclusion and always with one foot in the black world, it was easier simply to jump into blackness with both feet. Besides, being black was "bad," a new word for "good" that purveyors of black culture had created. My summer vacation in 1973 with my cousins, the Texas Cashins, "was the BADDEST week I've ever had!!" I wrote. The simple pleasure of going to a drive-in to watch *Cleopatra Jones* from the hood of my cousin Herschel's car was its own revelation. "Bad" described Tamara Dobson, the actress who played Miss Jones with butt-kicking exquisiteness. Her glorious Afro crowned a 6-foot, 2-inch frame that made her one fine tower of beautiful. Nothing in the white world could match her, I thought.

After we moved back to Lydia Drive, the Drek Set eventually collapsed along with the NDPA. "We were growing up and maturing and I was exhausted," Dad said of his closest political allies and friends during the NDPA years. Time moved on, and so did the members of the Drek Set, although Mama and Myrna remained close friends.

Our house on Lydia was less than half the size and much plainer than our castle on Owens, but it mattered little to me. A neighborhood full of caring black families placed me on surer social footing. Virtually all of the lots on Lydia had been developed by then. Dr. Hereford had moved his family there, as had his brother, Daddy's childhood friend, Thomas. Ministers, doctors, teachers, university professors, entrepreneurs, and other professionals called Lydia Drive home.

Lee Hereford lived across the street and three doors down. She became a true friend, as did Donna Booth, who lived next door to Lee. I delighted in having two running buddies on the block who looked like me, had the same concerns about how to tame their hair, and did not need cultural interpretations.

My brothers quickly turned our expansive driveway into a basketball court. Along with an undeveloped adjacent lot that was perfect for touch football, this rendered our house command central for Lydia's youth. Child's play unburdened by the vagaries of race politics was especially sweet. Each family had a long history with the others on the street and most doors were rarely locked. I spent so much time at Lee's that my parents could assume with assurance that I was there if I didn't come home. She shared my trundle bed just as frequently. Life would have been perfect, had it not been for my parents' troubles.

Mama started working for the Huntsville-Madison County Community Action agency, administering federal programs for poor people. The work was a continuation of her civil rights activism. She was making her own money for the first time in her life, and being paid to be of use to others. Daddy was still practicing dentistry, but she used *her* money to buy a new color TV for our den and pay for other minor improvements that freshened the house, lifting the museum-like quality Aunt Vivi had left it in. She and Uncle Tode had both died a few years before—his death, I think, caused by grief after losing her to a long illness.

I entered the sixth grade in the fall of 1973 at Highlands Elementary, which had a lot more black pupils than Blossomwood. Some of them asked me why I "spoke proper." I wanted to tell them, "Because my father insists on perfect diction," but I didn't. When I told them that my father owned an airplane, they didn't believe me. They thought I was bragging, and I was. I promised a few of my new school friends that my father would take them for a ride. That would never happen because his beloved Bellanca was sabotaged later that year.

He was scheduled to speak in York, Alabama. An intervening call from Abbas Rasul—Clarence Byrd, before he joined the Nation of Islam—his friend and national secretary of the Black Muslims, may have saved his life.

"Hey, man, get up here, I need you bad," Mr. Rasul had said. My father had learned not to talk business on the phone. In prototypical form, someone else's emergency became his emergency. Because Mr. Rasul had asked for help, my father canceled his appearance in York and headed to Chicago.

He called the Huntsville Airport where his bird was tethered and told them to get his plane ready in a hurry. Upon arrival, he noticed a large man he described as "a big old redneck" crawling out of the cabin. He thought the man must have been part of the maintenance staff that was fulfilling his request to ready his plane. When he landed at Meigs Field in Chicago, Rasul was waiting for him, briefcase in hand.

Actually it was "85 Victor," not Dad, that the Nation of Islam needed. My father was pressed into service to help the NOI make an important, discreet delivery. Rasul needed to deposit six well-oiled handguns—.38s and .45s—with some deacons of defense in Arkansas. One of the NOI's mosques was being threatened by the local constabulary, and Elijah Muhammad wanted his deacons to have some high-quality weaponry in the event they needed to defend themselves.

Mr. Rasul took his place in the front passenger seat and my father proceeded to the runway to position himself for takeoff. They were headed directly to Arkansas. Dad began to run through his pre-flight protocols.

I had never had any interest in this standard series of procedures until he told me this story. While going through the pre-flight safety checks, his right rudder pedal collapsed to the floor with a thump.

"Damn, what is this?" my father exclaimed. Mr. Rasul was edgy.

"Let's go back. We can't go anywhere like this," he said.

"We can't go anywhere period because I need my rudder pedal to steer the plane," Dad replied. He examined the pedal with a flashlight. The cotter key and safety wire had been removed, and the rudder pedal had been put back in position with nothing to hold it in place. It was a clever method for a would-be assassin to use, as detection of a missing cotter key was unlikely until after takeoff and there was a decent chance that its absence would cause a crash upon landing.

Had my father flown that evening to York as originally planned, he would have hit his rudder pedals quickly to brake after a high and fast approach above a grove of pine trees. If the right rudder pedal had collapsed while the left caught and held, he would have been tossed into the trees. With a hot engine and sixty gallons of high-test fuel, he might have been barbecued. In Chicago the runway was longer and smoother. He had landed without incident and now he considered his luck. His "85 Victor" seemed to come with a spiritual protector. A few months earlier, a tornado had touched down at the Huntsville Airport, smashing more than a dozen planes, while Dad's ship had merely rolled a few feet from its moorings.

On the ground in Chicago, my father improvised. He took the NDPA button he was wearing from his lapel and used the pin's wire to reassemble the cotter key mechanism. The wire held and felt so durable that Dad flew on to Arkansas, and then home, despite Mr. Rasul's nervousness. Like Rasul, he was convinced that someone had tried to kill him.

He may have been paranoid when he discerned surprise in some of the faces he encountered upon return to the Huntsville Airport. I always rolled my eyes at the conspiracy theories my father could weave. The more he told me about what happened to his airplane, though, the more I understood his paranoia. He reported his allegation of sabotage to the Federal Aviation Administration (FAA), the FBI, and the Huntsville Police Department, to no avail.

Relying on his own ingenuity and the good karma that came with an NDPA button, he flew several more times before entrusting his bird to a mechanic for repairs. Perhaps it was fearlessness that enabled Dad to continue to fly, or it may have been too difficult to give up a lifelong passion and the ability to jump into his own wings and go anywhere on a moment's notice, which he did, almost weekly. All that came to a halt on Election Day 1974.

At daybreak, he was returning to Huntsville after an election eve rush of delivering NDPA campaign literature and money to his candidates. In the previous twelve hours, he had made ten or more stops in the Black Belt and was returning home with the expectation of savoring victories later that evening. As he touched down, the left main landing gear folded. He hit the throttle, attempting to gain enough speed to take off again. It was too late. The left main wheel and the nose wheel failed simultaneously. They collapsed softly, like the air going out of a flat tire. As the plane lowered, the propeller sliced into the runway, and the plane skidded to a stop. He had badly scarred his bird but not himself. Faced once again with the specter of death, he knew at that moment that he would never fly again.

He sold his bird to the insurance company and focused on earthly pursuits. Six months later, he received a call from the mechanic who had been charged with rebuilding "85 Victor," who happened to be black. "Doc, I think there is something you ought to know," he reported. "I know why your wheels folded up on you. The O-rings were reversed on your left front, left rear, and nose wheels." An O-ring is used to seal a hydraulic cylinder. If it fails, hydraulic fluid escapes and the retraction cylinder collapses, which is exactly what happened to Dad's plane. Again, this appeared to be very sophisticated sabotage. It could not have happened accidentally, Dad argued.

He had no idea who did it but felt certain that the maintenance staff at the airport would have had the opportunity. Someone could have been placed on the maintenance staff for this particular purpose. Once again he reported his suspicions to local and federal authorities. This time he sought the help of a lawyer familiar with flying. Thomas Jefferson had been a Blue Angel in the U.S. Marine Corps. He earned a law degree from the University of Alabama, the law school that mattered most in the state. He had once served as the personal pilot for Bear Bryant, the football coach at UA whom many Alabamians believed could walk on water. Bryant called Jefferson the "Sky King."

Dad and the Sky King managed to arrange a meeting with a black attorney who worked at the FAA's regional office in Atlanta. They spoke to the gentleman on the phone and drove to Atlanta to meet with him to discuss the evidence Dad had collected in support of his claim of sabotage. When they arrived at the FAA office, they were told that the person they had spoken to a few days before did not exist. The phone number they had for him did not work. The Sky King looked at Dad and said, "John, somebody big and bad is after you and I am going to advise you to pull in your horns and be quiet for a while."

My father would have attracted fewer enemies had he been more diplomatic in his pronouncements. He was a taste that some people never acquired. Yet even a kind revolutionary attracts enemies, as the children of

Dr. King could attest. I have no proof, but it is possible that my father's treatment by the FBI and IRS was part of the federal government's infamous Counter Intelligence Program (COINTELPRO) operation— J. Edgar Hoover's hubristic attempt to neutralize a motley assortment of "radical" organizations from the Communist Party to nonviolent civil rights groups to the Klan. The FBI's methods included infiltration, illegal surveillance designed to harass, discriminatory and wrongful enforcement actions, and, some believe, assassinations. If Hoover viewed Dr. King and the SCLC as subversives, I imagine John Cashin and the NDPA would also have been viewed as such. But COINTELPRO was exposed in 1971 and, at least in theory, terminated that year. And my father had garnered his share of enemies within the state of Alabama. Whether federal, state, or local, his adversaries did more than knock him out of the skies.

In becoming a dentist, my father had done his duty as the second son, following the path ordained for him by his father and mother. He did not regret going to dental school. He could see that his father, John Sr., needed help in order to continue his dental practice and earn a comfortable living. Dad had also enjoyed "doing things right" in the dental chair, his friendship with patients, and, he admits, the prestige that came with the profession. Still he always said that *he* should have been the lawyer and his brother Herschel should have been the dentist. He was "mad as hell" when the City of Huntsville took his dental office by eminent domain in 1975 but figured it was an opportunity to transition to something else. He never practiced dentistry again, and his bail bond business and dental laboratory also folded with the condemnation. The "something else" became a series of professional and personal adventures and misadventures. Sometimes Dad had money, from unexplained "deals," an occasional consulting contract, and a rental property he had managed to retain. Most of the time he was low on cash. My mother became the primary breadwinner in our house, and our family of five often stretched her $17,000 salary to the breaking point.

Dad had fought the condemnation of his office and boyhood home. Like other black neighborhoods across the country, the Grove was targeted for "urban renewal," or "Negro removal" as the tribe called it. The homes owned by most blacks in central Huntsville would be mowed down, including

Grandma's house and the dental office next to it that my grandfather had built. The homes owned by whites one street and a universe away would remain, untouched and ultimately restored by historic preservationists.

Most blacks sold when the city offered to buy their homes. My father was the last holdout and the only one who fought the city in court—a case he lost. While his suit was pending, the city ran a six-foot trench immediately in front of his dental office, forcing his patients to trudge through the mud. The city offered him much less for the family compound than he felt it was worth. He did not want to sell and tried to save our property from destruction by deeding it to an ad hoc committee formed ostensibly to create a black culture center on the site. That never transpired, and the committee, rather than Dad, received the $200,000 the city paid as "just compensation." Once again, my father was undermined by his faith in a cause and by placing his trust in people who would betray him. He has always been a paradox, a man who could best conspicuous enemies with his brand of psychological warfare but whose altruism toward his tribe often led him to give and trust blindly.

Initially, the city put a parking lot for city vehicles on Grandma's land. I was glad she did not live to see it. The black asphalt was ugly, redeemed only by two large trees that had been in Grandma's front yard. They stand there to this day, a pecan and a magnolia, living monuments to the vibrant neighborhood they once inhabited.

Eventually, the land that our family had owned since 1930 was transferred to a local bank, which built an impressive headquarters on the site—probably the kind of "progress" the city hoped for. I would never have known the Grove existed, had it not been for Dad sharing his boyhood stories. By the time I was old enough to begin depositing my own memories, Negro main had begun to collapse under the weight of integration. The Princess Theater became a boarded-up relic before it was torn down. Howard Barley's Sweet Shop, Odell's Beauty Parlor, and the barbershop it abutted were among the few black-owned businesses that were still operating during my girlhood. Ironically, my parents were in the vanguard of a movement that hastened the demise of a community and culture they both treasured. A few months before my father's eightieth birthday, I asked him whether he had any regrets about their civil rights activism and what "integration" had wrought. "No! It was the fight of the century and we haven't finished yet!" he cried. For him, white supremacists were like schoolyard bullies who needed to be taught to pick on someone their own size. "That system of apartheid had to be destroyed," he concluded. I am confident that, were my mother still alive, she would have echoed my father's fervent sentiment about the seminal cause of their lives.

Independence

It never made sense to me that my father would entrust Grandpa Herschel's box to someone other than family, even at the height of his paranoia about the IRS. I keep hoping that I will unearth it if I continue to dig through all of the NDPA files, Aunt Vivi and Uncle Tode's mementos, and the accumulated stuff of my parents' lives that still occupies the furthest recesses of our attic on Lydia. That box was a treasure that held the secret to Dad's obsessions, and I was very sorry he never saw fit to show it to me. It hurt to think that my great-granddaddy's beautiful letters and other effects were lost forever. I would have taken good care of them because I have always appreciated objects with a history. I still use a baroque silver hand mirror that belonged to Grandma Grace. I remember watching her hold it up to see the back of her bobby-pinned hair reflected in the bathroom mirror, her final ritual before going out. Grandma had inherited the hand mirror from her mother, Idella Brandon. Dad recalled seeing his grandmother hold it up to gaze at herself when she wanted to look pretty for the world. Mama enacted a similar ritual with the mirror, which she kept on her dresser after Grandma Grace died. I am the fourth generation to use it this way. Sometimes I can almost catch a glimpse of Idella or Grace looking back at me in the glass. That is how it is supposed to be. These kinds of treasures are meant to be kept in the family, to be passed on with pointed explanations as to their provenance so that the next generation will know the guiding spirits that come with these objects and the purposeful lives those spirits lived. Thankfully, my father did preserve and pass on the family lore, one of his greatest gifts to me, besides his love.

I first heard the stories of our ancestors when listening to Dad share the family history with Johnny, my older brother. I didn't mind being an observer rather than a participant in these discussions because I was confident in my status as "the baby" and the only girl in our family. In time, Daddy's embellishments became my embellishments. He would hold his tattered copy of Grandpa Herschel's book, *Under Fire with the Tenth U.S. Calvary*, and rail about the injustices done to the Buffalo Soldiers. Teddy Roosevelt's Rough Riders took credit for their victory, he would say. He would rail even more about the Alabama Constitution of 1901 and how the white supremacists undid Grandpa Herschel's work.

He was home a lot more now that he was not practicing dentistry and no longer owned an airplane. I benefited most from his grounding. He loved science and would explain concepts to me such as "ontology recapitulates phylogeny," the discredited theory that as an individual of a species develops, it fully repeats the evolutionary development of that species. Or he would point out the patterns in numbers, hastening my love of and comfort with mathematics. Or he would regale me with the teachings of Thomas Paine, Buckminster Fuller, and Frederick Douglass.

He was rather proud of his first-edition copy of Douglass's autobiography, *The Life and Times of Frederick Douglass*. I opted to read his heavily annotated paperback of Douglass's shorter autobiography, *Narrative of the Life of Frederick Douglass*. That slim volume was more than enough to hook me. My father's hero became my hero. I was awed to learn that a former slave could teach himself to write and speak with such power.

My father would also entertain me with tales of his own exploits, especially as a student. Over and over again, I heard about how he simultaneously carried two heavy course loads and filled his transcript with A's, and about how he led his class at Meharry for four years. He demystified academics for me by talking about *how* he did it. I learned that there was a direct correlation between effort and excellence. Even my brilliant father had to exert himself, and he emphasized that he studied as many hours as were required in order to master a subject. I emulated his example, pursuing an A in every class and always getting it. I also emulated my father's tendency to play hard.

"You do too much," Mama would say in exasperation, probably because she was the one who would drive me to my activities, despite the obligations of her job, and pay for my multifarious uniforms. In seventh and eighth grades at Ed White Middle School I was a cheerleader, the only black one. I played volleyball, basketball, and ran track, all the sports that were available to a female athlete. I served on the student council. I played the saxophone, first chair, in Mr. William T. Robinson III's award-winning band.

Mr. Robinson was an erudite man who did not tolerate foolishness and dressed with precise sartorial elegance, choosing bow ties and tightly cropped hair over the fat ties, Afros, and sideburns that the other black male teachers and administrators sported. He modeled the rectitude of an earlier generation of Negro and demanded similar comportment from his students. It was a privilege to have Mr. Robinson, and Mr. Monroe, my caring social studies teacher, as instructors and mentors. They were my first black teachers. Huntsville in the mid-1970s was beginning to make good on the promise of the *Brown v. Board* decision. At Blossomwood, I had been one of a few integration pioneers, and there had been only one black teacher in the entire school. At Ed White, integration was three-dimensional. There were several black faculty and administrators, including Mr. Anthony, who became our principal. The student body was more than one-fourth black, and children from the projects mingled with middle- and a few upper-class children. There were no class distinctions because the school system had not yet discovered ability tracking. Through classes, sports, and physical education, we learned to deal with each other.

Most of my close friends were black, and several were poor. With rare exception, only a fellow race traveler would invite me to her home and it never occurred to me to invite non-blacks to my house. My relationships with whites were formed in the context of school and stayed there, although I became extremely close to a few of my fellow cheerleaders and we loved each other as much as was possible within that milieu.

After we moved back to Lydia Drive, my parents settled into an uneasy peace that proved ephemeral. They would fight, stop for a period, then fight anew. I abhorred conflict. When the screaming started, my intestines flared and I ran for cover. As the only person in the house with the luxury of a room to herself, I would close my bedroom door, lock it, and lie in bed, waiting for the argument to end while listening carefully in case their mutual recriminations turned from the usual script to brutality.

Eventually, their fighting became background noise to my adolescence. I learned to depend on their inevitable reconciliations, sensing from experience that peace would eventually return to the house. They *always* reconciled. Mama would never leave Daddy. She learned that from her mother. In Nana's culture, divorce was not an option, no matter how errant her husband, and that seemed to be my mother's attitude. My mother and grandmother accepted the deal they made: a husband who loved them with incredible tenderness and generosity at times but who could not be tamed.

My father had no intention of leaving his marriage, either. It struck me as odd, as much as he seemed to wander and as much as they fought, how resolute each of them would become when I began to suggest, at first gingerly, and later straightforwardly, that they should divorce. As an outspoken teenager, I told them they weren't doing me any favors by staying together. I longed for normalcy and a more dependable peace at home.

Divorce also was not an option in Dad's culture. His uncles and father had prospered within the institution of marriage; it was an unarticulated maxim: A Cashin man married for life. Nor did he want to leave his children. His response to the turbulence in his marriage was simply to bear down harder in his insistence that his wife "change her attitude," meaning accept his edicts and actions without protest.

Although I loved him dearly, I swore to myself and to my mother that I would never put up with such a ridiculous husband. My bravado never moved Mama. "I still love him" was the only reason she ever offered for staying, and clearly the only rationale she needed. I was developing an independence that Mama never possessed or wanted.

The violence ebbed with time. Perhaps it ceased as my brothers grew tall and muscular and could double up on him. Perhaps it was because Mama relented to a degree and stopped questioning him about where he was going, when he would call, when and how he would produce some money. Perhaps he finally took a cold look in the mirror. Of course, their verbal parries continued. They would be married nearly thirty years before their hostilities finally ceased and they achieved an unwavering peace.

Mama's battle with breast cancer made Dad realize that he would be utterly devastated if he lost her. Through a faith beyond my own understanding, Mama was vindicated in staying through the hard times. In the final ten years of her life, she enjoyed a husband who often deferred to her and occasionally took out the trash.

In the meantime, in my adolescence we all endured regular family strife. As the Cashin children became teenagers and hormones raged, everyone in the house seemed to be on edge. Someone was always arguing with someone—father with mother, father with son, father with daughter, sister with brother, but never, thankfully, did mother and daughter argue. Mama and I were always at peace with each other.

There was abundant laughter in the house in happy moments. As I got older, Dad ceased to hide his vulgarity from me. For this reason, I have never blushed in the presence of crudeness because no one could be more vulgar than my father. He carried a half century of black oral culture in his head. Whenever I wanted a break from the intensity of his bitterness about what Alabama had done to Grandpa Herschel or to him, I would ask him to tell me a favorite joke involving a man of unspecified race who frequented a saloon in a frontier town devoid of women. The story is unprintable. Once he got going, Mama and I would sit with him, talk and laugh through several easy hours as he mined a bottomless reserve of politically incorrect jokes he had collected since his time at Fisk. My father could make me laugh until it hurt and tears streamed down my face. Daddy's ego saved him. His sense of humor saved us.

Mama's fights with Daddy were often about money. Initially, my fights with my father were about boys. He trusted me implicitly, but he did not trust the hormone-induced intentions of my suitors. He dealt with a growing terror of his daughter's dealings with the opposite sex, mainly by intimidating any young man who came calling and lecturing me about doggish male behavior with which he was clearly familiar.

It had not mattered to my father that my first serious boyfriend lived in the projects. He was a star athlete and a serious student who was also devoted to me. My best friend, Lee, dated his twin brother. All that mattered to Daddy and Dr. Hereford was that their daughters' feet remained on the floor.

I had inherited my father's cultural and class dexterity. Lee and I thought the kids from the projects were cool, and they were. In 1976, in Huntsville, Alabama, the worst ills of the projects were weapons called "numchucks." A fight was resolved not with bullets but with fists or handmade sticks of wood connected by a chain that mimicked the weapons of Bruce Lee. It was a pre-AIDS, pre-crack, pre-Reagan era—a mostly innocent time in which the music we loved was about love, and the melody and lyrics were discernible.

After breaking up with the dependable boyfriend, any youthful insecurity I harbored was usually about unworthy knuckleheads who paid me just enough attention to drive me crazy. Otherwise I was quite confident. I moved easily through the mini-universes that existed at a predominately white public high school in which blacks had a 25-percent toehold. When elections for class officers opened at S. R. Butler High School, then the largest high school in the state, running for freshman class president seemed an obvious step. I relied on my friends in athletics, cheerleading, and honors English to spread my campaign literature and received 509 out of 700 votes with three other opponents—a final vote tally I proudly recorded in my diary. This was an election that was not engineered by my father. Through the family lore and the NDPA, I must have inherited an instinct for political engagement. Without much thought, I entered the race because I felt I was as qualified as anyone else and told my parents about it only after I had won. While Mama was very proud, Daddy took the greatest pleasure in my vote margin. It was at that moment, I believe, that he began to consider the possibility that his daughter might be destined to continue Grandpa Herschel's legacy. To the litany of variations on my nickname that he used, he now added "Senator Poo," dreaming that his daughter might one day be a U.S. senator from what had once been the keystone state of massive resistance. This seed he planted would soon take root. Running for public office would become the central ambition of my twenties.

I wasn't a particularly good class president. Our most notable activity that year was a newspaper recycling drive that netted $95. I must have made some impression, though, because no one ran against me for sophomore class president. I was ambitious, careerist even, when it came to high school. But my drive was also fueled by a fear of falling through the tatters of a shredded safety net.

Like Mama, I learned not to ask questions when Daddy was flush with cash. This was just how my father operated. He would leave town without offering much explanation about where he was going. Only much later did I realize that sometimes his excursions had to do with other women. Other times, he was off trying to make some business partnership happen. Even more often, he was on a political errand. He continued to be fervently involved in politics. Each election cycle brought new hope of blacks gaining more seats in the state legislature, and he never stopped strategizing and working through grass-roots black organizations to expand black political power. He often spoke of reviving the NDPA, but that was not to be.

"Your father's dreams keep him going," Mama once volunteered to me. Throughout the civil rights movement in Huntsville and the NDPA years, she had helped him turn what some viewed as idealistic folly into reality, and she knew that even his most harebrained ideas contained a kernel of possibility. She also knew that he could not live without a cause to champion. That knowledge did not dampen her frustration with our depleted finances, but I think it was part of why she stayed. She too believed in living *for* something, in being useful in the world. She had entered a pact with my father when she married him, and she intended to keep it.

Our financial troubles weighed on me. I wrote in my diary about the "things we need." The series of used cars my father bought were forever breaking down. Our weathered house badly needed a paint job. And my brother John was headed to college in the fall and would need to supplement the wrestling scholarship he received at the University of Alabama. It would take a while before I could articulate how I felt about my family's financial insecurity. Our dramatic reversal felt like a rug had been pulled out from under me, and it must have exacerbated my worst childhood fear. If our existence could change so radically, seemingly overnight, then the people on whom I most depended might cease to exist as well. "Every night before I go to sleep I think what it would be like to have somebody from my family die," I wrote.

I did become resilient about money, or our lack of it. I taught myself to sew and made beautiful sundresses and wrap skirts on Mama's otherwise dormant sewing machine. It didn't take much to look cute. Through sewing and layaway at a dependably cheap store called Lerner's, I could create several outfits from the $30 I occasionally extracted from Mama. At school I worked even harder, knowing that my performance was the only surety I had for the future I longed for. I began to dream of attending an Ivy League college and escaping our impecuniosity. I wanted to "squeeze life" and applied to be an exchange student to Barranquilla, Colombia, then Huntsville's sister city. This seaport on the Caribbean, I learned, was the golden gateway to South America's oldest democracy. I was elated to finally have the chance to live in another country, especially one that would allow me to utilize the foreign language I had been learning at school.

I stepped seamlessly into colorblindness the minute I left the United States in the fall of my sophomore year, becoming a *gringa* (American) rather than a *negra* at Karl C. Parish (KCP), a bilingual school to which affluent families sent their children as a sure route to college in the United States. Living with a kind host family in a high-rise apartment overlooking the Magdalena River, I escaped the worries of home for two months and liked how it felt.

Upon returning home, a week before my sixteenth birthday, I found it difficult to settle back into the racial balkanization at my high school. Context was everything in terms of my relationships. In Spanish Club, I was a Colombiana who organized parties and outings for exchange students and the curious souls who wanted to know them. In Omega Beta Upsilon (OBU), a black sorority, I was a sister-girl. In Math Club, chemistry class, and later physics, I was a girl nerd who cleaved to the few other (white) girls there. The only students who truly transcended race at Butler High seemed to be the army brats that lived on Redstone Arsenal, the military base that helped lead our national race to the moon. Army brats possessed a worldview that the rest of us, observing from the outside, could not completely understand or penetrate without the benefit of growing up in a military family. The only color that seemed to matter to them was army green, and they were the only source of interracial dating that I had observed since the days of my parents' Drek Set parties.

I also found it difficult to return to my parents' house, which seemed rather plain and beleaguered after I had lived among the "beautiful people" in Barranquilla, as I called them. My parents had begun an argument the night I returned, and I mourned the end of my two months of peace. My new friend for life, Nury Gallardo, had invited me to return to Barranquilla for a visit. Taking in the cultural riches of another country had left me starving rather than satiated, and I vowed to get a job so that I would have the funds to escape again.

I must have inherited some of Grandpa Herschel's work ethic and tenacity—the "Fuller Brush" mentality that Uncle Jimmy had foisted on his son Blinny. When my application for employment at Burger King resulted in a paying job, I exulted in my diary about my good fortune, considering myself either "born under a lucky star" or God's special child because I had been given an opportunity to work. Within four months, I had saved $475, every penny of my Burger King earnings. A bank account with a hefty balance became my psychic security blanket. It felt good to watch the numbers build with each paycheck, and as my cushion grew, so did my sense of independence. I began the summer of 1978 with a self-financed trip to visit Nana in Jersey City, which meant I was also headed to New York City. I took the cheapest route available, a Trailways bus ticket. For $88 and the sweat equity of a seemingly interminable, twenty-six-hour ride, I got out of town, with Lee as my fellow traveler, and fed my wanderlust.

I also used my earnings to begin financing my "self-improvement plan." I was not yet sure what I wanted to be, but I was certain that I wanted to get out of my parents' house and that going to college was my exit route. Earning an A in every class wasn't good enough in my estimation. As a rising junior, I committed "to study harder than I ever have in my life," I wrote in my diary, because I needed a scholarship. To that end, I focused on my deficits rather than my successes. Because I was a slow reader, I enrolled in an Evelyn Wood speed-reading course, gladly paying the $400 tuition that neither of my parents could afford. Because I thought my vocabulary was far too limited, I bought a workbook designed to expand it and tried to do more reading than usual that summer. I would leave nothing to chance.

Nana moved to Huntsville after Papa died, introducing a degree of normalcy into our lives because everyone in the family, including me, was on their best behavior in her presence. She also provided me with a quiet place to study. She brought the elegance of her former home to a nondescript two-bedroom apartment, which she decorated in various shades of her favorite color, pink. The chaise longue in her bedroom became my study spot. It was turquoise, her second-favorite color. And it vibrated, complete with controls for elevating one's feet or heating one's back. Her bedroom, like the rest of the apartment, exuded calm and order. There was no clutter in her space. Unlike my father, who had trouble throwing out a newspaper, Nana was not a Depression baby. She was born in 1908 and had seen America's abundance as a child. She didn't feel the need to hold onto every material shred.

Nana epitomized class. She enunciated her words like Audrey Hepburn and reminded me of the actress's exquisiteness, although most people who didn't know Nana did not realize that she was black. She wore the pale skin of her grandmother, a white German who immigrated to New York City, became a laundress to a wealthy family, and married its coachman, a black man. Nana would take umbrage at the notion that she appeared to be anything but a Negro, the label she felt most comfortable using for herself and her people. "Black" had been a pejorative to a generation that had started out in the world as "colored." By the time she had become comfortable with that word, the next generation had begun to propagate a new double-barreled moniker, African American, that was supposed to connect us to our lost roots. On Nana's side of the family, it was always said that it was the German in us that asserted a need for order. And I must have felt that on the occasions when I would retreat to Nana's hearth to get it.

As I entered my junior year in high school, Nana's positive aura seemed to be lifting everyone's spirits, especially mine. One of Dad's unexplained deals came through. He was "back in the money and everything seems to be looking up," I wrote in my diary. November 1978 brought the first gubernatorial election in twenty years in which no one named Wallace was on the ticket. Dad was excited about the possibility of blacks making more political inroads. He viewed the state legislature as his own private chessboard, chess being a game he had mastered and loved. He began to envision a campaign to bring the descendants of the Great Migration back to an Alabama that was moving slowly into the future. If these reverse-migrants responded to his "Homecoming" message and agreed to settle in districts in which a black person had a chance of winning, blacks could gain a majority in the legislature and earn the respect of the nation, he theorized. While he was strategizing about the future of *Africanus Alabamus*,

I was worrying about mine, and struggling with dissonant feelings toward my father.

He was plagued by bad headaches and vague ailments and was always threatening to die, sometimes with a morose tone and grand gestures designed to evoke maximum sympathy, especially from me, though this was more often done in jest. "You're going to miss me when I'm gone," he would say. *Yes,* I always thought, *I will—terribly.* It was a frequent riff he would hurl at me, Mama, or whoever might be giving him grief at a given moment.

Just once he told me he was contemplating suicide. We were sitting in our junky family room, my brother Carroll in a chair close to the television so that he could hear it well and I on a daybed on which Mama usually flopped each evening to vegetate before the television and forget her cares. Dad sat down next to me and talked quietly. It was a rare moment in which he seemed utterly defeated, by his reversal of fortune and a depression that may have been clinical. "I should just go on and kill myself," he said. There it was, my worst fear. I immediately began to cry and begged him not to do it, telling him I didn't know how I could live without him. Had I known he would still be alive thirty years later, I would not have succumbed so easily to his melodrama. At the time, I was not sure he meant it. But the specter of losing him was enough for me to extract a promise that he would not die by his own hand. I knew how seriously he took his promises and was comforted by his assurance.

Even without his talk of dying, I could see that he was hurting. He had been fighting for one cause or another most of his adult life and had given, and given, and given again to other people. Now his world had come crashing down and he felt unrecognized and unappreciated for what he had done. I knew my father needed my love and understanding and yet I felt hostile and angry with him, especially when he and my mother fought. Sometimes Mama exacerbated their tensions by reminding him of his mistakes, opening up old baggage that they had supposedly put away with their last reconciliation. He was worse, though, I judged in my diary. He didn't know how to defuse his anger and he turned his lacerating tongue, and sometimes his hand, on my mother when she challenged him. I could no longer compartmentalize my feelings about him. At some point, all teenagers begin to judge their parents' faults and rebel against them, and I was no different. It wasn't only his treatment of my mother that incensed me. I was terrified about how and whether I would be able to pay for college, and I resented the fact that he had not put aside some of his treasure for my education. Years would pass before I learned the full extent of his contributions to his causes and his misplaced trust in others. What little I did know made me seethe, even as I was proud of him and Mama for what they had done as activists. Dad exacerbated my anger by calling me his "old age insurance." *You didn't hold up your end of the bargain,* I thought. Increasingly, I viewed his commitments, to the Black Muslims, to E. D. Nixon, even to changing Alabama, as a form of betrayal because, it seemed, he had put his causes before his family. Now that seems like a childish, self-centered way of thinking. After years of digging for the truth about the lore and spending many hours interviewing my father, I have come to understand that his obsessions were imperatives he could not ignore, lest he cease being who he was. In searching for the truth, I would lose my anger and understand that he had fulfilled his destiny and that his altruism came from a positive, not a negative, place in his heart.

As a teenager, though, I vacillated between loyalty and rebellion, love and anger, sometimes in the same instant. I needed an outlet for my feelings, and for the time being that outlet was my diary. Hugs were therapeutic for Daddy, and he began to extract them from me when I no longer offered them voluntarily. I began to bristle at his bear hugs, enduring them but feeling a need to push him away. In moments when I needed him, though, it felt good to know that my father would always be in my corner. Mama never begrudged the closeness between her husband and her daughter, probably because my parents' romance was genuine, if tempestuous, and because there was an easiness between Mama and me.

Worrying about how to pay for college and how long my father would live contributed mightily to a weightiness I carried with me. On a night when I was exhausted by my job, my self-imposed pressure to succeed, and my fears about college, Daddy called me to him and I did something that I hadn't done in a long while. I sat on his lap and allowed myself to relax into his chest. When I began to tell him about my worries, I broke down and cried. As he had when I was his little girl, he made me feel much better. "Don't worry about it, Pooskie, I will find the money some kind of way," he said. Intellectually, I knew that I could not depend on him financially. Instead, I allowed myself to depend on him emotionally, and my father's infinite love always felt good. I told him that I was considering applying to Vanderbilt University in Nashville. He thought Vanderbilt was a good choice because it was the best school in the region—"the Harvard of the South," its alumni called it. And he liked the idea that I would be attending college nearby, in the same town he had conquered as a collegian and graduate student. He also thought it was important for me to imbibe a black culture, and I could experience some of that in the city where his three alma maters—Fisk, Tennessee State, and Meharry—were located.

Mama wanted me to consider applying to a historically black college. Unlike Daddy, she rarely attempted to press her views upon me. She was a laissez-faire parent who was content to leave her children to their own devices when it came to figuring out how to be in the world. On this subject, though, she was adamant. I could go anywhere for graduate school, she argued. College was the place where lifetime bonds were formed, where you made friends who stuck with you through every crisis.

I knew she was referring to Peggy, her roommate at Fisk. They had arrived on campus at the same time and had roomed together for five years. Like most Fiskites, Peggy had done well. She became a medical doctor and, after a divorce, raised a fine son who also became a physician. Mama did not share her pain with outsiders. At some point, I became the person she turned to on those rare occasions when she needed to unload about the stresses in her life. But Peggy was next in line. I appreciated the depth of their friendship because I had a similar relationship with Lee. Perhaps it had taken living on Lydia Drive, in a thoroughly black neighborhood, for me to form such a bond. Still, I was not convinced that the black world was the only context in which to make lifelong friends. I could not appreciate Mama's logic, or her nostalgia for Fisk. She wanted me to have "the black experience," and yet she and Daddy had done too good a job of integrating Huntsville's schools and other realms and raising us to believe we deserved to be there. After more than a decade of attending racially mixed schools, I lacked the ability to comprehend the benefits of attending a predominately black institution. I was ranked first in a majority-white class of 589 students. There was no question that I could compete with whites, and I was inclined to continue to do so because I was supremely ambitious and wanted to pursue the best educational opportunities available to me. In my dreams, I was headed to Princeton, maybe to study history or literature.

I had also begun to think that I wanted to become a lawyer. The lore had influenced me. I had heard my father say repeatedly that Grandpa Herschel was "the first black lawyer in the state of Alabama," and I had heard him say many times that he should have been a lawyer rather than his brother. My motivations differed from those of my father, though. He thought that he would have been better equipped to "finish Grandpa Herschel's job" as an attorney rather than as a dentist. My immediate motivation was to escape. International law appealed to me, simply because I had traveled abroad and wanted to do more of it. Law seemed like an exciting profession, one that I was capable of entering because my great-grandfather had done it at a time when racial oppression was the norm for most black people. My emotional inheritance had vested me with a great deal of family pride and a sense of obligation to make a contribution. For the time being, however, my fears suppressed my idealism. My instinct, borne of my father's unreimbursed altruism, was to save myself before saving the world.

I had been planning my college application since freshman year. On a crowded bulletin board in my bedroom, above a more crowded desk, I kept a roster of my honors and activities. The list assuaged my worries to a degree about how to pay for college. It was a security blanket that made me feel in control of my destiny. I would look it over often, thinking strategically about what other club to join and what office to run for to improve my chances for a scholarship. In my diary I kept a running account of my grades: "an A+ semester average in every class except Nobel Prize [on laureate writers], which was a 96," one point short, I groused, at the end of my junior year.

That summer I headed to Tuskegee Institute for the Minority Introduction to Engineering (MITE) program. My great friend Felicia Gardner led me to it. She was preparing to enter her freshman year at Tuskegee and was working on the campus. Her father was an aeronautical engineer who made "good money," and she was following in his footsteps by studying electrical engineering. When I told her of my desire to become a lawyer, she challenged me with the question, "Who pays a black lawyer?" Unwittingly, she had found my weak spot. I didn't have an immediate answer and it scared me. Felicia equaled or exceeded me in brassiness. Her forcefully articulated opinions about black lawyers who starved while waiting for their deprived clients to pay exacerbated my phobias about money, or our lack of it. I began to retreat from my dreams.

Had I reflected on what I did know about black lawyers, or discussed it with my father, I would have been comforted. There was Orzell Billingsley, whom I hadn't seen in years. Even as a "justice" lawyer he seemed to do reasonably well, or at least be able to live on his terms. And Uncle Jimmy, who had made a fortune as a lawyer and businessman in Chicago. Uncle Herschel, Dad's brother, had also made a decent living as a solo practitioner, adequately providing for five children.

And there was Grandpa Herschel, although Dad's mythology about him did not convey much about his life as an attorney. The family lore was an impetus for my interest in law, but it did not help me overcome my insecurities. It also hadn't helped that my high school counselor had not encouraged me when I spoke of going to Princeton. She was a nice woman, but she was not accustomed to her charges reaching so far beyond the universe of north Alabama and its public institutions.

My fears were not entirely irrational; they were borne of our great economic reversal. I watched what happened when my brother John called home to ask Dad for money for tuition or textbooks when the University of Alabama terminated its wrestling program. My parents gave him what they could, but it wasn't always enough to cover these expenses. I would not leave myself vulnerable to the vicissitudes of my parents' lives. Fear got me up in the morning. It motivated me to go from a grueling volleyball practice to an eight-hour shift at Burger King and then stay up until 4:00 AM to finish a research paper. Depending on myself became the way I attacked life. Even relying on God seemed precarious. I craved certainty and it made sense to explore engineering. It was a familiar profession in Huntsville, the Rocket City, and I had always excelled at quantitative reasoning. Scholarships designed to entice minorities into technical careers were abundant. Scholarships to study history were not. At Tuskegee, I was seduced by what I learned about starting salaries for engineers.

That summer I was also enrolled in a pre-calculus class at the University of Alabama at Huntsville. The same university that denied Mama entrance to an extension course seventeen years before had admitted me as a high school student. Again I paid for the course with my fast-food wages. It was part of my plan to raise my math score on the ACT and SAT as well as prepare me for the advanced mathematics class I'd be facing as a senior. I was heartened to learn that I could compete with college students. Ultimately I earned an A in that class, too.

While fear motivated me, my inherited work ethic sustained me. Daddy didn't have the resources to pay for my education, or to ease my path into adulthood. But he had given me everything I needed to succeed. His abundant, unconditional love had instilled a confidence that propelled me. And he had given me the lore. One of the most important lessons I had internalized from his many stories was that a Cashin persevered. If a test required six, eight, or even ten hours of study, I did it.

As I entered the fall of my senior year, again I brought that intensity of purpose to my classes and my college applications. I settled on Princeton, Vanderbilt, and Washington University in St. Louis, applying to engineering programs at each school. In our school counselor's office, I scoured the reference books looking for scholarships. My parents continued their episodic battles, and my anger with my father was intensifying. It was not lost on me that both Mama and I were working and he was not. On occasion I even lent my father money, usually to cover an exorbitant telephone bill that he ran up talking to anybody who would listen about his ideas for the next election cycle. He always paid me back, with interest, and laughingly called me cheap. Although I had no trouble spending $600 for a return trip to visit Nury in Barranquilla over the Christmas holiday, I did hoard my earnings with an embarrassing stinginess that I would overcome only after earning a few degrees and finally feeling that I had an inviolable economic foundation.

In the meantime, I voiced my frustration in my diary about why my father wouldn't "go out and earn money the same way everyone else does." He claimed that he could not work because of the IRS. I didn't know enough about it to know whether this was true or an excuse. In retrospect, I think a confluence of forces kept him at home. He had once reaped more than $500,000 from a stock deal, and he was looking to make a similarly big score that would place him back on the kind of financial footing he had once enjoyed. He had never worked for anyone but himself and therefore becoming someone's employee was beyond his imagination. And he didn't return to dentistry because he didn't want to, and he lacked the resources to open a new dental office. A deal that would "make us millionaires" was always looming but never materialized.

On New Year's Day 1980, Mama and Daddy had another blowout. Holidays were always fraught with peril, except when Nana was around. The revelry could lead to reminiscing and drinking and an errant statement by one or the other of them about what had once been, and then the recriminations would begin. On this occasion the fight was about who really owned our house on Lydia. He had built it and paid for it. She now had title to it. Perhaps he wanted to mortgage it to finance one of his deals. Whatever the source of the argument, my father had entered what I viewed as the danger zone, and his rage was uncontrollable. I sided with Mama. "You don't own this house," I shouted at him. He could not accept this direct challenge from his daughter or his wife. For the first and last time, he turned "the violence" on me, slapping me hard across the face. His ugliness hurt as much as the sting. I ran out of the house in my bare feet, down to the Hereford's house, and sat on their garage steps for a long time before I rang the bell. In the cold of winter, my feet had begun to turn blue. I could not bear to return home and decided I would rather face the embarrassment of exposing my family's dirty laundry to the Herefords. Lee's older sister, Kim, answered the door. Fortunately, her parents were out of town and no one else was there to see me in this state. I was crying uncontrollably, but Kim calmed me down, never once asking me to explain what had happened. We talked about other things and soon I was laughing. By the time I returned home in borrowed shoes, my parents had entered another temporary truce. Ever the peacemaker, Mama had agreed to sign a paper stating that he owned half of the house and this had assuaged his pride.

At some point a child declares independence from a parent and this was my moment. It reinforced my resolve to escape. Henceforth, I would keep my opinions about their madness to myself. "They can kill themselves if they want to—but they're not going to take me with them," I wrote of my parents' fights. I also vowed that upon leaving for college I would never return to stay in their home for more than a few weeks, and I kept that vow, filling every summer with a job in another city until I completed my education. I never stopped loving my father, but I needed some distance, both physical and emotional, from him. Daddy's love was like the sun. The warmth of it felt good, but if you tarried too long under its intensity eventually you would burn.

After he struck me, Dad broke my silent treatment of him with a gift of a beautiful Princess telephone, ostensibly for the good grades I received on my latest report card. Like all my previous reports, this one was filled with A's, but this was the first time I had ever been rewarded with a gift, other than the nickels Grandma Grace had given me when I was in elementary school. Like Mama, I could not stay mad at my father, and the Democratic presidential primary season soon gave us a project to work on together.

We did not have many regular family rituals. Initiation to voting was one of them. As he did with my brothers, my father took me to register to vote on the day I turned eighteen. He was uncharacteristically quiet as he drove me to the county courthouse. "We need your vote," was all he said. The collective "we" meant Democrats, state and national. The NDPA was dead. Daddy's obsession with politics was as fiercely alive as ever. The Alabama Democratic Party was no longer the enemy. Instead, he reserved his ire for "those damned Republicans," his epithet for the party that was emerging as a force throughout Alabama and the South.

In the solemn act of accompanying me to register and take my place as a fully engaged citizen, he conveyed a powerful message. Voting was both a sacred act and an utmost responsibility. Dad's passion conveyed the impression that my vote truly mattered and that I had the power to change the course of an election. I wanted my classmates to feel the same way and convinced my fellow Student Government Association officers to sponsor a voter registration drive at Butler.

The Alabama Democratic Party had adopted rules to create the kind of delegation to the upcoming Democratic National Convention that the NDPA had offered in 1968 and 1972—one in which women, men, minorities, and youth were represented in critical numbers. The party approached my parents about campaigning to become delegates, and together they hatched the idea that their daughter should run instead. The idea excited them. As parents of one of the youngest elected delegates to the convention, they could send a message to Alabama and the Democratic National Committee that they were still agents of change. Local Democratic operatives were also delighted at the prospect of engaging a new generation of voters. Dad immediately began to strategize for my campaign. His daughter would receive the most votes among delegates from north Alabama, he pledged, while I pledged my allegiance to Jimmy Carter on my candidate declaration. I was running for myself, not my father. The family lore had become my lore and I was eager to get involved in politics because, as with excelling at academics, it seemed this was what I was supposed to do. I did not know then that I was about to become the third generation of Cashins to join an Alabama delegation to a national political convention. The road to these conventions had been rocky for Grandpa Herschel and my parents. Now I was being courted and encouraged by a new, inclusive Democratic party that my parents and their compatriots had forced to reform.

My father was my campaign manager and stage parent that spring. He engineered television coverage of our voter registration drive, and Mama delighted in watching her daughter explain, at first timidly and then more forcefully, that young people would care about elections once candidates began to speak directly to them. Dad also arranged for me to speak at Alabama A&M and Oakwood College and to appear on a locally televised talk show. At each appearance, he counseled me to be more assertive and to say things that I would not choose to say. My father was too confrontational and often controversial in his edicts, I thought. At A&M he followed me with a few comments of his own and I was appalled when I heard him for the first time refer to himself as a "black supremacist." I bristled at the divisiveness of the term, even though I knew he was trying to boost the students' race pride, and make them believe, as he had always told me, that they could do *anything* they set their minds to.

My last campaign appearance was in a crowded auditorium at Oakwood, the same place where Dr. King had spoken to rejuvenate Huntsville's sit-in movement. I shared the stage with Robert Kennedy Jr. He was there to speak on behalf of his uncle, Edward, who was challenging Carter for president. My father prevailed upon university officials to put me on the program for five minutes right before Kennedy, the main event. My right leg shook uncontrollably as I approached the podium to speak to the largest audience I had ever faced, a sea of mostly black faces that seemed to number in the thousands.

"Good evening. My name is Sheryll Cashin. I am a native Huntsvillian and a senior at Butler High School. I am eighteen years old and I am running to be a delegate pledged to Jimmy Carter!" I exulted. The crowd erupted with applause and smiles, clearly pleased to encourage a youthful upstart. The applause continued as I explained my support for Carter. I don't remember what else I said, only that I spoke through barely suppressed nervousness. Upon sitting down, overcome with adrenaline, I watched Bobby Jr.'s worn black cowboy boots move him to the lectern and then raised my eyes as he expertly roused the crowd with an oratorical skill he clearly had inherited from his father. He invoked my name several times, vowing that ultimately Sheryll Cashin would be voting for Ted Kennedy because he would give life to the aspirations of my generation. I was not swayed, but I hoped that one day I could mount and ride words the way he did.

March 11, 1980, was primary day. The weekend before, my OBU sisters and I had papered all the cars at the local mall with flyers my father had printed about my candidacy. The night before I had prayed to God that I would be elected. I knew that ultimately I could be appointed a delegate through party diversity rules and the strings Dad could pull. But winning at the ballot box was what most mattered to me. I wanted to prove to the world (and myself) that I could win an election.

Wanting to savor the import of voting on my own, I drove myself to the polls. As I entered the booth, I looked for the Alabama Democratic Party. The white rooster was still its symbol. Directly under the bird, I pulled the lever beside Jimmy Carter's name, not realizing how much my parents had fought for this simple privilege. Then I scanned the list of candidates for delegate and found my name in small black letters. As I pulled the lever I laughed excitedly. I had voted for the first time, and I had voted for myself.

NOTES

CHAPTER 7

1. General John A. Logan's biography offers several clues as to why my great-grandfather might have named a son after him. A native of Illinois, Logan was a member of Congress and a premier volunteer general in the Civil War who helped turn southern Illinois from secessionist leanings to strongly pro-Union. He also served as a U.S. senator and an unsuccessful vice-presidential candidate on the Republican ticket in 1884. (The head of the 1884 Republican ticket was James G. Blaine, Uncle Jimmy's namesake.) Above all, Logan, like my great-grandfather, was a passionate, radical Republican partisan and an instrumental advocate for public education.

2. In a storied career full of accomplishments, one item in James Blaine's dossier suggests why Herschel was so enamored as to name a son after him. Although Blaine had served as Speaker of the House, U.S. senator, secretary of state, and unsuccessful Republican presidential nominee from Maine, Herschel would have been most appreciative of Blaine's advocacy during Reconstruction. As a member of Congress in that era, he advocated aggressively for impartial suffrage and was the primary proponent of the Fourteenth Amendment to the U.S. Constitution. Herschel could thank Blaine for the provision that reversed the *Dred Scott* edict that Negroes were not entitled to full citizenship.

CHAPTER 12

1. The Lowndes County Freedom Organization (LCFO) became known as "the Black Panther Party" because its founders chose a black panther as their ballot symbol. It was distinct from the organization Huey P. Newton and Bobby Seale started in Oakland, California, and possibly more important in terms of the seed its founders planted. Inspired by the Mississippi Freedom Democratic Party, which had actually been a political caucus without official ballot position, the LCFO was a genuine political party that fielded a roster of candidates in November 1966 in Lowndes County.

SOURCES

Memory is elusive, and my memories are episodic and sometimes vague. Had I not kept a diary from age eight to twenty-six, I could not have written this book. I also could not have written it without the benefit of my father's memories and those of other family members and friends who shared their recollections with me. In addition to my own memories, this book is supported by the sources listed below.

CHAPTER 2

Cashin Jr., Dr. John L. ("Daddy" or "Dad"). Interviews by the author, August 17, 1999, and November 15, 2005. On file with the author.

CHAPTER 3

J. Mitchell Brown conducted archival research in Georgia, and Kenneth W. Milano conducted archival research in Philadelphia. In addition to archival documents referenced in the text, this chapter is supported by the following sources:

Cashin, Edward J. *The Story of Augusta.* Augusta, GA: Richmond County Board of Education, 1980.
_____. *Old Springfield: Race and Religion in Augusta, Georgia.* Augusta, GA: Springfield Village Park Foundation, 1995.
Johnson, Whittington B. "Free Blacks in Antebellum Augusta, Georgia: A Demographic and Economic Profile." *Richmond County History* 14:1 (Winter 1982).
Leonardo Andrea Collection. Pages pertaining to the Cashin family of Richmond County, GA. Available at the Thomasville Genealogical, History & Fine Arts Library, Inc., Thomasville, Georgia.
Williamson, Joel. *New People: Miscegenation and Mulattoes in the United States.* Baton Rouge: Louisiana State University Press, 1995.

CHAPTER 4

Along with conducting archival research in Philadelphia, Kenneth W. Milano provided the author with a private tour of Historic African-American Philadelphia on March 17, 2006. In addition to archival documents referenced in the text, this chapter is supported by the following sources:

"Annual Report of the Managers of the Institute for Colored Youth." *Christian Recorder*, October 8, 1864.

Catto, Octavius V. "Our Alma Mater: An Address Delivered at Concert Hall on the Occasion of the Twelfth Annual Commencement of the Institute for Colored Youth, May 10th, 1864." Available at http://www.afrolumens.org/rising_free/waskie2.html, last visited May 19, 2006.

"The Dedication of the Institute for Colored Youth." *Christian Recorder*, March 17, 1866.

Douglass, Frederick. *Life and Times of Frederick Douglass.* In *Frederick Douglass Autobiographies.* New York: Library of America, 1994.

DuBois, W.E.B. *The Philadelphia Negro, A Social Study.* Philadelphia: University of Pennsylvania Press, 1996, originally published 1899. Relevant excerpt available at http://www2.pfeiffer.edu/~lridener/DSS/DuBois/pnchiv.html, last visited May 20, 2006.

"John Pendleton King History." Available at http://www.augustaga.gov/departments/trees_landscaping/pendleton_history.asp, last visited May 20, 2006.

Lane, Roger. *William Dorsey's Philadelphia & Ours: On the Past and Future of the Black City in America.* Oxford: Oxford University Press, 1991.

Objects of the Institute for Colored Youth, With a List of The Officers and Students and the Annual Report of the Board of Managers, For the Year 1864. Philadelphia: Sherman & Co., Printers, 1864.

Pizzulo, Karen, and Vincent Pizzulo. Interview by the author and tour of the home of these residents of historic Clifton Street, Philadelphia, March 17, 2006.

Waskie, Andy. "Biography of Octavius V. Catto: 'Forgotten Black Hero of Philadelphia.'" Available at http://www.afrolumens.org/rising_free/waskie1.html, last visited April 27, 2006.

CHAPTER 5

J. Mitchell Brown conducted archival research in Georgia and Alabama, and Kenneth W. Milano conducted archival research in Philadelphia. In addition to archival documents referenced in the text, this chapter is supported by the following sources:

Bailey, Richard. *Neither Carpetbaggers Nor Scalawags: Black Officeholders During the Reconstruction of Alabama, 1867–1878.* Montgomery, AL: Richard Bailey Publishers, 1995.

DuBois, W.E.B. *Black Reconstruction.* Millwood, NY: Kraus-Thomson Organization Ltd., 1976.

Foner, Eric. *A Short History of Reconstruction, 1863–1877.* New York: Harper & Row, 1990.

Journal of the House of Representatives of the State of Alabama, Session of 1874–75. Montgomery, AL: Barrett & Brown, 1875.

Journal of the House of Representatives of the State of Alabama, Session of 1876–77. Montgomery, AL: Barrett & Brown, 1877.

Lacey, Marguerite Dobbins. "The Social, Economic and Political Life of the Negro in Madison County from 1880–1900." Master's thesis, August 1963. On file in the local history archives of the Huntsville Public Library.

Manning, C. Max. "Colored Lawyer in Montgomery Ala." *Christian Recorder*, February 28, 1878.

Walton Jr., Hanes. *Black Republicans: The Politics of the Black and Tans.* Metuchen, NJ: Scarecrow Press, 1975.

Williamson, Joel. *New People: Miscegenation and Mulattoes in the United States.* Baton Rouge: Louisiana State University Press, 1995.

CHAPTER 6

J. Mitchell Brown conducted archival research in Alabama, and Kenneth W. Milano conducted archival research in Philadelphia. In addition to archival documents referenced in the text, this chapter is supported by the following sources:

"Alabama, A Call for a Masonic Convention." *Christian Recorder*, August 1, 1878.

Bailey, Richard. *Neither Carpetbaggers Nor Scalawags, Black Officeholders During the Reconstruction of Alabama, 1867–1878.* Montgomery, AL: Richard Bailey Publishers, 1995.

Banks, Athelyne. Interview by the author, November 8, 2005. On file with the author.

Booker T. Washington Papers. Vol. 2, 1860–1889. Quoting Horace Mann Bond, *Negro Education in Alabama: A Study in Cotton and Steel.* Washington, DC: Associated Publishers, 1939. And quoting August Meier, *Negro Thought in America: Racial Ideologies in the Age of Booker T. Washington, 1880–1915.* Ann Arbor, MI: University of Michigan Press, 1963. Excerpts available at http://www.historycooperative.org/btw/Vol.2/html/308.html, last visited June 19, 2006.

Cashin, Herschel V., et al. *Under Fire with the Tenth U.S. Calvary.* Niwot: University of Colorado Press, 1993; originally published London, New York: F.T. Neeley, 1899.

The Colored American Republican Text Book: A book of Facts and Figures, showing what the Republican Party has done for the Afro-American. Washington, D.C.: Colored American Publishing Company, 1899. Available at http://dbs.ohiohistory.org/africanam/sample/pamphlets.cfm, last visited June 20, 2006.

Douglass, Frederick. *Life and Times of Frederick Douglass.* In *Frederick Douglass Autobiographies.* New York: Library of America, 1994.

Flynt, Wayne. "A Tragic Century: The Aftermath of the 1901 Constitution." In Thomson Bailey, ed., *A Century of Controversy: Constitutional Reforms in Alabama.* Tuscaloosa: University of Alabama Press, 2002, relying on data from the Alabama Official and Statistical Register.

Franklin, John Hope, and Alfred A. Moss Jr. *From Slavery to Freedom: A History of African Americans.* New York: Alfred A. Knopf, 2004.

Jenkins, William, and John Knox. *The Story of Decatur.* Decatur, AL: Mayor and City Council of Decatur, 1970.

Lacey, Marguerite Dobbins. "The Social, Economic and Political Life of the Negro in Madison County from 1880–1900." Master's thesis, August 1963. On file in the local history archives of the Huntsville Public Library.

"Land Office to Close, Orders From Washington to Abolish Huntsville Office." *Morning Mercury*, January 4, 1905.

McDaniel, Deangelo, and Martin Burkey. "Pair of Decatur Pillars Fall; Educator Athelyne Banks Dies at 98." *Decatur Daily News,* online edition. Available at http://www.decaturdaily.com/decaturdaily/news/060208/banks.shtml, last visited August 3, 2007.

Official Proceedings of the Constitutional Convention of the State of Alabama, May 21st, 1901, to September 3rd, 1901, vol. 1. Wetumpka, AL: Wetumpka Printing Co., 1940.

"Radicals Split." *Atlanta Constitution*, April 29, 1892.

"Receiver H.V. Cashin, Retires From Office and Will Practice Law at Decatur." *Morning Mercury*, January 8, 1905. Also printed in the *Huntsville Weekly Democrat,* January 11, 1905.

"Report of the Proceedings of the Convention of Colored Masons National and Independent Held in the City of Wilmington, Del., May 8th, 9th, and 10th, 1878." *Christian Recorder*, May 23, 1878.

Smith, Michael David. Interview by the author with this north Alabama historian, December 9, 2005. On file with the author.

"To the Members of the Alabama Constitutional Convention." Alabama Secretary of State Constitutional Convention Proceedings, SG17778, Alabama Department of Archives and History, Montgomery, Alabama. Available at http://www.archives.state.al.us/teacher/ccon/lesson3/doc2.html, last visited June 19, 2006.

Walton Jr., Hanes. *Black Republicans: The Politics of the Black and Tans.* Metuchen, NJ: Scarecrow Press, 1975.

Williamson, Joel. *New People: Miscegenation and Mulattoes in the United States.* Baton Rouge: Louisiana State University Press, 1995.

CHAPTER 7

J. Mitchell Brown conducted archival research in Alabama, and Telette Roberts conducted archival research in Decatur, Alabama. In addition to archival documents referenced in the text, this chapter is supported by the following sources:

Bailey, Richard. *Neither Carpetbaggers Nor Scalawags, Black Officeholders During the Reconstruction of Alabama, 1867–1878.* Montgomery, AL: Richard Bailey Publishers, 1995.

Booker T. Washington Papers. Vol. 6, 1901–1902; Vol. 7, 1903–1904. Available at http://www .historycooperative.org/btw/Vol.6/html/371.html, last visited August 9, 2007.

Carter, Dan T. *Scottsboro: A Tragedy of the American South.* Baton Rouge: Lousisiana State University Press, 1969.

Cashin Jr., Dr. John Logan. Interviews with the author, November 17, 2005, and March 10, 2006. On file with the author.

Cashin Jr., James Blaine ("Blinny"). Interview by the author, March 16, 2006. On file with the author.

Daniell, F. Raymond. "Negro Defense Gets Test of Juror List; Judge in Scottsboro Case Grants Right to Inspect Roll for Racial Bar." *New York Times*, March 31, 1933.

DuBois, W.E.B. *The Souls of Black Folk.* New York: Penguin Books, 1996; originally published Chicago: A. C. McClurg and Co., 1903.

"Land Office to Close, Orders From Washington to Abolish Huntsville Office." *Morning Mercury*, January 4, 1905.

McMillen, Elizabeth Cashin ("Betty-V"). Interview by the author, March 6, 2006, and subsequent e-mail correspondence. On file with the author.

"Negro Attorney to Be Buried Thursday." *Albany-Decatur Daily*, March 27, 1924.

Norris v. Alabama, 294 U.S. 587, 597 (1934).

"Receiver H.V. Cashin, Retires From Office and Will Practice Law at Decatur." *Morning Mercury*, January 8, 1905. Aalso printed in *Huntsville Weekly Democrat*, January 11, 1905.

Walton Jr., Hanes. *Black Republicans: The Politics of the Black and Tans.* Metuchen, NJ: Scarecrow Press, 1975.

Wedding invitation of Minnie Vivian Cashin and Carroll Napier Langston, July 31, 1906. On file with the author.

Wesley, Charles H. *History of Sigma Pi Phi: First of the Negro-American Greek-Letter Fraternities.* Washington, D.C.: The Association for the Study of Negro Life and History, 1954.

CHAPTER 8

Cashin Jr., Dr. John L. Interviews by the author, August 5, 1999, August 17, 1999, August 29, 1999, November 17, 2005, December 9, 2005, and January 5, 2008. On file with the author.

Holloway, Mrs. Velma. Interview by the author of this Lydia Drive resident and former schoolteacher, March 10, 2006. On file with the author.

CHAPTER 9

Cashin Jr., Dr. John L. Interviews by the author, August 29, 1999, July 9, 2005, November 15, 2005, and January 5, 2008. On file with the author.

CHAPTER 10

Cashin, Joan Carpenter. Interview by Dale James, *Huntsville Times* reporter, January 30, 1995. On file with the author.

Cashin, Joan Carpenter, memo, April 21, 1962 (describing her arrest with her baby daughter and subsequent jailing). On file with the author.

Cashin Jr., Dr. John L. Interviews by the author, November 17, 2005, and January 5, 2008. On file with the author.

Cashin Jr., Dr. John L. Interview by Dale James, *Huntsville Times* reporter, January 30, 1995. On file with the author.

Cashin Jr., Dr. John L. Interview by Hardy T. Frye, conducted in 1972. On file in the Hardy T. Frye Oral History Collection, Auburn University.

A Civil Rights Journey: A History of Huntsville's Civil Rights Movement as Seen Through the Eyes of Sonnie Hereford, III, M.D. Documentary film produced by Dr. Hereford and Calhoun Community College, Waymon E. Burke, executive producer.

"Dr. Carpenter's Daughter Held in Sit-In Case." *Hudson Dispatch*, April 13, 1962.

"Free Pregnant Alabama Sit-In Without Bail." *Jet*, April 26, 1962.

"Freedom Is a Family Affair." *Southern Patriot*, March 1963.

Hereford III, Dr. and Mrs. Sonnie Hereford. Interview by the author, December 9, 2005. On file with the author.

"It's Time to Call a Halt." Editorial. *Huntsville Times*, January 9, 1962.

"Marc Carpenter's Daughter Arrested at Ala. 'Sit-In.'" *New Jersey Herald News*, April 28, 1962.

Morgan Jr., Charles. *A Time to Speak.* New York: Holt, Rinehart and Winston, 1964.

"Trio of Negroes Choose the Jail Instead of Bail." *Huntsville Times*, April 26, 1962.

"White Man Beaten, Doused with Chemical." *Birmingham News*, January 23, 1962.

CHAPTER 11

"Arch Timeline." Compiled by the *Post-Dispatch* Reference Department. Available at http://www.stltoday.com, last visited January 18, 2006.

Cashin Jr., Dr. John L. Interviews by the author, February 3, 2006, March 10, 2006, and January 23, 2008. On file with the author.

"Cashin's Race Gets Clocking of 97 M.P.H." *Montgomery Advertiser*, September 1, 1970.

Copeland, Myrna. Interviews by the author, March 12, 2006, March 19, 2006, and January 25, 2008. On file with the author.

Freeman, Roland L. *The Mule Train: A Journey of Hope Remembered.* Nashville, TN: Rutledge Hill Press, 1998. Including 1968 interviews with Joan Cashin and Myrna Copeland, and a 1998 interview with John Cashin.

CHAPTER 12

Borenstein, Audrey. *Chimes of Change and Hours: Views of Older Women in Twentieth Century America.* Cranbury, NJ: Associated University Presses, 1983. Featuring an interview with Sallie Mae Hadnott.

Branch, Reverend William. Interview by the author, February 13, 2006. On file with the author.

Branch, William. Interview by Hardy T. Frye, conducted in 1972. On file in the Hardy T. Frye Oral History Collection, Auburn University.

Cashin Jr., Dr. John L. Interview by Hardy T. Frye, conducted in 1972. On file in the Hardy T. Frye Oral History Collection, Auburn University.

Cashin Jr., Dr. John L. Interviews by the author, February 1–3, 2006, January 5, 2008, and January 23, 2008. On file with the author.

Cashin Jr., Dr. John L. "Unrecognized Heroics in Alabama: The Hadnott v. Amos Story, Part I." *Speakin' Out News*, May 29–June 4, 1991.

Cashin Jr., Dr. John L. "Unrecognized Heroics II: Sallie Hadnott / Fannie Lou Hamer." *Speakin' Out News*, June 5–11, 1991.

Cashin Jr., Dr. John L. "Unrecognized Heroics III: The Greene County Special Election." *Speakin' Out News*, June 12–18, 1991.

Copeland, Myrna. Interviews by the author, March 12, 2006, March 19, 2006, and January 23, 2008. On file with the author.

Douglas, Carlyle C. "Black Politics in the New South: Emerging Black-Dominated Third Party Movements May Prove More Effective Than Dixie Versions of 'Liberal' Coalition." *Ebony Magazine*, January 1971.

Durr, Virginia. Interview by Hardy T. Frye, conducted in 1972. On file in the Hardy T. Frye Oral History Collection, Auburn University.

Edwards, Bill. Interview by the author, January 7, 2006. On file with the author.

Frye, Hardy T. *Black Parties and Political Power: A Case Study*. Boston: G.K. Hall & Co., 1980.

Frye, Hardy T. Interviews by the author, February 27, 2006, and February 1, 2007. On file with the author.

Gilmore, Reverend Thomas. Interviews by the author, February 14, 2006, and January 23, 2008. On file with the author.

"Greene County, Ala.: Change Comes to Courthouse." *Time*, February 1, 1971. Available at http://www.time.com/time/magazine/article/0,9171,909744-1,00.html.

"Greene County Inauguration." *Eagle Eye*, February 1971.

The Greene County Special Election. Pacifica Radio documentary, 1969. On file in the Hardy T. Frye Oral History Collection, Auburn University.

Hadnott v. Amos, 295 F. Supp. 1003 (M.D. Ala. 1968).

Hadnott v. Amos, 394 U.S. 358 (1969).

Morgan Jr., Charles. *One Man, One Voice*. New York: Holt, Rinehart and Winston, 1979.

Swift, Wesley R. "The National Democratic Party of Alabama: The First Year." Unpublished paper, August 25, 1984. On file with the author.

"Three Inaugurated in Lowndes County." *Eagle Eye*, February 1971.

Waldron, Martin. "Six Negroes Win Alabama Offices." *New York Times*, July 30, 1969.

Walton Jr., Hanes. *Black Political Parties: An Historical and Political Analysis*. New York: Free Press, 1972.

CHAPTER 13

Cashin Jr., Dr. John L. Interview by Hardy T. Frye, conducted in 1972. On file in the Hardy T. Frye Oral History Collection, Auburn University.

Cashin Jr., Dr. John L. Interviews by the author, February 3, 2006, and January 23, 2008. On file with the author.

CHAPTER 14

Cashin, Dr. John L. Interviews by the author, February 3, 2006, and February 11, 2008. On file with the author.

Hardy, David M. Letter to Dr. John L. Cashin Jr., from Section Chief Hardy, Records Management Division, FBI, June 30, 2006, including attached redacted records concerning past investigations of Cashin (response to Freedom of Information Act request). On file with the author.

ACKNOWLEDGMENTS

Many people made this book possible. First and foremost I must thank my father, Dr. John L. Cashin, Jr., for loving me so very much and for answering all my questions. I will always treasure our trips together in 2006 to Decatur, Hunstville, Birmingham, and Greene County where we relived history. I love you Dad.

My mother is deceased but I must thank her anyway, for holding on to the mementos of her life, and Dad's, and for holding us together.

Heartfelt thanks also to those who took the time to share their memories and memorabilia with me: Athelyne Banks (deceased), Rev. William Branch, James B. Cashin, Jr. ("Blinny"), John M. Cashin (my brother), Myrna Copeland, Bill Edwards, Hardy T. Frye, Rev. Thomas Gilmore, Martha Hereford, Dr. Sonnie Hereford III, Velma Holloway, and Elizabeth Cashin McMillen ("Betty V"). I am especially grateful to Hardy Frye for having the forethought to deposit his wonderful interviews of NDPA activists in an oral history collection at Auburn University and for writing a definitive case study on the NDPA.

Thank you to the professional and amateur historians who imparted their knowledge and/or mined archives for me: J. Mitchell Brown, Kenneth W. Milano, Karen Pizzulo, Vincent Pizzulo, Telette Roberts, and Michael David Smith. Mitch and Ken, you were both especially amazing in discovering hidden gems about my great-great-grandmother, Lucinda, and great-grandfather, Herschel. Thank you to Beth M. Howse, head of Special Collections at Fisk University, for confirming the educational background and contributions of my great Aunt Jack, Lillian Cashin.

Thank you to my dear cousin Dorothy Reed, who read the entire manuscript and pushed me to make it better. Thank you to my "probable cousins," Joan E. Cashin and Edward J. Cashin (deceased), for reading and providing reassuring feedback on the historical chapters. Thank you to my newly discovered cousin James A. Cashin, for invaluable assistance in confirming our common lineage.

Thank you to Alex Aleinikoff and Carol O'Neill of the Georgetown University Law Center for affording me a sabbatical and much emotional and financial support in the writing of this book. My research assistant Elias Salameh and the terrific staff at the Edward Bennett Williams Law Library at Georgetown also provided important research assistance. My assistant Deborah Bays was a cheerful aide and ally. I am also grateful to the faculty support staff, especially George Belton, who aided me in scanning and archiving photographs.

Thank you to the great team at PublicAffairs, for believing in me and patiently shepherding me through all stages of the production of this book. Clive Priddle and Mindy Werner were fantastic editors. Melissa Raymond and Michele Wynn were especially adroit with the rush to final printing.

Many thanks, again, to Peter Osnos for offering me a book deal when no one else would, and to my agent, Esther Newberg, for enabling me to be a writer.

Thank you to my darling sons Langston and Logan for enduring so much time away from mommy. Finally, I cannot thank my wonderful husband Marque enough for suffering with me through the writing of another book. From our first foray through the mouse droppings in my parents' attic, to the many evenings and weekends when you cared for our twin baby boys, you made it possible for me to do this. I love you.

Rhoda Baer

Sheryll Cashin is the author of *The Failures of Integration*. A summa cum laude engineering graduate of Vanderbilt University, and the recipient of a Marshall Scholarship to study in the United Kingdom, she also graduated with honors from Oxford University and Harvard Law School, and is now professor of law at Georgetown University Law Center. She lives with her husband and sons in Washington, D.C.

PublicAffairs is a publishing house founded in 1997. It is a tribute to the standards, values, and flair of three persons who have served as mentors to countless reporters, writers, editors, and book people of all kinds, including me.

I. F. STONE, proprietor of *I. F. Stone's Weekly*, combined a commitment to the First Amendment with entrepreneurial zeal and reporting skill and became one of the great independent journalists in American history. At the age of eighty, Izzy published *The Trial of Socrates*, which was a national bestseller. He wrote the book after he taught himself ancient Greek.

BENJAMIN C. BRADLEE was for nearly thirty years the charismatic editorial leader of *The Washington Post*. It was Ben who gave the *Post* the range and courage to pursue such historic issues as Watergate. He supported his reporters with a tenacity that made them fearless and it is no accident that so many became authors of influential, best-selling books.

ROBERT L. BERNSTEIN, the chief executive of Random House for more than a quarter century, guided one of the nation's premier publishing houses. Bob was personally responsible for many books of political dissent and argument that challenged tyranny around the globe. He is also the founder and longtime chair of Human Rights Watch, one of the most respected human rights organizations in the world.

·   ·   ·

For fifty years, the banner of Public Affairs Press was carried by its owner Morris B. Schnapper, who published Gandhi, Nasser, Toynbee, Truman, and about 1,500 other authors. In 1983, Schnapper was described by *The Washington Post* as "a redoubtable gadfly." His legacy will endure in the books to come.

Peter Osnos, *Founder and Editor-at-Large*